SOMEDAY YOU WILL UNDERSTAND

Walter C. Wolff in Paris, December 31, 1945.

Someday You Will Understand

My Father's Private World War II

NINA WOLFF FELD

Arcade Publishing • New York

First Edition

The author wishes to thank Jeff King for his kind permission to reprint an extract from his blog.

Arcade Publishing books may be purchased in bulk at special discounts for sales promotion, corporate gifts, fund-raising, or educational purposes. Special editions can also be created to specifications. For details, contact the Special Sales Department, Arcade Publishing, 307 West 36th Street, 11th Floor, New York, NY 10018 or arcade@skyhorsepublishing.com.

Arcade Publishing® is a registered trademark of Skyhorse Publishing, Inc.®, a Delaware corporation.

Visit our website at www.arcadepub.com.
Visit the author's site at nwfeld.com.

10 9 8 7 6 5 4 3 2 1

Library of Congress Cataloging-in-Publication Data

Feld, Nina Wolff, author.
  Someday you will understand : my father's private World War II / Nina Wolff Feld.
      pages cm
  Includes bibliographical references.
  ISBN 978-1-62872-377-9 (hardcover : alk. paper) — ISBN 978-1-62872-399-1 (ebook) 1. Wolff, Walter C. 2. Jews—Germany—Biography. 3. Jews, German—United States—Biography. 4. Jewish refugees—United States—Biography. 5. Holocaust, Jewish (1939–1945)—Germany—Biography. I. Title.
  DS134.42.W68F45 2014
  940.53'18092—dc23
  [B]
  2014016696

Cover design by Brian Peterson

Ebook ISBN: 978-1-62872-399-1

Printed in the United States of America

For Jacob, so that Grandpa will always
be in the room with you.

Contents

Author's Note

This book is a work of nonfiction and is based in its entirety on the collection of letters written by my father to his family during his World War II service, which he saved for the rest of his life and entrusted to me not long before he died. All of the names of family, friends, soldiers, or Displaced Persons mentioned in this book come from those letters and in some cases from my own subsequent research for this book. The translation of the letters from their original French was done by me, and I have made every effort to be as accurate as possible. Any letters written in German or that have German writing in their letterhead were translated by scholars or friends. No historic work of this scope and nature can be free of error, but it is my hope that the reader will recognize the effort to achieve accuracy while trying to paint a full picture of my father's experiences during his childhood and early manhood before, during, and in the early aftermath of World War II. All of the dialogue and gestures are drawn from the letters or in some cases from my father's personal vernacular and body language as I knew him. All of the archival material, whether letters, postcards, Nazi propaganda material, or photographs, has been reproduced from my personal collection given to me by my father.

Preface

The Maginot Line of Memory

Long before he was the man he would become, he was a boy running for his life. With a discriminating eye for detail and the inner mechanisms with which to cope, my father was lucky enough not only to survive but to remember moments with a certain fondness. Later, while he served in the US Army, he wrote with humor and dry wit in such vivid detail that a present day reader of his letters feels as though immersed in a newsreel. Some of the persecuted from that time returned to prosecute. My father, Walter C. Wolff, was one of them. He sent war criminals to their fate.

Sometimes that which is precious shines through the misery of the continuum. As soon as there is an opportunity for normalcy, normalcy takes over so that recovery can begin. He almost never spoke to me about those years when I was growing up. Is silence needed to recover from the nightmares of war? Only gradually, and only after my father had died, did I begin to understand.

His elegant, cultured demeanor hid dark secrets of a childhood lost to time. He carried his memories like a lockbox for valuables. Occasionally, pieces were brought out, but his chosen memories were happy. They didn't reveal any of the terror his family had lived through, fleeing the onslaught brought about by Hitler's quest for world domination and ethnic cleansing. From conversations with my father, I had no idea what they had experienced; but if September 11 was one day of terror in my past, for him living that fear on a daily basis until safety was assured was certainly formative. When he reached me by phone from Italy on September 12, 2001, there was no disguise for his emotions or the significance of that date. I had only heard him cry like that once, when my grandmother died.

We were lucky that day; we lost a legacy but were very fortunate not to have lost any family or friends. The legacy was the Twin Towers. My father-in-law, Lester Feld, had been the chief structural engineer on the original Trade Center project. He went to Japan to inspect and select the type of steel used to build them. Since the towers were his life's work, we always referred to them as "Grandpa Lester's buildings" when we pointed them out to our son. Lester died almost a decade before Jacob came into the world, and this was one way to give him a sense of who his paternal grandfather was. On the night of September 11, my then three-year-old son sat at his alphabet table in our old kitchen and wept over his strawberry Jell-O. He somehow understood that he would never see those buildings again and that the planned trip to visit them with his cousins on their next visit to New York would never come to pass. We had wanted to make it a special occasion, to make a day of it. The loss was devastating. War was at home. September 12 often recurred as a significant date in my father's letters.

Silence is its own kind of mask. Yet, though silence and reserve were a constant while I knew my father, I grew up with a lot of love. I always felt thankful, for with that came the security to enjoy life and in turn return the love. Before he died, I even taught him to say, "I love you," back to me. At the end, my father's heart lost its strength, but I like to believe he used that muscle a lot in his life. It may have hardened to survive his childhood, but I knew it to be a soft and fiercely loyal muscle. He was a complicated man whose love was unconditional. I returned the favor. Even after their divorce, my parents could still find a way to love one another and never throw that to the wind. It meant everything to me. When he called me from Florence that day, he cried, "How is your mother?" It was for her that he opened his eyes one last time before dying, as she whispered into his ear that she loved him and always would. She kissed his feverish forehead before she said her last goodbye. Poetry.

I always felt the wonder of privilege. A great part of my education came from traveling.

When I look back to my childhood, I understand why we spent so much time in Europe. There was no need to discuss the past with the children; my father was too busy building a life—busy with family and business. He had become a very successful furniture designer and retailer in New York after the war. He built his business around his lifestyle, and Bon Marché, his company, was the vehicle. All of the furniture was produced in European factories. We would travel back to what he had left behind because he found comfort in the familiarity. Yet, we never had a second home there. It would never be in the right place; it was too cumbersome and a weight. We had one home, where my mother still lives today. If there were any questions pertaining to his past, the answer was always, "Someday you will understand."

We never had to fight for our lives or search for the food that we put in our mouths, as he did. Our charge was to be good children, study, and do well in school and never to worry because we received everything that we needed.

*   *   *   *

I loved how my father could switch between languages without skipping a beat. I inherited this gift. Dad was strict, business-like, and hard to reach. His stubbornness was renowned; that quality was a survival tool. He was also a most elegant man, with the finest taste. I looked up to him, I feared him, and finally, toward the end of his life and well into my own, I was able to stand my ground with him—no small victory.

I am a lot like he was. My father had a guileless love for so many things, perhaps because life had been so tenuous during those early years. I have never lost my childlike love for most things. With every sip of espresso, with every bite of a delicious pastry, with every sniff of a fine wine, with every scarf that I wear like his ascots, so he is everywhere in me. When I lean a certain way, when I speak another language, when I see his lasting impression in a design.

As I write, my son Jacob is approaching bar mitzvah. Something of his grandfather has passed into his looks, his demeanor, and most certainly his approach to Judaism, which is to act in line with tradition as he questions the veracity of what he is learning. This is completely, but exactly, as my father did. Only, when my father was bar mitzvah at the Grande Synagogue in Brussels, Hitler had been in power for four years and any act of religious tenacity was a brave act of resistance. Though Belgium wasn't under occupation, the threat of persecution was ever-present. My father adored Jacob and moved beyond his reserve to show affection in the most comfortable way he knew how, through "goodnesses"—pastries and chocolate, toys, and the occasional and most loving brush across his little nose or lift of his chin or tweak at his ear when Jacob was little. He was funny, though. Only my father would run out before afternoon tea with Jacob to buy coffee ice cream for a three year old! When we sat down at his dining table and the "goodnesses" were served, I looked at my father and said, "Dad, ice cream from Starbucks for a three year old?!"

"Why, it's *latte*," he said in a pronounced Italian accent, pointing to the word written boldly in green across the container.

"Dad," I sighed, "latte has caffeine in it. *Caffe* latte. Dai, Papa?!" I said in Italian, hoping he would catch my drift.

"Nini, *latte* is 'milk' in Italian."

"Really, but here in America it's coffee ice cream from Starbucks!"

He was oblivious, always. It was part of his aloof charm. He was, and remains still, a force in our lives, whose influence reaches Jacob on levels both great and small. We are after all the product of a man whose silence spoke of a generation of children who survived narrow escapes to live very full lives, their masks intact to the end.

Someday You Will Understand

Prologue

Several months before my father died, I visited him at the apartment he shared with his second wife on West 96th Street. It had been a long hot ride uptown on the subway.

The sun was shining through the window as I faced him, its warm rays settling on us while we talked quietly. My throat ached as I fought back tears, thinking of the inevitability of pending loss. He didn't need his gold and sapphire stud set anymore. It was part of a life he no longer could lead. My fingers went over the tooling of the metalwork and the coolness of the deep blue stones. This feeling of a last goodbye would replay between us in the months to come, as my father's body gave in to his enlarged heart and weakened lungs.

Dad told me how much he loved me, making a difficult moment sweeter. He was always very private with his thoughts. When he summoned his strength, I helped him off the bed and walked in front of him in case he should fall. It would hurt, but I'd rather he fell on me than hit the floor again. This time it really might kill him. The last time that happened, I stood over him in the ER at Mount Sinai and directed the plastic surgeon as he rebuilt my father's nose. It had been crushed when his six-foot frame fell face first to the floor after he had lost consciousness, flattening his nose. The surgeon immediately asked for a photograph. I didn't carry one in my wallet, so I pointed to my nose and told him to copy it exactly; they were identical. Though the operation was not for the faint of heart, I volunteered to stay and hold my father's hand while the doctor realigned his features. As the doctor began the reconstruction, he pointed out each aspect of his injury. At one point he pulled up a broken white band and showed me a severed artery. He said that had my father not been found in time, he might have died from the fall.

As the surgeon manipulated my father's nose, I knew Dad would remember none of the experience later. At the time, it reminded me of moving a piece of furniture into place: a little to the left, a little to the right. It was a remarkable moment, and my very vain father was forever thankful that he didn't wind up looking like Rodin's sculpture of a man with a broken nose. All of that money spent on a Beaux Arts education was finally put to good use. I didn't let the surgeon stop until the shape had been restored to a hair of what it had been. It was always about one thirty-second of an inch off. The surgery left a faint scar down the middle, but my father never got over how great the result looked and would often tell the story of how his daughter the artist helped a plastic surgeon restore his nose.

As he walked to his suit closet in the makeshift office, his lips pursed together, he let out a little whistle through every labored breath. He said, "I want to give you something."

While he opened the door to his closet, I took a good look at the books lining the rosewood bookcases that had once lined the library at my mother's apartment in Greenwich Village. I made a mental note of where my favorites were kept. I had always felt proprietary about them. Someday these would be mine, and I would cherish them as he had. Atop the bookcases were his old radios, each design more modern than the last. A timeline of sorts. He reached up to the shelf just above his suits and carefully removed a green metal file box from his army days.

"Here, you may as well have these," he said, and handed it to me.

Having never seen the box before, I had no idea what was inside. I opened it and coughed, choking on the dust that coated the exterior. There were letters and newspapers that gave off the musty odor of history. When I leafed through the letters, I saw that most were in French. Over the many months to come, I began the painstaking process of archiving them and sorting through the newspaper articles and photographs that told his story. It would be years before I would begin to translate those letters, but a title came to mind immediately.

"If this were ever a book . . . ," I would say.

On a late summer afternoon several years later, I lay on the couch, dictionary in hand, struggling to translate a chapter of a manuscript written by a friend, an Italian writer. If I could give his writing an English voice, I would be invited to translate his whole novel. For whatever reason—where sometimes only fate can lead us—I felt I was translating the wrong person's words. I crossed the living room and picked up one of the hundreds of letters that I had so carefully archived, then bounded up the stairs to the computer. Try, I thought, just see what happens. In contrast, the words flowed like water from a faucet. I found my voice. It was my father's.

Jews on the run in war-torn France in June of 1940. Surely the situation surrounding my family had to have been more terrifying and damaging than my father let on. The weather had warmed; the heat was already intense during the day. They had no choice but to continue; they couldn't go home. As they scrambled to safety under their car, the fabric of my grandmother Lisa's handsome tweed suit got caked with mud. She clutched the alligator bag that would accompany her all the way to the safety of their new American lives.

Not long ago, I was looking for something in the handbag she carried with her throughout their escape, and I found a very old set of keys. She clearly thought they would return; my father said as much. My grandmother kept those keys, and when she died in 1981 they were still in her purse, where they've remained to this day. She kept them as a reminder, perhaps as a talisman.

When she looked at them, what did she let herself remember? She never went back to Europe again. Never returned to any place that held the keys to her past. I have since turned the three keys into a piece of jewelry.

Every Sunday, we visited my grandmother at the Park Royal Hotel when I was growing up. She waited for us in her upholstered chair. She learned that kind of patience during the war. Of that I am certain. There was a lot of time spent waiting, wondering, worrying. As her polished, orderly life spun out of her control, all that Omi held dear and familiar was ripped away in a moment. The threat weighing so heavily could have, in an instant, delivered its crushing blow. The elegance of her former life vanished, and she was left with few belongings, memories, and tireless anticipation of a son's visit, with wife and children in tow. He lived a full life. She could no longer allow herself that privilege, for she had broken with her past, and the depth of loss was too great to overcome. It was as if part of her soul had frozen, so encumbered was she. Loss, like a fingerprint or a scar, is a permanent marker, leaving one to forever compensate. She left living to youth and found comfort as the passive observer in her blue chair, where war could no longer impose its warped rules and break her.

Mr. Kresser was this family's human talisman. Perhaps if my father had allowed himself, he would have acknowledged that some force greater than himself had brought them together by an accident of fate, sealing their chance for a future.

My grandmother Omi with the handbag she carried
during their escape.

PART ONE

Hidden in Plain Sight

CHAPTER 1

Walking My Father's Labyrinth

*119 Moselweiserweg, Koblenz: the house where
my father was born.*

His early childhood was spent cloistered in a large four-story Victorian building in Koblenz, Germany. He didn't have a lot of friends and played only with his sister and cousins. Times had become dangerous, and he was kept apart from other children. My grandfather was a wine maker and merchant. One of his wineries was located

behind the house. They were Conservative Jews; my grandfather was
an active community member. They were quite wealthy, and he gave
generously to the Socialist Party. My father used to say, "The enemies
of his enemy were his friends." It was well known that he gave money
to one of the many parties that opposed the Nazis.

August 1933 was the last time the family would see their home.
They never returned. My grandparents fled Nazi Germany through
Luxembourg and settled in Strasbourg, while the children were put in
boarding school. My father was only five when he was sent away. His
parents used a bout of tuberculosis as an excuse to send him, along
with his sister, Ellen, who was three years older, to Switzerland. Eventually, with permits as tight as they were, they could no longer stay
in France. My grandparents moved once again, this time to neutral
Belgium.

Ellen, Omi, and my father taking a spring break from
Belmunt, on the slopes of St. Moritz, 1932.

From 1933 until 1939, my father's formal education was at
Belmunt, an exclusive boarding school in St. Moritz, Switzerland.
Photographs from that time show an active and happy boy. For both
my father and Ellen, school represented a safe haven and a secure

home. There was no fear associated with being Jewish. In fact, the school's director, Monsieur Shoch, was a Dutch Jew. My father and Ellen kept in touch with him and his family for the rest of their lives. Not knowing their history, I could never fathom the bond that my father had with his sister and his cousin Pierre. If I had, I would have respected and nurtured it more as an adult. I can hear my father's voice begging my brother and me to get along as children, because we might really need one another someday. I understand now that Ellen and my father's bond was their lifeline. They depended upon each other for survival. Rivalry was not an option.

While at boarding school, they took advantage of all the school could offer. My father became fluent in French, continued learning to read and write in German, and learned to speak English. He made life-long friends who included his sister and the cousin of the king of Spain, Fernando Zobel, and others who would pass through their lives for decades to come, such as Henry Arnhold and even the now notorious Claus von Bülow. As children they had a sheltered sense of freedom in St. Moritz, surrounded by the wonderful caring atmosphere at Belmunt. It was there more than any other place that my father considered his spiritual and ancestral home.

All of this, before the real running began. A childhood sprinkled with charm all the way through, or so it might seem.

CHAPTER 2

Bombs, Bullets, and Lies

On or about May 6, 1940, my father's family began their sixteen-month odyssey of escape through France, ending with their safe arrival in New York on September 12, 1941. Sixty years to the day later, I would hear my father's halting voice, choked with tears when he called to see if my family and I were safe after the fall of the Twin Towers. As devastated as I felt, I found myself comforting him over the phone like a child in my arms. It broke my heart.

Several years after his death, I sat watching the video testimony about his family's escape that he gave for the Shoah Foundation's Visual History Archive. He had consented to do the video as a gift to Jacob, his grandson, and the foundation had granted me permission to edit it for use on my website. My father sat with his arms at his sides, almost passively. His eyes move down and to the left, as if he's watching his own scratched memory in his mind's eye. His words come slowly, evenly, as he thinks carefully about what he is going to say on camera, mindful not to show any emotion. I watch his every gesture; I try to understand more than he is willing to say. When he slows down or hesitates, filling time with uncharacteristic disfluencies, I edit him, forcing him to clarify his thoughts. I have an hour and a half of video to work with, and it is up to me to pull the best of him out of the footage to build around his story from the details I uncover.

He says, "Times had already become dangerous; we fled from Brussels. We left when the German armies were approaching." During the four days before the Nazis rained bombs on Brussels, my family drove away from the city. They took a head start. Approximately two million Belgians joined them and flowed south into France as Paris herself was being evacuated. In his book *Diary of a Witness,* Raymond-Raoul Lambert describes the course of events: "We were conquered by Germany in the course of ten days. May 10: Belgium was invaded. May 11: they broke through the Ardennes in Belgium. May 12: bombing of the roads in Belgium, with fleeing civilians hindering troop movements. New tactic: target first the nerve centers from which morale and motivation stem. May 13: the Germans crossed the Meuse [the Belgian border with France]."

Before their escape from Brussels, they carefully packed up their belongings at La Résidence, the elegant residential building where they lived, and left them with the concierge, Monsieur Hubert. They took only the necessities and stored the rest. With a trailer in tow and an American friend, Lewis Kresser, at their side, they traveled literally one step ahead of the enemy, with the Germans at their heels. From the windows of their car they watched Rue de la Loi and their adopted city disappear. City turned to country as they inched towards the coast.

Mr. Kresser, a retired intelligence officer, had been part of the American army during World War I. Why he was in Belgium for the Wehrmacht's invasion is a matter of speculation, though some in my family say he was my grandmother's lover. When I

My grandfather Arthur, Omi, and an unidentified woman. This
may be the car they used in their escape.

read through my father's letters, I found a paper luggage tag with Kresser's Baltimore address on it and a couple of letters that my father sent him while he was in the army. Remarkably, Kresser must have given those letters to my grandmother as a keepsake.

The five—my father, his sister Ellen, my grandparents, and Kresser—drove along the coastal road toward Dunkirk. My father continues in his interview: "We were in Dunkirk at the time of the first bombardment, in a restaurant having dinner." Food was scarce, and increasingly hard to find. They took cover in the restaurant and finished their meal. Once they left Dunkirk, they continued along the coastal road toward Normandy. My father recounted the many times he sat on the hood of the car at night with the headlights off and would act as my grandfather's eyes leading him down the road. He wore the Jaeger-LeCoultre watch with the glow-in-the-dark face that he had worn as he stood at the Bimah in Brussels' Grande Synagogue in July 1939 for his bar mitzvah. Long ago, my father gave me that watch, which I had restored to its original luster. On the occasion of Jacob's first birthday in 1999, and my adult bat mitzvah, I wore it as I read my Torah portion.

"There was no more border control; refugees were flooding the road. You could barely drive. There were carriages and cars and bicycles," said my father. They were traveling at the rate of about five-to-ten kilometers per hour. Old footage shows civilians silently moving in one direction as the troops moved past them. People are on foot, on carts, in cars; they are stopped by the edge of the roads, eating or just watching. The roads are narrow; everything and everyone moves slowly. Escape was not fast. It seemed orderly, like columns of ants moving toward a destination. The muted, shocked people were following each other, but where to? They were expressionless, homeless, and soon to be stateless refugees. I always look for my family in the footage.

Newsreels show rumbling lorries, tanks, enemy fire, and the ensuing explosions. At times German Stukas wailed through the sky, piercing the silence to announce imminent bomb attacks. Nazi bombs indiscriminately hitting civilian as well as army targets. This is a detail my father chooses to overlook during his account of their escape. Inasmuch as they could, they took control of their situation by planning their route away from the masses.

When night fell, my family would either sit in their car or find a farmhouse where they could spend the night. Along the way, the French police stopped them and brought my grandparents and Mr. Kresser to the station for questioning, while nineteen-year-old Ellen and my fifteen-year-old father were left in the car to wait. This is where my father betrays some emotion, as he remembers the possibility that he could have lost his parents. I cannot imagine what that must have felt like for a child. My father said, "Luckily, they came back."

Reunited, they continued along the Normandy coast. By this time, Mr. Kresser had devised a plan that would ultimately save their lives. They rehearsed it well, and everyone knew their role. Along the road they ran into a British regiment, the North Umberland Fusiliers, who were lost. Ever the intelligence officer, and the only one who spoke perfect English, Kresser befriended them. The soldiers were in need of maps, and my family needed gas. A trade was made. The family declined an offer to put their car in one of the army's trucks because they feared that if caught they would all be killed on the spot. Once they filled their car with gas, my grandfather got back behind the wheel and led the regiment's column with his car until they arrived near the village of Noyelles-sur-Mer, a small town facing the English Channel. Once again they were stopped, this time by the French police, who warned them, "The enemy is near. All civilians off the road!"

My father remembers, "Regardless of the pleading of the British, who said, 'These are friends of ours, they are helping us,' the French repeated, 'All civilians off the road,' and that was that." Stuck on a country road near a river, they could not have known they were in the shadow of General Heinz Guderian's 2nd Panzer Division. They shimmied under their car to shield themselves.

The roads were overcrowded with fleeing refugees as the troops approached. Within an hour of the order to clear the road, firing started and the battle raged around them. The warmth of the car engine tempered the chill they felt from the cooling night air and dried the sweat from the fear that was shaking them through to their core. Moisture in the ground from the previous week's rain dampened my grandmother's tweed suit. She wore that suit every day for six months. There was an unmistakable odor of battle in the air, which mixed with the smells of spring in France. With every round of machine gun fire or tank blast, sound reverberated against the evening sky and shook the ground.

While they lay under their car, the Nazis fought toward the channel coast, leaving casualties in their wake. It was a defining moment in the war. The small French force was hiding across the small river, the Dien, when the firing started. Darkness fell and the French were rapidly outnumbered. They suffered no injuries. Others around them were not so lucky.

"Some people were hurt." My father tells the story calmly. Once the French lost, they found themselves in enemy territory. The battalion of the 2nd Panzer division had passed through Noyelles-sur-Mer on that night, May 20, 1940. They were the first German unit to reach the Atlantic and had moved so far, so fast, in breaking through the French lines, that even they were confused about how to continue their advance. They were so close that the troops could see the estuary of the Somme flowing into the English Channel. In his memoirs, Guderian remarked very dryly that as he passed columns of his advancing troops, they drove through "crowds" of refugees. Five of those refugees were my family—four German Jews—and Mr. Kresser.

The morning after the battle, Kresser sought out the German commander and told him that his troops had behaved like maniacs. Soldiers had broken into their car and stolen their passports and jewelry. "Forget the jewelry," said Kresser. Their stolen identities were the real issue. He asked the commander for the name of his superior in order to lodge a complaint against him for failing to control his men. The commander explained that he couldn't watch his soldiers every minute and that this can happen during a war. With that, a carefully thought-out, well-rehearsed plan was set in motion, and the Germans fell for it.

What actually happened was this: My grandparents had purposely destroyed all of the family's passports and documents that would show their real identities or give any clues to their being Jews in what was now Nazi-occupied France. Mr. Kresser held an American passport, and therefore his identity was secure, since the United States and Germany were not at war yet. The Germans believed our ex–intelligence officer's story, and, to appease him and move them along, the commander issued them a laissez-passer (which literally means "let them pass") that listed all of their new names on it. At some point during the many hours and days spent in that car, they had come up with a plan for taking on new identities. My father describes what happened next:

"I became Walter Kresser. I was from Baltimore, I knew what high school I had gone to, and I knew what courses I had taken. Mr. Kresser was thorough, good at that. . . . My sister went to a different high school; we knew that too. Both of us spoke English by then, quite fluently with British accents, but I don't think the Germans would have known the difference. My mother became Mr. Kresser's wife. My father became Mr. Kresser's French chauffeur; his name remained Arthur Wolff. He claimed to have been born in Alsace-Lorraine, which would have been okay. The only thing that might have given him away was his accent, which was of a slightly different variety. We destroyed our real passports. We had papers giving our correct birthplace and everything else. We wouldn't get caught that way. Remember, Mr. Kresser was an ex–intelligence officer and didn't make such mistakes."

With their identities changed, they stayed in Noyelles–sur-Mer for six weeks. They were able to find shelter at a local farmhouse for several days and then moved into the Château de Noyelles, which belonged to French fascists, who had abandoned their home. My father even remembered the family's name but never told us. The château is now a lovely inn. It soon became headquarters for the German army, and everyone was living under one roof, giving a new twist to the expression, "Keep your friends close and your enemies closer." My father's family lived on the top floor. Omi, my grandmother, never said a word; she was pretending to be shell-shocked and mute. The children spoke only to Kresser.

On September 12, 1991, the Wolff family was honored to have an article published in the *Congressional Record* commemorating the fiftieth anniversary of our arrival in the United States. The article mentions part of what happened when my family came face-to-face with the German army. "Ellen Wolff Ducat remembers one particular event during their journey, when they were quartered in a castle in Noyelles-sur-Mer, a coastal village northwest of Paris. Platoons of German soldiers also inhabited these grounds, for the estate was being used as a staging area to fan the army throughout the region." Perhaps it was General Guderian himself, who had posted his troops at the château.

One day Ellen returned to the family's car and found that it had been searched and their possessions ransacked. Among the items now left out in the open by the soldiers, she discovered the Hebrew prayer book that had belonged to her grandmother. Although they had destroyed their identities, they couldn't forsake the most incriminating evidence. The *Congressional Record* continues: "Ellen hid this prayer book, and kept it with her for the rest of the journey. Fortunately, the soldiers who were responsible for the raid were suddenly relocated and the Wolffs fled to safety again." While they were living in Noyelles with the Germans at the château, an officer who was a former actor was rather taken with my aunt Ellen and flirted with her. He eventually told her he understood their story but that he was civilized, and people like him did not make such distinctions. He must have discovered their true identities. They were betrayed by an heirloom.

Château de Noyelles, Noyelles-sur-Mer.

One afternoon during the early summer, my father was in the garden doing what he loved more than anything, picking berries. Wherever we traveled throughout my childhood, this was something we would do, even if it meant stopping along a highway on the road to St. Godknowswhere! In St. Moritz we would come down from the mountains, go straight to our favorite pastry shop, Hanselmann's, and take afternoon tea. We covered the pastries with the berries that we had collected and thick whipped cream.

The warmth of that afternoon in June 1940 was interrupted when RAF planes came from out of nowhere and dropped their one-ton bombs down from the sky. It was quiet; people were going about their business around the château. To the passive observer, nothing was out of the ordinary. The noises of summer, buzzing bees collecting pollen from flowers, worms turning the earth, birds, other imperceptible sounds bound together, creating white noise. My grandmother and aunt were hanging wash out to dry in the hot sun. On hearing the approaching planes, they looked helplessly out toward the garden at my father. My grandfather was under the hood of the car, checking the engine as every chauffeur does. He was stopped, frozen in time. Mr. Kresser stood watching the carnage as the moment unfolded before his eyes. He yelled out the window of their quarters to my father to seek shelter. The problem with hearing my father tell this story during his video testimony is that he is so relaxed that anyone listening must surely have the cartoon-like image that I have long held onto. One cannot grasp the sounds, or the smells and the feeling of dirt spraying, or the fear that takes over you as you look to the sky while bombs fall, at first silently, then with the loud unmistakable screech flooding the ears as they reach the earth. There is a vacuum of silence just before the explosion. With his telling, I missed the mental chaos they must have experienced, not knowing who was hit, whose body parts were flying through the air, mixing with the other debris shattered by the explosion. No one could protect them. The strafing did not last long, though they wouldn't know that.

When the firing stopped and it was clear that the planes had gone, my father found himself dangling in a crater. His neat clothes were covered in dirt that had rained down, entering every exposed orifice. The bomb hadn't exploded. With the blood drained from his face, shaken and dazed, and his ears ringing with sudden but temporary deafness, he thanked the God that he no longer believed in for sparing his life and staggered to safety. The bombing kept their secret safe and bought more time. The Nazi with a crush on Ellen lay dead a short distance away. Dad could remember the garden and the berries, but whatever else—the blood and dirt, smoke, the acrid smells of burning machinery and burnt flesh, the fear, his family's terrified screams, the yelling of the Nazis—was repressed long ago. My father was unharmed—the irony of war.

During the interview, he rubbed his chest through his gray-and-white-striped shirt. I vehemently disliked it, perhaps because I found it curiously reminiscent of a concentration camp uniform.

"I had several victims." His laughter broke through his wry smile, the mischievous one that showed there was a hidden side to him. He liked to recount the German's drinking escapades in the cellar of the château throughout the six weeks that they stayed there. Dad points to a photograph: the window on the upper floor of the tower is where my family slept. The fifteen-year-old Walter Wolff is revealed as he begins his story again. The Germans were drinking like crazy; they spent their evenings in the wine cellar. He noticed that the French people had bottles of oil stored on one side in wine bottles labeled "*huile*," and the wine was in bottles on the other side. He said the Krauts in their drunken stupor never bothered with a traditional uncorking. They broke the neck off each bottle and guzzled. He switched the bottles; he thought it was a funny thing to do.

Down to the cellar during the bombings: a family of Jews with a bunch of drunken Nazis leaning on each other, their laughter hiding fear, their odor of sweat and alcohol permeating the darkness, through walls of bottles. Those soldiers were ready and stoked to fight their war, their advance momentarily halted by Hitler himself. My family watched with loathing in their eyes as the soldiers sat drunk in the darkness, singing songs and leaning into each other the way drunk men do. And my father had the audacity to play tricks. Did they sit opposite each other? Was plaster falling from the ceiling with each thud of explosives? How did my father keep from laughing? Had the thunderous sounds of war become so routine that evenings in the cellar were as mundane as an evening spent around the hearth? These questions all have very clear answers. The answers simply cannot be discovered because the participants in this story are all gone. What remains is washed of detail. The château has been restored. The walls plastered over, faded paint given a fresh coat, flowers replanted to blossom in their perennial beauty.

Later, as a soldier himself, my father wrote hundreds of letters to my grandmother Omi. Most begin "Chère Mamo." They are written on scraps of dossier paper, army stationery, his bar mitzvah stationary with "WW" in the upper left-hand corner, even Nazi stationary. He experienced war and its beastly rage on the soul but possessed a very special approach and sensibility toward life. Besides a marvelous sense of humor, he had magic, perhaps something he himself wasn't even aware of. It was an innate ability to compartmentalize, to quickly adapt to any situation or circumstance and function in the realm of that given moment. That aspect of his personality worked to his advantage. Throughout his life he had a singular capacity to draw out the best that life had to offer during the course of a devastating experience. Perhaps this is why this story is so unique. So many millions suffered, but somehow my father's coping mechanisms made him enjoy what he could and come away with some very charming and, strange to say, fond memories.

The family left the Château de Noyelles after armistice was declared in June 1940. Decades later, my parents returned during a last trip to Europe together as their marriage dissolved. It should have been something that brought a family together. Instead it was as if my father needed to go back to Noyelles one last time. Before moving on to a different stage, he shared this deeply private moment with my mother. I too wanted to walk the grounds with him to see the strawberry patch, go down to the cellar, and see the room. Didn't he think it mattered to his children?

My mother and father went up and visited the room he had occupied half a century earlier. The view out the window—what memories did he see before him? The room absorbed the summer light, making everything bright. Everything had stayed the same. They stopped at the garden. My father pointed to the spot where a boy's life had once been spared when he was left quietly stunned in the crater of an unexploded bomb. When they were leaving the grounds, the caretaker's wife ran after my mother, presenting her with a deeply felt gesture: a bouquet of flowers. If I had been there, I would have looked for clues in his face, deep in his tender eyes, that offered an opening into his reserved, quiet exterior. My own family will go someday and stay in that very room. I wish for a marker, carved initials into a hidden floorboard, something to reveal their presence during those chaotic weeks. We were always looking for a way into that reserve, a way to bring him out. No one ever really knew what it was. I can only guess that it took a lot of energy to hide the vast quantity of emotion and fear that he felt. In order to be successful, he pushed ahead with all of his emotional might.

CHAPTER 3

Vichy, Lyon, and the Flag of Rags

France capitulated to Germany, and they left Noyelles-sur-Mer before their true identities could be discovered. Before they continued on, they did several things: Mr. Kresser had the idea that they should make the vehicle look as official as possible. One of them found a brush and some white paint and carefully painted "USA" all over the car, the roof included. Omi made an American flag out of rags, and they attached it to the car's aerial. They needed gasoline, and my father, Ellen, and Mr. Kresser found a way to siphon gas from the abandoned cars, trucks, and tanks that littered the road. They took rubber tubes and sucked on them, transferring the gas to the bottles they collected, and filled their tank. My father mimes the action during his interview; an incredulous smile breaks through as he recalls what an unpleasant task it was. They went to abandoned cars, ignoring the carnage and the wreckage. Just the fumes from the gasoline must have made them ill, but they filled their tank and headed toward Vichy.

At Moulins, the border to the zone under French control, the *zone libre*, Mr. Kresser pulled out his American passport and screamed out the window at the German guard, "Embassy, embassy!" Bewildered, the guard looked at the oncoming car with its makeshift flag and paint job, and said, "I can't let you through, but I'll let you go to my colleague down the road. He's my superior. If he lets you through, it's fine with me."

As they pulled up to the second guard a little farther down the road, he screamed once again, "Embassy, embassy!" and pointed to his passport. This time the guard looked at the passport, saluted, and let them through the demarcation line to so-called unoccupied France.

This was nothing short of miraculous, because if their ethnicity had been discovered, they would have been shot on the spot, no questions asked. Besides that, border closings were at the Nazis' whim and might last days or weeks. From one day to the next, no one knew if they would be allowed to cross. At times there were hundreds to thousands of cars and people lining the road, waiting to cross, with no place to sleep and little food to be had.

Having crossed many borders in my life, I know it to be an unnerving process. There is always a fear of being searched and questioned, even if one has nothing to hide. As a young teenager, I was once pulled aside and searched at an airport in Italy. I have never forgotten how scared and unnerved I felt. As children, we were never to fool around while crossing a border. On at least one occasion, this proved impossible. We were crossing into Lugano, and my father decided that the guards would take less notice if he played being an "Americano." He rolled down his window and smiled at the guard while handing him our passports. He looked at the man, and deadpan, in the most American accent I ever heard come out of that man's mouth, he practically yelled, "Luggaanno!" Whereupon my brother, mother, and I fell to pieces in the car, trying not to laugh as he slapped his car seat to shut us up. This, of course, made us laugh more. We had tears rolling down our cheeks as we tried to contain ourselves. Never did we laugh harder.

After the Germans let them through, a wave of relief must have passed over them long enough to look back and laugh at the gullibility of the young Nazis in charge. My family was now in the unoccupied zone in the center of France, less than sixty kilometers from Vichy. Jews were being rounded up no matter where they were found, though, and it was dangerous. When they finally approached the outskirts of Vichy, with the car decorated as it was, they were greeted by a line of applauding bystanders who mistook them for American dignitaries. Years later, as he would watch the parades and floats slowly move down Fifth Avenue in a sea of color and sound, perhaps my father allowed himself the luxury of a memory of a thousand days before. A young man and his family were the center of attention, with their painted car a beacon of hope for the occupied masses. For just a moment, they could believe that help was on the way, that the Americans had finally stepped in. My great uncle lived in Vichy. They found the keys he left for them before he fled. They stayed as long as they could, decamping six weeks later when it became too dangerous for their cover to be secure. It was Vichy after all, the epicenter of French collaboration with the Nazis. The Gestapo was everywhere, so they left.

They packed up and headed to Lyon, a two-hundred-kilometer drive that would have taken at least three tanks of fuel. They must have sucked on a lot of rubber tubing to fill their tank when there was none available for purchase. What did they see on the way? How long did it take for them to get to Lyon, on those narrow roads, at the end of the summer of 1940?

No longer able to use the German "laissez-passer," they reclaimed their original identities and dropped their American ones.

My father on the run in Lyon, France, age sixteen.

My grandfather must have started to contact relatives in New York to get sponsorship for visas. My father recalled that they were never completely aware of what was happening to European Jewry at the time. They had seen people being arrested. He had a short-wave radio that he always called his TSF (*télégraphie sans fil*, a French term for a radio), and he would listen to it every night, hiding the sound of its crackling static under his blankets. After he separated the propaganda from the truth, he would update family and friends with news. Even as a teenager on the run, Dad kept a portable radio that was powerful enough to get the BBC, the only truly trustworthy source. Informed, they had a pretty good idea of how the war was going, where and what battles took place. The local newspapers were of no use. Garbage, he said.

To replenish their shrinking resources, my grandfather sold the escape car. Life on the run required capital, probably access to even more funds than usual. Everything had its price. In Lyon, life was anything but normal for them. There was no school, no work. Food was rationed, scarce, and extremely costly. There were curfews. There was anxiety. The children's principal occupation was to find food for the family, but Mr. Kresser saw to it that my father had something else to do with his free time. The head of the Resistance was a friend of his, so he introduced my father to him and put him to work at night. At just sixteen, he became a runner for the Resistance. I am sure that my dad felt duty bound.

His footsteps, made louder by his worn leather soles, clattered on the stone streets. Rainy nights only amplified the sound. They walked and talked casually, just like old friends winding through the nighttime streets, darting into the *traboules*—covered walkways that were hidden behind unmarked doors. Once used by silk merchants, they now led to safe houses in the old city. It's all a blur really, the innocuous chatter, shadows clinging to walls. The British airmen nodded as my father babbled at them in French, telling them irrelevant stories while leading them to safety after they had parachuted down from the skies over Lyon. When need be, the sound of his breath was barely audible now. My father had learned to control his breathing. One wrong move could attract attention. If caught, he would have been tortured to betray his loyalties and his comrades and then shot. Lyon was a stronghold for the French Resistance and, as such, was fertile ground for rounding up anyone who went against the regime in deed or in thought. The authorities would have shown absolutely no mercy.

I think of Omi sitting with her hands clasped, waiting at in their hotel room on Rue Gasparino, utterly terrified that my father would never return, acid in her stomach a reminder of their never-ending fear of being caught. Mr. Kresser sat with her, reassuring her that she would see her son again. Decades later, we would often hear Omi say, "I am my own master," repeating it as if a mantra with that very distinguished accent of hers. As age pulled her farther away from the life she once knew and the heart-throbbing fear that was her past, she would remind those around her that her dignity was very much intact and never to be taken for granted. Their lives had been so diminished, fighting every day to stay alive, even willing to make the sacrifice of allowing my young father to do his part for the Resistance. The warmth of summer faded, and they spent the fall and winter of 1940 in Lyon. I can never picture my grandfather beyond the photos that I have seen. No one ever really spoke about him. Mr. Kresser, though faceless, looms larger than life.

They needed to get out of Europe. They had already been warned to leave while there was still time. On her way to Amsterdam, Aunt Hedwig had taken a detour with her young daughter, Doris, and visited them in Brussels. On more than one occasion, Hedwig pleaded with her brother, but for whatever reason they were not ready. My grandparents knew the regime in Germany was trouble; laws against the Jews had forced them to move out of Koblenz long before they settled in Brussels. They simply thought Hitler was a passing phenomenon, that he couldn't last, and in neutral Belgium they were safely out of reach. How much more of a hint does one need, though, when they still mourned the loss of a family member murdered on the way to a concentration camp shortly after Hitler was appointed chancellor?

In February 1940, Omi received word that her father had died sometime during the weeks before. My aunt Mete, a nurse, had stayed behind to care for him in Mannheim, Germany. It almost cost the former national tennis champion her life. Shortly after her father's death, Mete was deported to Gurs, the notorious internment camp in southwestern France, where the conditions were deplorable. As with many stories handed down within families, there may be inaccurate nuances here and there, but Aunt Mete was on some kind of line and a guard recognized her.

Unbelievably, he was Mete's mixed doubles partner from their tennis days. In order to save her life, he beat her as a cover for his plan to help her escape. Once free, she made her way to Paris where she tried unsuccessfully to locate some family members. Strangers told her that if she stood on the Champs-Élysées, she might be filmed for a newsreel and then spotted by a relative. According to the story I was told, that is exactly what happened! While at the movies in Brooklyn, her sister, Erna, and daughter, Lore, spotted Mete and had the projectionist replay the film until they could stop it and be sure. They were able to secure a visa for her, and she spent the remainder of her life in New York. Amazingly, we lost just one relative to the Nazis.

My aunt, Meta Bach, playing in the Reich Championship.

While she was interned at Gurs, Mete's house in Landau was seized and sold. My father returned to Landau as a soldier in July 1945. The road into town was a sea of red, white, and blue flags.

Having not been there for quite some time, my father asked a soldier and three civilians for directions to the house. They found that only the windows had suffered damage. The house was one of the few left intact amid the devastation. They pulled up to the front gate in their jeep and rang the bell. As soon as it sounded, all the lights in the house were turned off, so my father screamed: "Ich gebe Ihnen genau zwei Minuten zum Aufmachen, dann schiesse ich die Tür nieder!" Translation: "I will give you exactly two minutes, and then I will shoot the door down!"

Thirty seconds later, a trembling man opened the door and asked him what he wanted. Losing patience, my father told him that he was the nephew of the legal owner and to let him through immediately. These people were in such shock when my father explained who he was that they were left standing with their mouths open. He was told by the "new owner," an elderly woman called Frau Kopf, that Aunt Mete had ceded the house and that she was the legal owner. She showed my father the contract she had signed at the Polizei Praesidium between her and the Nazis, which mentioned the laws of expropriation. She paid 65,000 marks for it. He requisitioned the house and, before turning it over to the French government, he had the two families, Kopf and Maatz, taken away. From the remaining occupants, he demanded two beds with fresh linen and kept them up until midnight lecturing them on the morality of buying stolen goods while he calmly played with his revolver. They did indeed remember my aunt Mete, especially the elderly Madame Hertel. Dad found the whole incident so amusing that he pressed them further and demanded six eggs for 9:00 a.m. the next morning. He "requisitioned" approximately forty bottles of wine before heading off to find the governing military body the next day, after a very satisfying breakfast. Later that day, after meeting with the governor, he wrote him a formal letter describing in detail the background of the situation and that since the property was in fact expropriated under the laws of the Third Reich, that the house should be surrendered to him as per his aunt's wishes.

CHAPTER 4

No Exit: Marseille, Fascist Spain, and the Nightmare Ocean Crossing

In December 1940, after six months in Lyon, the Wolff family left and made their way to Marseille. Finally, after months of frustrating negotiations with American embassy officials in Marseille and the help of relatives in the United States, they were granted visas to America. There are no details about where they lived during that time, but we had relatives in Marseille. By then, Mr. Kresser had returned to the United States. They kept in touch, and my father occasionally wrote to him while he was in the army.

In order to be granted a visa to the United States, they must have had to go through the Joint—the Joint Distribution Committee, created to help Jews in distress overseas, whose European office was headed by Joseph Schwartz—or through Varian Fry, the American journalist who ran a rescue network in Marseille during the war. His heroic efforts alone helped save the lives of thousands of Jews otherwise destined for the death camps. In August 1941, my father along with his sister and my grandparents boarded a train heading southwest from Marseille to Seville, Spain, a distance of 1,600 kilometers, in the blazing heat of summer with no air conditioning. My grandmother wore the same suit and carried the same alligator handbag that she left Brussels with the year before. The trains were patrolled by armed German soldiers, who were checking papers very carefully. If there had been any kind of delay on the train, for any reason, their visas could have expired and they would not have reached Spain in time to buy passage on the SS *Navemar*, leaving from the port of Cádiz. The Joint chartered as many ships sailing to the United States as possible and bought all available berths on regular passenger ships. My father's family bribed the *Navemar's* captain, who was asking for $2,000 per head for as many people willing to pay the exorbitant fee to fit into his quarters, one of the few spaces on board with a port hole. They were four among seven who secured a cabin on this famed voyage to America. The incredible story of the *Navemar* was told by Pulitzer Prize–winning author Herbert Agar in his book *The Saving Remnant.* He described the ship as:

> an ancient freighter with no facilities for passengers, not even toilets. Tiers of bunks had been fitted into the airless holds. Passengers took turns on the meager deck for a breath of air. There they found themselves in competition with five live oxen, the commissariat for the voyage. . . . By the time *Navemar* sailed, the American visas of the passengers . . . expired. . . . Joseph Schwartz in Lisbon cabled New York to ask the Department of State to extend the visas, and told *Navemar* to drop anchor in the River Tagus, the Joint paying the demurrage. Mr. Schwartz then induced a reluctant Portuguese government to allow the passengers on shore, so long as the Joint was responsible. . . . But when he boarded *Navemar,* and pointed out that no one could live in such conditions, and to take care of anyone who went ashore until the next regular sailing to the United States, nobody would leave ship. The Joint, as they well knew, could not possibly promise that another vessel would ever sail from Lisbon with a passenger list, which had not been vetted by the Gestapo. . . . The Department of State had generously sent word to the American consulate at Lisbon to extend the visas. But this proved impossible because the consulate did not have enough typewriters to make out the new forms in time. *Navemar,* with slave-ship conditions below decks, could not lie indefinitely off Lisbon. Yet the passengers were still too frightened to disembark. Here is a problem which no government is equipped to solve. If you do not have typewriters you cannot do the necessary paperwork for hundreds of new visas. A pity, but, come what may, the forms must be completed.

What happened next is phenomenal. There were hundreds of refugees still in Seville whose visas were expiring. The American consulate was willing to extend them, but due to the shortage of typewriters they were incapable of helping. In a decisive act that saved hundreds of lives, the Joint in Lisbon sent two Portuguese Jews with enough funds to acquire as many typewriters as they needed to fill out the new forms. Money was no object.

The only story that I ever heard my father tell of his final escape aboard the *Navemar* was that when the ship came to port in Bermuda, before continuing on to Cuba and then New York, he noticed the way the Bermudan men were dressed and thought to himself that he had long shorts and knee socks. He changed his clothes and snuck off the freighter in search of oranges to prevent scurvy. According to him, he snuck back on board minutes before the ship pulled out of port. The extremely long and arduous journey to Brooklyn Harbor was anything but enjoyable. Varying reports say that the freighter could accommodate between fifteen to twenty-eight passengers but was crammed with anywhere from a thousand to more than eleven hundred passengers in its cargo holds.

In an article on his website, Jeff King wrote this about the *Navemar*:

The Spanish freighter, equipped to carry 28 passengers, crammed 1,000 people into its cargo holds. The conditions were so horrible when it arrived in Cuba in 1941 that Manuel Siegel of the Joint Relief Committee in Havana wrote to the JDC that "everyone seemed to be fighting everyone else for the privilege of living. The relationships seemed more animalistic than human." Victor Bienstock, a writer for the International Jewish Press Bureau, gave this grim report: "It was a nightmare spectacle—Hollywood could have used it for a setting in a new production of Dante's Inferno. The great, gloomy caverns, the tiers of bunks rising on all sides. Old men and women gasping for breath in the insufferable heat, lying motionless on their bunks, while children tossed and cried. Everyone hungry, everyone thirsty, everyone dirty. . . . The captains on the old slave ships saw that their human cargoes got better treatment than this—and over a half-million dollars in passage money was paid on this ship." The overcrowding was so dangerous that the *Navemar* was labeled "a flowing Gurs," referring to the Gurs concentration camp in France. Six Jews died on the voyage.

Many were stricken by food poisoning. The only relief came when the *Navemar*, nicknamed the Nevermore by passengers, reached New York in 1941. Dr. Joseph J. Schwartz, the JDC's European chief, admitted that the agency knew about the condition of the ship before it set sail, but that it was under pressure to get the refugees out at any cost. "Several thousand people in Germany, Austria, Czechoslovakia held U.S. visas which were about to expire. Unless the people left prior to the date of expiration of those visas, the chances for renewal were remote," he wrote in a memorandum on the *Navemar*. "We tried to clean the ship up as much as possible, but try as we did, it was impossible to make the *Navemar* a decent ship, and we knew when the ship left the harbor that there would be much suffering and privation." Schwartz said the urgency was a result of the "fear which exists all over Europe today, of the horror of remaining behind, of the almost certain doom that people expect unless they are able to emigrate."

The *New York Times* of September 13, 1941, quoted passengers as saying: "[A]s freight we were treated satisfactorily, but just freight not passengers. . . . [W]e could only stand this trip because it meant our salvation." No words could have been spoken with more truth than those uttered by the passengers aboard.

During the six weeks of their voyage, the danger for the Jews and other people at grave risk increased drastically. The Nazi siege on Leningrad began, all Jews were ordered to wear yellow stars, and preparations for the Final Solution were put into effect to eradicate the Jews. Experiments with the use of gas chambers started at Auschwitz, and the industrialized mass slaughter was put into effect with the issuing of the infamous letter from Göring to Heydrich dated July 31, 1941, while the *Navemar* was crossing the waters, escaping the war and leaving behind the many who would soon perish at the hands of Hitler's armies.

Berlin, July 31, 1941
To: Gruppenführer Heydrich:
. . . I hereby charge you to carry out preparations as regards organizational, financial, and material matters for a total solution

[*Gesamtlösung*] of the Jewish question in all the territories of Europe under German occupation.

Where the competency of other central organizations touches on this matter, these organizations are to collaborate.

I charge you further to submit to me as soon as possible a general plan of the administrative material and financial measures necessary for carrying out the desired final solution [*Endlösung*] of the Jewish question.

Göring

Time magazine of September 22, 1941, shows a photograph of people crammed into the lifeboat wrapped in blankets and as close together as sardines in a can. The ship arrived on a typically hot and humid twelfth of September, almost three months to the day before Pearl Harbor. Waiting on the dock at Brooklyn Harbor, amid the chaos of government officials, police, families, friends, journalists, and photographers, were my grandmother's sisters and their children. Once my father's family disembarked and passed through customs and on to a safe welcome on American soil, they stayed in Brooklyn for a short time before moving to the Upper West Side of Manhattan. Incredibly, my father and his family were staying a half a block away from where my mother and her family were living on Ocean Avenue, but their paths would not cross again until one afternoon at the Museum of Modern Art fifteen years later when they met and fell in love.

After Brooklyn, my grandparents lived in various hotels and never resettled in an apartment or home. My grandmother lived at the Park Royal Hotel on West 73rd Street around the corner from the Dakota until her death in 1980. My father resumed his formal education after a two-year hiatus and was enrolled first at the Rhodes School, where he met Monroe Rosenthal, his best friend and, as we often teased, significant other. Together, they switched to the Dwight School and graduated in June of 1942.

On January 23, 1942, an enemy U-boat attacked the *Navemar*. It sank somewhere in the Madeira archipelago off the coast of Portugal. The German propaganda machine claimed a British submarine sank it, which only underscores the acute danger the refugees were in during their harrowing journey across the Atlantic four months earlier. In a race against time, they won their freedom while the fast-moving tsunami of organized genocide enveloped and annihilated 17 million other souls. Although exact figures are impossible to determine, upwards of 56 million people, civilian and military included, died during the course of World War II. The world had never imagined such a catastrophe could become a reality.

CHAPTER 5

Unraveling the Chaos: A Kid at the Dwight School

On February 27, 1942, just six months after arriving in New York, my father presented his essay, "A Survey of the Military Situation," to members of the faculty and his fellow students at the Dwight School. Having been swept into the vortex of history, he used his paper to impose order on the chaos of his past by analyzing the machinations of the enemy as the Allied Forces pushed forth to crush the Axis. What is remarkable about the paper is an eloquence that can be earned only through experience, and the depth of his knowledge of geopolitics. Worthy of a seasoned journalist, it was delivered by a boy of seventeen, whose third language was English, only five and half months into his new American life. He used the only sources he had: the radio, American newspapers, and those around him who had survived the same circumstances he had and who had some perspective to offer. This is the speech he delivered, with his grammar and punctuation intact:

February 27, 1942 4:30 PM

Members of the faculty, fellow students:
It is very difficult nowadays to be accurately informed. Through a continuous barrage of false news, sent out by hundreds of radio stations, we must detect the facts. But, with a little study of propaganda methods we are, most of the time, able to obtain a fairly accurate picture of the war.

This war is very different from previous wars, because it is not merely being fought between armies. . . . [E]verybody is involved, civilians as well as soldiers. We can even go so far as to say that civilians are just as much in it as the soldiers are. Here in the United States, naturally, this does not apply literally, as it does in England and in Russia, China and in Serbia. But we too are affected.

But let us leave the totalitarian aspect and come to the war between the armies. I think we all realize that there are no separate battlefronts. What happens in the Pacific is closely connected with Libya as we have seen. What happens in Russia is closely related to the problem of whether the Turkish army is to remain passive or not. Consequently, let us begin by examining our own position in the Pacific, now that more is known about what is termed the Pearl Harbor Disaster. I think we can do away with that term. It would be wrong to minimize the damage done and the losses; but Uncle Sam's fleet is far from destroyed or erased from the map, as the Japanese have loudly proclaimed. The darkest point about the matter is actually . . . that it happened.

The series of Japanese successes in Asia is incontestable. The Nipponese grabbed Indochina, until then under the control of the so-called Vichy government, swallowed Thailand, knocked out Hong Kong, swept through Malaya, took Singapore, parts of the Netherlands' Indies, and New Britain as well as part of the Philippines, but only part of the Philippines! There General Mac Arthur, who fully realized how difficult it would be to defend the islands when he accepted such responsibility, is giving Japan a sample of the steel of which America is made! His gallant 20,000 are fighting without either sea or air support, an enemy more than ten times their number, an enemy well provided with tanks, aeroplanes, artillery and ships. Not only are our gallant 20,000 holding their own, they are plugging ahead! The other day we heard the most startling news: General Mac Arthur is counter attacking, advancing 6 miles along the coast of Manila Bay. He is hacking away at the enemy after a sudden slackening of Japanese attacks. Observers believe that the Japanese commander has abandoned temporarily the plan to take Batan peninsula; another Tobruk! Furthermore, the Japanese only occupy the most important of the 700 islands, and as long as the American troops will be there, the Philippine islands will be of absolutely no use as a supply base for the invaders. The price they paid so far is greater than most of us hoped. On the sea, the Japanese knocked out, in addition to the losses at Pearl Harbor, which as I said before were to some extent exaggerated, 2 British battleships and 2 dozen or so United Nations ships of all kinds. We have now reviewed what the Japanese have taken. Let us now consider their losses: official Washington figures published in February show that 112 Japanese troop transports and warships have been sunk or put out of action during the last 3 months by the UN.[1] The American Army, Navy and Air Forces alone have shot down 245 enemy planes as compared to 48 US planes lost. These figures do not include the enormous losses inflicted by the US squadrons with the Chinese army.

This shows that whenever American planes are in action, most often one against six, their crews and pilots are superior in quality. Whenever there has been an equal fight, it has ended in a disaster for the Japanese. On land they suffered a terrible defeat at the hands of the Chinese at Changsha. With the town and surrounding area they lost about 46,000 men. Then came the battle of Macassar Straights in which Dutch and American surface and under water craft as well as bombers were said to have sunk or badly damaged more than 100 ships, the entire convoy. The enemy not only lost ships, but, what is equally important, great masses of war materiel and thousands of troops. They took Macassar and parts of other islands, but at what price?

When we look at a map we may see how valiantly and effectively the Dutch were and still are fighting. Not everybody realizes what they have been courageously sacrificing by ruthlessly destroying what they built up in years of toil, sweat and labor, rather than leave it to the invader who wanted to exploit it. At this time, the Japanese are attacking Java, but only after many futile attempts have they made a successful landing. It is there, too, that the US Navy had great victories.

In Burma, things are not going too well; apparently there is not enough materiel available, and Chinese forces have to be brought over a very long route, it is always the old story: too little, too late and not enough air support. The Burma road itself can be written off as a supply line for the time being at least. This, however, does not necessarily imply the loss of the road proper, but the proximity of the enemy makes the use of the road impracticable. Thus the Allies will have to find another way to supply China. Either to complete new road through India over the Himalaya to China, or through

Russia. This latter arrangement seems to be the one agreed upon right now.

There may even be a way to save Burma by a Chinese counter offensive, a thrust into Thailand, or what would even be better, into Indochina. In the latter, the Allies should not have any scruples concerning Vichy, which in that area has not feigned to keep up its so-called neutrality. Furthermore there would be a fifty-fifty chance that the French garrisons there would join the UN and turn their arms against the enemy. Talking about Vichy, there is another very important spot the Allies should closely watch: Madagascar! Diego-Suarez, a harbor on the northern tip of the island, is the only major naval base left in the Indian Ocean which can accommodate ships up to 26,000 tons. There are excellent dry docks and repair shops. Last week, rumors were circulating already, that the Japanese had demanded naval bases there. What happened through Vichy's sell out of Indochina ought to be a warning! Furthermore, I don't think the French would ever fire at the Americans! As to the French fleet and North African Empire and Martinique, the puppet government of Vichy is said to have given assurances to the US not to give aid or support to Germany. But, what are assurances of men under the Nazi heel?! Actually, I have talked with people having seen the German officers' military missions, economic missions, armistice commission and tourists (or whatever they call themselves), spread all over Dakar, Casablanca, and Tunisia. As for Martinique, there is persistent suspicion that German U-boats are operating from there, the nearest European base being too far away, unless the Germans have built special long range U-boats. So much for Vichy.

Let us now turn to Russia. When Germany attacked the Russians in June 1941, things looked pretty dark right from the first day on. German reports dealing with millions, with the Russian air force wiped out completely. At least twice a week, many people gave up all hope. Others said: "Let's see what happens when the Germans will have reached the old Polish border where the famed Stalin line was supposed to be." But, when the Germans smashed their way on and on, meeting considerable resistance, but always advancing steadily, those too thought it was all over; a revolution would break out in Russia and a peace treaty would be signed. That was the general belief at least. Well history has proved since that they too were wrong! The war went on in the old style, according to the German communiqués. Moscow was caught in an enormous pincer movement. The government and foreign legations have moved to Kuibyshev. Leningrad was about to fall, Rostov, Odessa, Karkov, and Orel fell. In the Crimea, Russian resistance was said to have been finally broken and Sevastopol was about to be taken. But suddenly, as if by magic, the Germans were stopped. The Russians had thrown into battle fresh troops of the Serbian armies. The Germans began to admit stubborn fighting, and suddenly on or around November 28th, as one was waiting for Moscow's fall, Rostov was retaken by a victorious Russian Army. German communiqués were reassuring, saying that it was merely a strategic retreat, "caused by Soviet Guerrillas," but Sevastopol did not fall; and the Germans, ready to leap over into Caucasia were thrown back. The Nazis began to grumble something about winter lines and bad weather, and Russian stubbornness. They bitterly complained about "senseless Russian destructions," the Scorched Earth Policy, which by the way was very effective. But, the Russians decided to make the most of winter. Moscow was relieved: the Huns had to take a terrible beating and were thrown back, Leningrad was freed, Mohaisk was reoccupied and today the Russians are about 30 miles from Smolensk and have reached the Latvian border.

Last Tuesday a Soviet communiqué announced the closing of a giant trap, locking up about 96,000 Germans. One arm of the pincers runs roughly along the coast of the Gulf of Finland, the other covers the area near Staraya Russa in the direction of Lake Peipus: a second pocket, horseshoe shaped, is limited by Nevel near Vitebsk which is in German hands. Rzhev in the middle and in the south is limited by a point approximately 30 miles from Smolensk. The latest reports say that the Soviets are systematically cutting the Nazi armies to pieces and destroying division after division. So far, the Germans have refused to surrender, obviously in hope to break out. In the south, the Russians are meeting stiff resistance in the Karkov area, but further below, they were reported to be advancing in the direction of Dnipropetrovsk. In the Azov Sea area they were reported to have outflanked the Germans by driving a one-hundred-mile wedge into Nazi lines, evidently to close a pocket around Stalino. Russian guerrillas are playing havoc in the rear of the German lines and are a great nuisance to the Nazis.

The Russian air force, far from being doomed, is said to blitz the Germans in their good old, own way. All this must have made a good impression on General Field Marshall Adolf Schikel Gruber, because he made up his mind to fire his general staff and take over "personally." Immediately following this, a total of eighteen generals, if I counted right, were officially reported to have either died from heart failure, or something. But, since the great general took over personally, the Germans advance to the rear has been considerably accelerated. . . .

That is the situation today in Russia. The German reverses do not mean that they are permanently beaten. No, but the invincible Germans have been beaten. It is true, when the British smashed a German invasion attempt with their RAF in August 1940, they had enormous casualties. But they have never even admitted that they tried. In Libya, the Nazis got some beating from the British RAF, but this was no disaster, as they suffer right now from the hand of the Russians. As to further developments of the Russian offensive, it is hard to make a forecast based on facts. The Russian aim, naturally, is to kick out and destroy the German armies. As the Russian ambassador to Washington said the other day, and I quote "We do not insist on exclusive rights," he declared when talking of Russia's pride to have been first to take the initiative from the Germans, "We are quite prepared to let others have a share of our pride!" unquote. He also predicted that, if the Allies could open another front or two, Hitler would be through by summer. This statement, however, should be treated with caution. Such an opportunity, he went on to say, should not be missed, because errors made in diplomacy should not be repeated in strategy, the peace having been lost! So much about Russia.

Now what about England and the British Empire? The British are at a great disadvantage: they are spread over the whole world, and when their forces are concentrated on one spot, the enemy is likely to attack somewhere on the opposite side of the globe. If they spread their forces equally over the world, they would be weak everywhere, and would lose everything. Thus, England has to sacrifice something, so that she may not lose everything. It is not merely a problem of manpower, but also of long supply lines and supplies. But, time does not allow for a discussion of this very important subject. The problem of manpower could be relatively easily solved, if the British were willing to grant political independence to India. Not only is England reluctant to grant the freedom, but also in London one is not inclined to give arms to India's millions. Russia and the whole world however are appealing to England to open another front, so as to forestall an eventual Nazi spring offensive. When Stalin appealed last winter to the English for a second front, Prime Minister Churchill despite heavy criticism, turned a deaf ear to all pleas. We can now see that the English would have taken a great risk, had they opened a second front. They would have been unable to send simultaneous reinforcements to the Far East and Lybia, to keep enough troops in the Middle East to helps the Turks in case of need, enough in the homeland to block any desperate attempt to destroy the English in their home. Thus, it was wiser to wait.

But, there is one possibility, which could be very successful, would not need too many troops, or too much material. I am thinking of the indomitable Serb armies under the Yugoslavian war minister, General Draza Mihailovic. It may not be commonly known, but the Serb patriot troops occupy between two and three fifths of Yugoslavia. The Germans, too busy or unable to destroy these troops last summer when the Serbs reoccupied large parts of the country, have now before them a well trained fanatical army which is estimated to number more than 100,000 men. Where these men are supplied from, is a mystery. There were reports saying that Russia was supplying these troops by air. Mihailovic is said to be using Russian aeroplanes. Latest reports indicate that the Yugoslav armies have opened a general offensive. So far they are said to have reoccupied the area around Sarajevo. In the southwestern tip of Montenegro and in Bosnia, the Italian armies are reported to "have hastily left" the towns of Podgorista, Cetinje, Bar, Rogatisa, and four more towns of names I am unable to pronounce. Would that not be the ideal place to establish a front? It is easier to stir glowing coals than it is to start a new fire . . . Especially when matches are scarce . . . The establishment of a front there would have the great advantage of hitting the enemy at his weakest spot. The words "Balkans" and "sudden explosion" are often named together. Furthermore, it would leave open two possibilities: an attack on Italy or in the direction of Rumania Czechoslovakia, or even in an effort to make a junction with the Russian front. Considering reports coming in from Italy, this ought to be not too difficult.

The question of a spring offensive brings us again to England, to the battle of Dover Straits. To many, it has been a riddle why the Germans transferred their ships from the Atlantic to the North Sea. One of the ships is even reported to be in the Baltic, being repaired. The official explanation from Germany was simply that the ships were withdrawn from Brest, where they were of no use; to the North Sea, in view of the spring campaign. One of Germany's reasons was naturally to get the ships out of Britain's bomber range. As we have seen already, it did not help them much because RAF bombers have been blasting Kiel for the past nights, and Germany has admitted considerable damage in an official communiqué. But the other reason is not clearly perceivable. There have been persistent reports about heavy German fortifications being built along the Norwegian coast. On Friday the radio reported that German newspapers were discussing the possibility of Allied attack on Norway, apparently trying to prepare the Germans for something of the sort. By the way, the RAF is giving considerable attention to the port of Trondjem, and a British submarine was reported to have sunk a German cruiser of the Prinz Eugen class, off Norway. Although the submarine has been named, there were no further reports on the subject, however, the attack on Norway is a possibility.

Thus we conclude this survey of the military situation. The vastness of the topic made it impossible to give a more complete report in a relatively short time, but I hope to have given you the most important facts.

Thank You.

Fifteen months later, my father was drafted into the US Army. This opened a new chapter for him, a chance for some autonomy from his parents and a place to really adapt to his new country. Happy to be part of history as it happened, he painted in his letters home an often touching picture of life in the army, with beautiful descriptions of war-ravaged Europe, food, friendship, and camaraderie. Both an outsider looking in and an insider looking out, he ofttimes felt like a war correspondent with a duty to describe life as he saw it happen.

I, as an armchair traveler accompanying my father on his whirlwind journey through his letters, often have had a sense of voyeurism. His memories were my path; his story holds the clues to the mystery of his youth. Details can be researched with such ease nowadays that I could place myself where he was and bring up the most minute of artifacts. One of the most striking things to observe was the silence of the refugees as they passed the oncoming troops during the occupation of France in the old newsreel footage. The muteness of the victims as they advance toward their unknown destinies is intensely powerful, contrasting with what my imagination conjures as I listen to my father tell his story in the Shoah Foundation interview. In reconstructing his experience as I translate his letters, in the truest sense I am my father's ghostwriter.

PART TWO

The Long Road to Ritchie

CHAPTER 6

Drafted

News reports from CBS and NBC radio echoed in his head as my father left his family residence at the Clarion Hotel on West 79th Street and walked downtown on a lovely Memorial Day morning. Farther west, the oldest living Civil War veteran led the parade up the FDR Drive. My father's draft noticed warned: "Willful failure to report promptly   at the hour and time specified is an offense punishable by military authority. Bring with you sufficient clothing for three days. Draft Board 31." Since he was early, he decided to pass by Carnegie Hall to see what he would miss. Posters for upcoming events lined the wall on 6th Avenue. The New York Philharmonic was hosting a memorial concert for Rachmaninoff that week and on June 21 a memorial rally was scheduled for the Jews lost in the Warsaw Ghetto Uprising. Satisfied, he picked up the pace and walked the rest of the way to the draft office on East 59th Street.

Not yet a citizen, he was summoned by the US Army to report for duty on May 31, 1943. No doubt he was out late the night before, carousing with his best friend, Monroe, and discussing geopolitics, a debate that would continue throughout their lives. Early wake-up calls were never a part of the routine. They would often carry on these conversations from their respective bathtubs, talking to each other over the phone and smoking with their eyes closed as they governed the world and solved its problems. He was never the robust athletic type, and other times he must have set forth with pipe in mouth and an ascot tucked into his open collar. What must they have thought of this long and lanky eighteen-year-old boy from another country with a very proper continental accent, when he arrived at the induction center?

The small group from Draft Board 31 was sent by train to Fort Dix, where they arrived by two o'clock that afternoon and were placed in Company M. His first impressions were good, and he was happy enough. They were assigned four men to a bungalow. By the next day he found time to write home for the first time, describing his experience. I suspect no one had any idea that my father's need to communicate would amass in a collection of over seven hundred letters! And that was only the beginning of reassuring my grandmother that he was not being starved or worked to death, that all manner of food was available to him and what he ate was his choice and his alone! In fact, on that day they were the first to be fed. In stark contrast to his family's sixteen months on the run when they scavenged for food, at the mess were sandwiches, fruit, donuts, Coca-Cola, ice cream, and creamy milk, all for the taking. Next they were given their equipment: four uniforms, raincoat, mess kit, and toiletries and sent straight to medical for a physical and vaccination. By the time they were done with the preliminaries he was exhausted. Lights out!

For at least the next three weeks, communication from and to the outside world was not an option. His transition into the army would be made easier by two contacts whom he was to look out for. One was a Mr. Ohren, and the other was Robert Oppenheimer. Who they were exactly has never been clear, but from the letters they seemed to have held important positions in the military. It was probably our old friend, Mr. Kresser, the ex–intel officer who put my father in touch with them. He held on to these contacts and waited to use them to his greatest advantage.

It had already been recommended that my father become a translator. He took tests, making sure he scored as low as possible on anything other than the intelligence test. He scored 42 percent on the radiotelegraph test and demonstrated that he had no talent for mechanics. This would be his pattern as he tried to control his destiny in the army. Fort Dix was a way station, and he would leave within a week. During a routine interview exam he made a point of describing his past health issues in hopes of not having to go straight to basic training. Use my mind, not my body, and I'm all yours, he thought. He found himself among other Europeans and befriended a Hungarian and some veterans of the French army who had been there for a month. The Hungarian had experience and could show him the ropes. He found it surprising that a bed could be made so perfectly and that, if it was a off by even a millimeter, it was wrong. I never knew that my father could make a bed.

The first week consisted of working in the bakery and volunteering at the "Orderly Office." Every day was a learning experience and a new way to avoid rigorous training. A blister on his foot was an opportunity. Lance it, answer to "sick call" in pain, and be exempt from duty. A voracious news buff, he spent the day devouring the *New York Times,* paying attention to troop movements and biding his time until his real training started. He was so quick to come up with excuses that he developed a reputation amongst his peers. The next day he developed a deep need to see the chaplain. Since he was on the army's time now, my father tried to work around their schedule to fit his needs, which meant that he was not above a little religious comfort if this meant he didn't have to train in the heat of the day. He felt stimulated by the company of the other refugees. It didn't take long before he met three Russian coreligionists with whom he spent his free time. One was a psychologist, and the other two worked with G-2, the Intelligence Service. He garnered more vital information from them than from anyone he had encountered thus far: temporary camp had no importance, and once placed in a more permanent camp, their treatment was better and the most qualified were of value.

June brought with it the smells of summer in the country, in contrast to the heated canyons of the city that offered his family little relief. Fort Dix remained pleasantly warm, and my father often found himself left to his own devices. He quickly learned that if no one told him exactly what to do, he should keep his head down and stay out of sight of acquaintances and superiors. The free time that this afforded him allowed him to read, do his laundry, and drink beer! So far, it was a vacation. The "Jeeps" (new recruits) wore zoot suits or the more formal "sun-tan" uniforms. The former were their work uniforms, and my father wrote that they looked like convicts or that they had escaped from the circus. The official response to "Are you a soldier?" was "Hell no, we're just Jeeps and that means shit!" It was their official salute. Officers didn't like to be saluted by the new recruits, so ever the provocateur, my father saluted every bar he saw outside of his company area. He seemed overjoyed to wear a properly pressed uniform that highlighted his sun-tanned features.

My father reported all of this in his letters home. When he wrote, he literally dressed the set: "Please excuse the way this letter is written, but I am at the Service Club, sitting on a couch and writing on my knees. A radio, 4 ping-pong games, 2 arguments and a general brouhaha are also responsible for the salad my letter is!" He concluded with what became his motto, "Qui vivra verra!" (Time will tell, or, literally, "He who lives will see").

Food was an issue between my grandmother and my father from his first days in the army and would continue to be throughout his service. As her control slipped away, and stories of the raging war on the continent blanketed newspapers and newsreels alike, I can only think that some kind of post-traumatic stress manifested itself. Her suffering continued as her only son was now off to war, and a future for which they had almost lost their lives was once again uncertain. What must it have felt like to send a child off to the same war that caused them to flee their homeland in the first place?

The *New York Times* seemed to slant its views in favor of world opinion that somehow the Jews were to blame for the scourge. The front pages from that May reveal article after article reporting the "over reaction" of American Jews to the Warsaw Uprising, and that this behavior would have grave humanitarian consequences. It was a rough political climate for a refugee entering the army. People were systematically slaughtered, and to stand and fight was wrong?

Before long, my grandmother started to send cream-filled chocolates, prunes, and fruit. Dad was unable to stop her, and this routine of an excess of love in the form of care packages and exasperated protestations would happen so often that, as I translated the letters, I found myself laughing out loud. If he truly needed something, he would describe it in such detail that very often there was an accompanying sketch.

My mother remembers that, after the war, when she and my father were first married, her mother-in-law would arrive for a visit with bags of delicacies from Bloomingdale's and the Eclair bake shop. As she would empty one bag, my father would refill the other so she could take it back. My mother would stand there and watch this odd match, wondering: Why?

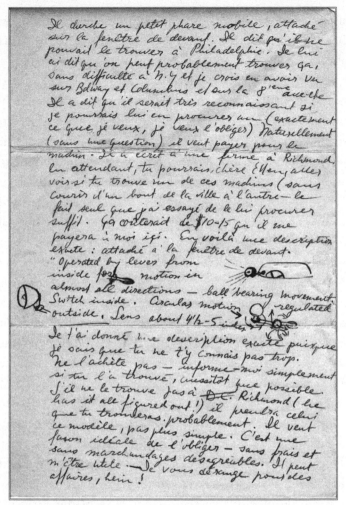

My father often included sketches in his letters home.

* * * *

They left Fort Dix too early and he missed his chance to speak to Robert Oppenheimer the night before. The sergeant wouldn't let him. Dad was supposed to contact him to see if he could get around the traditional training route, but then transfer orders came suddenly, and they packed up and left camp. His deep Asiatic eyes stared out of the troop train window as it rumbled past the many small towns on its way south. Since most of his comrades were bilingual, they were almost sure they were headed to the top secret military intelligence training center, Camp Ritchie, near Frederick, Maryland. When they passed through

Baltimore, they were sure it must be the camp near Washington, DC; then they passed through DC and were left wondering if perhaps the destination was Missouri, where a lot of his comrades were.

It was 7:30 when they pulled off the main track onto the rail spur that connected to the camp. His perspiration dampened his new uniform and formed a Rorschach pattern on his back as he stretched and gathered his gear, before descending the metal steps into the evening heat of a Virginia summer, weighed down with equipment. Their destination had been Camp Pickett. As my father got off the train, he noticed how out of the way the camp seemed. Trucks were waiting for them at the railhead. Looking around, there was nothing but nature in sight. As the trucks pulled forward and he began to focus, he saw that the camp was as big as a city. Their commander greeted them with a friendly smile, surprised by the mixture of languages he heard, as the new recruits entered the mess hall. He apologized; there was no fresh meat to feed such a large crowd. No fresh meat, but an assortment of food with unlimited portions. My father could always make do whatever the circumstances, but this camp reminded him of Lakewood, the famous New Jersey resort. It was clean, air-conditioned, and enormous. Free time meant waking up at eight o'clock to a hotel-style buffet, complete with morning papers. The open-air theater seated hundreds of soldiers. This camp was brand new and had every amenity.

The recruits were all assigned to the medical corps, qualified or not. That was the army's way of administering the refugee soldiers. They got new uniforms that resembled those of the African Corps: they looked for all the world like German soldiers, some of whom would later be held as POWs at Camp Pickett. The men settled into their new air-conditioned barracks. My father put his radio on his footlocker and tuned it until WOR came through the static. The big band sounds of Duke Ellington filled the barracks and wafted out the windows into the night. All he wanted to do was get to the "Chairs With No Middle Club" and sit on the latrine and read in quiet. Instead, the place was packed, with everyone snap-snapping and foot-tapping to the beat of the music while he fought for space. Café Society was a distant memory.

The "Latrine Society of the 3rd Company C" at Camp Pickett was the army at its best: six toilets facing each other, the boys on the thrones in various states of undress, a big game of dice in full swing. If a table was placed in the middle of the toilets, the soldiers could play poker, which they often did, especially after payday, betting their military wages. At 9:30, lights out, the club was filled to capacity. They went there to read, write, and smoke, and sometimes even for personal reasons. In the latrine, there was equality among the ranks, and sometimes even a "social" encounter with the sergeant. On that particular night, the guys passed around a photograph, and when his corporal got an eyeful of my Aunt Ellen, he said, "Pffs . . . she's really a knockout, gee!" He begged my father to write to her mentioning him and arrange a date for when he went to New York on leave. Sure, why not work that to his advantage too? Total strangers, many of whom were away from home for the first time, in the shared climate of an army bathroom. My father finally found a spot and read the *Baltimore Sun*.

Morning came and with it reveille. Well, at least it was at a more civilized hour than at Fort Dix. After a full breakfast, he took a twenty-minute jeep ride across camp to the hospital for an X-ray and urine test. They gave him a "light duty" slip, which didn't expire until nearly the end of his tenure at Pickett.

CAMP PICKETT, VIRGINIA   June 11th, 1943
    Today I was at the hospital for an examination—by order of the Sgt.—who after having heard my history and read my letter (which the commander of the company kept) was very nice. Everyone tells me that he's a nice fellow. They took an X-Ray and a sedimentation rate. Until there are new orders and the test results are back, I'm on "light duty."

Just as well: the thought of exerting himself made him hungry and in need of a nap. He found a patch of grass and wrote a letter home until it was time to get together with his bunkmate. Usually spot on in recognizing accents, for some reason my father couldn't place the source of this fellow's. It turned out he was Parisian and had been a photographer for *Life* magazine. More often than not, my father found himself surrounded by other refugee soldiers. He and the Frenchman wound up being "fire wardens" together, which was advantageous: in case of emergency, all the others had to deploy to the woods, while the fire wardens were left behind to file a report with the office.

He played up his tubercular past until he felt it was becoming a potential roadblock to a promising future in the army. It was too much of a good thing, and he was afraid that if he overused this excuse it might actually derail his aspirations. It had been a tool; time to put it away. He was called to headquarters for reclassification. That night, the honorary president of the Latrine Society of the Third Company C squeezed out a spot in the latrine, propped his writing paper against his knees, and wrote to Mr. Kresser. The man had taught him well during nearly a year and a half on the run. My father loved him and felt indebted to him. He wanted to share news of his progress:

June 16, 1943

Dear Mr. Kresser,

We have here Turks, Danes, Greeks, Italians, South Americans, French, Canadians, and—lots of Germans (non-Aryan and Aryan, and there some of the latter are anything but sympathetic). Well, when my turn came, I "let 'em have it!" I made good all my claims, especially in French, on which I put great emphasis for several reasons. The Frenchmen there told me that only 10–15% of the people who claim French really know it. When I sat down at his table, I started out full blast. He saw on my record that I was not French-born and was quite startled. He went over to the table with the "Spaniard" and said: " Listen to this one, he's GOOD!" The Spaniard answered: "Didn't I tell you?" With the Frenchman, as always, I did the most business. It's funny; I have had the same experience many times now. . . .

Mais revenons à nos moutons.

They asked me and about ten other fellows—out of an initial group of ca. 30–40—maybe more—to write a short biography, especially mentioning background, education, traveling experiences—and all that in the claimed languages. I started my letter in <u>French</u>—naturally (it's pretty rare—most everyone there knew German), alternated paragraphs in German and French and wrote one paragraph in Spanish. They wanted me to write in Italian too, but I explained in the letter that I couldn't write it. (I was interviewed in 4 languages.) I think I made a very good job of it— considering the short time I had. I wrote in very concise, accurate language.

. . . I gave a good picture of Belmunt as a 1st class school (International with a capital I) and sanatorium at the same time. They said that they're first going to check my medical record at the hospital. But since the report filed there states that I'm, at present, in good health, this probably won't jeopardize my transfer to Camp Ritchie in about 3–4 weeks—I hope!

Everybody here in the office tells me (I talk to everybody, or rather listen to everybody) that I am as good as there— in Intelligence. There are 2 grades of linguists: translator and interpreter. Translator is the higher and I was originally recommended for that.

I'd like to "talk" to you about so many more subjects, but time is worth gold here. I hope I'll soon find time again. I am glad that your family—civil war—is subsiding. My mother writes me that you want to get operated. I suppose you know what's best in your situation.

Sincerely Yours,
Walter

P.S. Your impression of Camp P. does not seem too good. I can assure you that this part of camp is just about the "jackpot" as far as camps are concerned. Everybody says that.
W. W.

He was almost nineteen now and had grown into a tall young man, looking almost like a descendent of a Hong Kong Chinese, with his slicked-back hair and those exquisite eyes that had just the right slant. He was a quiet listener, absorbing information. He had a personal stake in the outcome of this war. He had suffered and been tested long before his American comrades were drafted. His mind was on strategy. For now, Europe was as in a dream, recalled by a small breeze or when the sun gave off a certain light. These moments would remind him of how much they had left behind. He was listening for a way back. He wanted to go home again.

The brittle yellow pages of his letters brim with life. Every Coca-Cola stain, smear, or cigarette hole has an explanation and an accompanying apology. Any scrap of paper was used to fulfill his need to write. And he would write anywhere, at any time he could, sometimes standing on the troop train traveling to and from leave, always describing where he was and in what position while he was writing. As I translated the dizzying stack of letters and read the newspaper articles folded among them, I also played the music and watched the films to which he referred. It was all there, soundtrack included. If he fell, I dusted myself off.

At Camp Pickett, army life took on a routine of work and evasion of said work. Free time was spent at the Service Club, a show, or a movie, or simply honing his laundry skills by scrubbing his underwear against a washboard to whiten them. He was particularly proud of this accomplishment and joked that he would make a good husband someday because of it. He never did his own laundry again—God forbid! The entertainment at Pickett was phenomenal. It's no wonder he felt as though he was at a resort. He saw Fred Astaire and Jane Frazier live. He was safe, extremely well fed, was making new friends, learning, and enjoying himself—all while earning a salary and receiving a stipend from his parents.

Boredom was my father's nemesis. During classes, he often pulled his sunglasses over his eyes, leaving one ear perked just in case his teacher dropped a nugget of information that would be of later use. Sometimes he complained that he was so bored he could fall asleep standing up. During one anatomy and physiology class, hearing that blood was made up of red and white cells, he perked up just enough to find that the guy in front of him had fallen asleep and slumped forward in his chair with a thud. The sound jolted him out of his daydream, and the whole class got punished. Information was carefully packed away to be used once on an exam and then, in the case of the blood cell lesson, not for six decades until he was ill, when white cells were of keen interest as their count rose and fell, an indicator of just how sick he was.

My father was bursting with a certain kind of enthusiasm, and he had the charisma and gall to take full advantage of his situation. After all, as a civilian he had been chased, shot at, bombed, and yet lived, never really to speak of it again. So, coming from where they had been, having seen some of the worst of humanity, this was a cakewalk. He had attitude and elegance and played the part of refugee soldier like a professional. He wrote home about the "right way, the wrong way, and the army way," was undeterred, and showed confidence early on that he would serve at a higher level. Image was everything. He could not be thought of as a momma's boy. He had already made enough of an impression with his health issues and mail call. He was clearly dependent on his family and deeply devoted to them, but they needed a bit of control imposed upon them. They had definite ideas about how he should proceed with his military career and the expectation that he would remain as close as if he were living under the same roof. His letters were their lifelines. Not one to be fussed over, he nourished a seething antagonism toward his mother in particular because of her overabundant attentions. He included his parents in the process through his letters, but ultimately he was directing this show and would have to live with the outcome. As soon as he felt smothered, acrimonious words flowed from pen to paper, marking his determination to keep his family at bay.

Shortly after his arrival to Camp Pickett in June 1943, he wrote: "This is not a Boy-Scout camp; it is a military installation. . . . I don't get passes to visit my parents, if my parents come and visit me . . . and I would not make this request . . . and have no intention of making a fool of myself in the eyes of my superiors. . . . Don't get the idea to come to the village nearby. There is no fence from which you can see me even if only for ten minutes."

Up at 5:30, KP duty until noon, the rest of the day spent wearing a gas mask on bivouac, eating rations that were not to his liking. By the time they reached their barracks, it was 10:30 that night. There was something appealing about bivouac that was so contrary to what he knew. My father felt a sense of freedom in breaking away from the protected cocoon of his mother's constant and fearful worry about his health. It tested his manhood. It gave him strength and inched him closer to being a regular American guy. In the woods near the base, he put up a tent with a medical student from Baltimore, happy to have found an intellectual equal. They talked the entire time. It reminded him of a picnic at his Swiss boarding school—Europe never far from his mind. Then the news: all of his friends were going to be reclassified and sent to Camp Ritchie the following week. Number C173900 would be the only Jew left in his barracks, and the only European left in his company. Useful action had to be taken, so he filled out an application for citizenship. What a birthday!

To add insult to injury, the deluge of cards, letters and packages from home kept coming. He complained that it was enough to open a small store. Thankful for the check that fell from one of the cards but outraged by the embarrassment of riches, he had a lot to say to try to staunch the flow. Free time was becoming more precious as his training began in earnest, but every letter, telegram, or package needed a response. He had been away seven weeks and had written home at least fifty pages worth of letters. In turn, more telegrams, packages of chocolate, mandel bread, wool socks, fruit, and even a zoot suit came to him at mail call. He felt like a complete fool when he received eight such packages in one day. Half of them contained rotten food: he threatened to send the packages back unopened if he ever received such a thing again. In one package, he found two prayer books, one large and the other small enough to fit in a pocket. With a more courteous tone, he explained to my grandfather that he unfortunately had no use for them and would bring them home on his next visit, which had been delayed because ten men went AWOL and returned the next day at noon. The entire platoon was punished. Passes were earned and easily revoked; a thirty-six-hour weekend pass was a luxury.

Anyway, the prayer books were symbolic relics of a life not of his choosing. His strong-willed atheistic tendencies were supported by newfound freedom contrary to the orthodoxy of his father. During his boyhood, there had been structure to his religion. He would hold his father's hand as they walked to temple on a Sabbath morning. On the High Holy Days, my grandfather wore the customary high hat of the observant Jew. My grandfather's principles were supported by five thousand years of religious history. My father's principles were based in part on the five thousand years of survival skills that Jews have acquired from being under the constant threat of annihilation. Zionism became the religion to which my father held a steadfast allegiance. Atheism was his choice, a badge of merit earned from the courage it took to survive anti-Semitism:

June 20, 1943

. . . I made some really interesting observations on the subject of anti-Semitism here—and I learned a little about the character of the "rishes" in the working and peasant classes (in the North). The enemy propaganda has done irreparable damage. The guys I'm talking about were rustic and without education; their "ideas" on the origins and the goals of this war are from the authentic "D.N.B" [died not battle]. What is worse is that one cannot even have a discussion about their conceptions, because these people have no intelligence and do not and cannot follow an argument to prove the absurdity of their ideas. It is later than we think.

My grandfather remains a mythic figure in my mind. Having never met him, for he died long before I came into the world, I know little about him. He was an elegant, stern-looking figure with a restrained smile that barely shows in photographs. Some say he helped the poor and needy but would not help a family member if they had the finances in their background to help themselves. The overriding detail that surfaces is that he was not kind to my grandmother. They led separate lives, living in the same hotel, and he went as far as to bring his mistress to the United States after they came. The philanthropist was a philanderer.

Antics and evasive behavior aside, my father was in the army to do a job. This was an opportunity to contribute to the demise of those who so profoundly affected the course of their lives. His fellow American soldiers could not have understood, let alone empathized, and they were beginning to get on his nerves. They were being trained to fight and protect a world away from their own. After all, the last battle fought on American soil was the Civil War.

The army was an education on the finer points of being an American. Concealing his origin, his ethnicity, was a matter of self-protection. He worked on being a real American by studying his comrades' gestures and accents. My father found himself surrounded for the first time by people from all levels of American society, amid behavior that was uniquely American, and he was clearly not used to it. They ranged from humorous to outrageous, and he fought against the constant threat of mediocrity. At times, there was blatant anti-Semitism. He was something of a loner, which is of little surprise. When he was small, he was protected behind walls of safety against the rising wave of anti-Semitism. He developed his inner resources and enjoyed his own company. He had to, and was happiest with his eyes focused on the newspaper or a good book if he was not engrossed in challenging repartee. When his American comrades became too much for him, he thought nothing of going off by himself. He had no tolerance for seeing how many glasses "Johnny Dope" could put under the table. He was happier going into Blackstone to a good restaurant and seeing a movie like *One of Our Aircraft Is Missing*. On the one hand he spent a lot of energy trying to fit in and be one of the "guys" in the army. Later on, when we were children, he did not want us to present ourselves as if we were a typical American family when we spent time abroad. He was a chameleon, and we were expected to follow in his footsteps.

Before they came to the United States, the refugee soldiers had suffered different degrees of victimization, which varied from escaping the Nazis to actually having survived a concentration camp. They were a special group of people, with very useful skills that could not be replicated by their American comrades. They knew intimately the cultures from which they had escaped. They spoke the languages fluently, their native customs were a part of them, and they could blend in with the enemy. Many of them would be granted citizenship while in the army. When these men returned to Europe, more often than not as Ritchie Boys—intelligence men trained at Camp Ritchie—the rescued became the rescuers. These boys were not necessarily used for their physical prowess. Among the most educated of the soldiers, they were valued for intellectual gifts as well as their backgrounds. Most importantly, they possessed a desire for revenge, and this was a chance for them to prove in a very anti-Semitic climate that they were indeed proud to serve their new homeland and supported the ideals of our democratic society. Although avoiding as much mindless work as he could get away with and proud of his skill at it, my father was very serious about accomplishing the task at hand, and nothing was going to get in the way of that. Though he wasn't a pacifist, he felt he could accomplish more using his mind as his weapon.

Finally, the news that he had been waiting for arrived: the Field Selection Board for the Army Specialized Training Corps (ASTP) accepted my father, contingent upon his completion of basic training. Following that, he would be sent to a college of the army's choosing. It was unusual for a nineteen-year-old to qualify for anything but basic or an engineering course in the first place, but due to his special qualifications, he applied for a more advanced series of language courses. He was up against heavy competition and was skeptical of the army's red tape. He sensed there would be a catch. There was always a catch, as Joseph Heller famously illustrated after the war. He would fill out as many applications as he could for different positions, and whichever ball fell first he'd grab.

Meanwhile, menial tasks would be repeated countless times over the twelve weeks at Camp Pickett, until training ended on September 12. Whether he was peeling potatoes, waiting tables, or spending an entire morning bandaging and transporting the "wounded" to the mock barracks hidden in the woods as a stretcher-bearer for his squadron, he turned light duty into an art form. He made the monotonous daily grind an adventure in relaxation. Instead of carrying the soldiers on the stretchers, they made them walk the twenty meters, taking the shortest path to the medical station. They sneaked around the sergeants guarding the path and arrived weighed down and swearing, pretending to gasp for air: "Damn, these guys are heavy!"

Eventually, it was his turn to be wounded. He slept for half an hour, comfortably hidden and tucked in under the cooling shade of a large tree. Then, after having his leg bandaged, my father was taken to the station, where he waited for his bandages to be inspected. It was just another opportunity to read the headlines in that week's edition of France-Amérique. De Gaulle had become the permanent chairman of the new committee for national defense. "A victory for the Jews," he wrote.

He would actually look at the week's schedule and plan his sick calls. This practice allowed him ample time to think of excuses. While some of his fellow soldiers became enraged at his ingenuity, he "rose 20%," as he said, in the eyes of his two Italian bunk neighbors, who appreciated his "gold bricking." Again and again, he would skillfully avoid laborious tasks. If he wasn't stretched out on the night guard's mattress as acting air raid warden, he was on phone duty, answering calls. And if it wasn't that, then he volunteered to guard while the others were on a twelve-mile march: two hours on, four hours off, from 5:00 p.m. to the following morning at 6:00 a.m. On KP duty, he arranged boxes of jam in rows while reading the *Times* all morning. When he had a rendezvous at headquarters after lunch one day, he arrived back at his barracks to find his corporal standing with his chest inflated to capacity, blocking his entry. "What have you been doing all afternoon, Private Wolff?"

He thought better than to tell him that his meeting had taken only an hour and that during the rest of the four hours he was gone he had had a great afternoon getting his hair cut and relaxing in the cafeteria enjoying coffee, ice cream, and soda while reading. Instead he said, "Corporal, I went to seven different offices and was kept waiting at each one, but you should have seen the terrific blond WAC at HQ!"

When in doubt, redirect. My father embodied the expression, "Don't work hard, work smart." He had heard it said that the desire to reduce or avoid one's work is characteristic of a civilized man. Don't look for mountains where there are valleys. In the meantime, worried that he was being overtaxed, his mother suggested he check himself into the infirmary for a rest cure.

In answer to her suggestion, his response was, "Don't worry, and don't make up stories that I'm sick. Only the 'Führer' has intuition, and his aren't paying off these days!"

In some ways he is an accidental observer. Not there by choice, he'll stand as far back as he can get away with in order to go as far ahead as possible. He cuts the figure of a soldier in silhouette, looks just like the others, yet in his own mind he's different. If he stands apart and alone in the crowd, it might be enough to move ahead. Where he will go in the army isn't yet clear, only where his motivation stems from and the seemingly distant goal of becoming an intelligence officer. Barely two months in, he quietly bucks against the routine imposed on him, by going out of his way to spend as much time as possible at his leisure— and succeeding. He eats, drinks, reads, and seeks out entertainment at the base as if he's in charge. He seems to move through Camp Pickett as if his superiors were there to serve his pleasure. No matter what his assignment on a particular day, he is somehow off on his own, left of center and marveling at the ease with which he makes the best impression with those who can advance his position, while fooling them into thinking he is right there performing with the pack.

He remained that dashing figure later in life, a quiet, impressive presence whose intellect was his shield, a barrier to the world and his family. It was respected and at times even reviled when we couldn't compete with it. I know why. I've read over his class notes from high school, the army letters, and the notebooks he saved from Columbia University, where he majored in business after the war. I have looked at the doodles in the margins, seen the voraciousness with which he consumed, digested, and used his knowledge and breadth of experience. He could hold himself back or move ahead by choosing the quality and quantity of the information required of him. Where others excelled in order to be placed, he excelled to engineer his placement.

Accommodating new ideas, aspirations, and thoughts, and with the certainty that he would soon be protected by the cloak of citizenship, his youth swatted away the demons from his past. This in stark contrast to my grandmother, for whom those demons must have persisted long into her every night, pushing her closer to the stillness of her old age. His mother's unrelenting anxiety propelled him to succeed. America had its own deep-rooted racism, but for this young Jewish refugee, freedom held the promise of a bright future.

He also would have high expectations for his children. My father provided us with the best tools but didn't show us how to achieve success, just as I was given a metal box that left its new owner with a million questions and no father to answer them. His method was quite Socratic. The simple term of endearment, "Chère Mamo," and the words that followed told only part of the story. The letters at face value are a charming account of the everyday life of a young soldier, until the reader realizes what led to their innate simplicity. Weepy eyed, I occasionally reach out for my father as I grow to understand that when we are faced with great pain, we build a hard, protective shell.

My mother remembers my grandmother taking her aside before their first-born son's funeral to soothe her tragic loss: "You will have other children." Omi clasped my mother's hands in hers, offering those quiet words of strength, a buoy in a sea of despair. War had hardened her resolve enough to lead another down a path toward strength. My father, hardened with pain, was always cool and distant. It was easier to stand strong and straighten his neatly knotted paisley tie and his perfectly pressed hand-made shirt from Hong Kong, tucked perfectly into the pants of his three-piece Harris tweed suit, than offer the warmth that could save an emotional life and build a lasting bond. He was afraid. That made him vulnerable. He relied on his intellect and grace to carry him forth.

* * * *

Craning his neck, leaning out over the platform, he could see into the distance the lights of an ultramodern train appearing. White beams broke through like two moons from dark clouds. It pulled into the station. He boarded the steps and walked into the air-conditioned car, stowed his gear, and settled into a seat. Civilian trains were infinitely more modern and comfortable than their military counterparts. What seemed like moments later, my father took off his makeshift blindfold and opened his eyes to the bright morning sunlight beaming through windows.

"Breakfast!" called out the MP.

He took a deep breath and repositioned his seat from its fully reclined position to the fully upright one. The mere motion of it still caught him by surprise. It was so modern and so American. He slipped his glasses back over the bridge of his nose and glanced at his watch. Six a.m. What a night! He had twisted and stretched. They had left Camp Pickett at eleven the night before and were left standing outside with their gear for the better part of an hour before the trucks came and brought them to the station. It was after one in the morning when the wheels of the train headed north. The steady sway in tandem with the rhythmic music of the train cutting through heavy, humid night air had pushed and pulled his thoughts in and out of dreams.

He arranged himself, brushed his dark hair back with both hands, and pulled his uniform tight. He straightened his tie and regained a more formal composure. As soon as he opened the door to the dining car, he was hit with the dense aroma of the meal to come. His stomach protested, loudly rumbling, hunger recalling memory. He briefly thought of Lyon, where the only food to be found in abundance for a family of stateless Jews hiding in plain sight was the salty ham that became their mainstay. He found a seat at a table among the other twenty-five soldiers. The ceiling fans rotated softly above them, pushing the artificially cooled air. He ate, intermittently staring out the picture window while chatting with the others. Sipping from the thick-rimmed cup, wishing the Americans would call this warm watery drink by any other name. If he couldn't stand his spoon straight up, the coffee would never earn his approval. Shortly afterward, the train whistled into the station and slowed to a grinding halt. The only one from his company, and only one of three from his battalion at Pickett, he walked into the station waiting room, sat on a wooden bench, and dozed off. At nine o'clock, he was awakened from a fitful sleep.

"All ABOOOARD!" the conductor yelled as the soldiers approached the train in loose formation. This one was so old that it seemed to date back to at least the Civil War. They reached Blacksburg, Virginia, at ten and were greeted by a smiling lieutenant. "Men, your orders were revoked last night. I have no idea of what to do with you."

During World War II, Congress passed an act whereby the US Army was running the nation's single largest educational program in the country's history. Created in 1943, it was a short-lived program that ran for less than a year. The Army Specialized Training Program (ASTP) and the STAR unit were established to make sure the army had enough college-educated men to fill more technical and intellectually demanding positions. More than 200,000 soldiers passed through the programs, given at over two hundred colleges and universities across the nation. Yale's enrollment fell so short during the war that bankruptcy threatened to shut the school's doors. Courses were offered in everything from engineering and medicine to personnel psychology and in thirty-four different languages. Campuses were turned into makeshift army camps, where the soldiers interacted with other students but were required to adhere strictly to military rules and dress codes at all times. The regular military population frowned upon these soldiers, who were generally thought of as not experiencing the "real army." They studied hard and played equally hard, using breaks to play cards or catch up on the many activities offered at the campus service clubs. Not surprisingly, the soldiers in ASTP programs were to a great degree Jewish. Once their training was finished and they were placed, their technical abilities were so strong that prejudices harbored by the rest of the military fell away and they earned the respect of their comrades. The end of the program came suddenly, because it failed to gain the political and public support needed to continue. The general opinion was that ASTP was a way of protecting the soldiers who came from the wealthier classes from real combat duty.

Rumors circulated that they would be sent back to Camp Pickett, to New York to the City University, or maybe even to Penn State. The Georgetown unit had already closed. Finally, at noon, the higher-ups decided to keep the soldiers on the Virginia Tech campus, test them, and place them. They spent the afternoon filling out forms and scheduling tests they would be given the next morning.

Reveille sounded at six twenty the following morning. "Tant pis," my father thought as he rolled out of bed. Too bad. Left to his own devices until seven, when breakfast was served, he tuned the dial on his radio until a local station with the morning news and weather broke through the silence. He heard the reporter say, "Temperatures are cooling, leaving the dog days of summer behind us."

Since Virginia Tech was also closing, the soldiers would only be given refresher courses before transfer orders came through. He filled out the required forms and requested placement somewhere closer to home. His superiors promised to make every effort. Unfortunately, in the army nothing was certain. As he filled out the paperwork, my father ran across a stumbling block: he did not have enough college. He was just nineteen. Since he had spent the year prior to being drafted attending night school, he wrote down one year and left the credit box open. The issue would be addressed at his upcoming interview.

For now he was subject to placement tests. To determine their ability to learn a foreign language, soldiers had to translate English to an artificial language and vice versa. He also took a French test. This exam he found insulting. He breezed through it and smoked a cigarette at his desk and wrote a letter until the others were finished: "I pity the poor chap who'll interview me if he can't speak the language. I'll speak so fast that he'll understand every third word. . . . After that, I'll have an interview, after which, if all goes well, I'll take tests for two other languages, provided it's not Japanese. . . . It takes two to learn a language, a student who wants to and a teacher."

First thing Monday morning, he met the poor chap whom he pitied. She was actually a nice woman. He spoke slow enough for her to follow, but she eventually asked my father if he wouldn't mind continuing the conversation in English. Scheduled to have a hearing, he armed himself with a letter of recommendation from France Forever, Charles de Gaulle's agency in the United States during the occupation. It was founded eight days after the armistice with Germany in June 1940. My father had worked for France Forever for a time before leaving for the army, and he had brought the letter with him as proof positive that he was up to task.

Virginia Tech was as enormous as it was magnificent. The college had dozens of buildings spread out over a well-tended green. They slept three or four to a room, with a bathroom down the hall. Hot and cold running water too! Again, the army was like a vacation destination. My father was so charmed by his new surroundings that he sent half a dozen postcards home from the university, showing the various buildings. The Service Club at Virginia Tech was in a building that looked like a French château and felt like one of New York's chicest hotels. It had stores in the basement that sold civilian and military clothes, two drugstores, a post office, barbershop, bookstore, game room, and billiards. There was an enormous dance hall and rooms with club chairs, and radios. At the dining halls, they ate at tables covered with white mats. He found Army, Marines, and ROTC dressed like the cadets at West Point among the civilian students. His group was organized in paramilitary fashion, with insignias on their shirt indicating their name and company. Beyond the buildings, he found a little lake, tennis courts, and lawns for games. The town of Roanoke was small but neat, with bus connections to Washington, DC. As usual, he found ample free time.

Finally, by the end of September, he had been accepted into the language division of the Army Specialized Training Unit (ASTU) and was taking some classes at Virginia Tech:

September 22nd, 1943
"I'm writing you a letter from one of my most interesting classes—this one being English. I just had a really interesting class, on the French military. I'm one of the youngest in the class; there are Sgt.

1st, Sgts., etc.—all intelligent men, who have a pretty good knowledge of French; the instructor knows the language in depth, but
there are students who know more. Before that, I had an American
history class. It's good to be in a classroom again! To live with and
listen to intelligent men!"

My father was relieved to be placed with the more advanced
group of students ranked in the top 5 percent. The other 95 percent,
he said, wouldn't find an enviable destination on completion of their
more grueling training. He would rather have sweated over books
than a stretcher! For the moment, though, the atmosphere was relaxed,
and he boasted that during classes students were permitted to read
newspapers, write, sleep, smoke, or chew. The civilian professors didn't
care in the least. He lived almost as a civilian. School ended at four p.m.
and at noon on Saturdays.

The cooling temperatures of autumn brought rain. The
monochromatic blue-gray stone buildings lining the paved paths and
avenues on campus took on a more dramatic tone. With the change of
season came a sea of political change, as Italy capitulated to the Allies
and Mussolini was forced to surrender. Hitler's impenetrable wall was
crumbling. The shield of propaganda had created a sense of safety so
formidable that the German people and the Allies believed the Reich
to have the strength of a fortress, and that had aura had also weakened. "The Mediterranean was now an Allied lake," wrote a columnist
in *Time* magazine, September 20, 1943. "Militarily, the Allies were not
now pacing fretfully around Festung Europa—they were on the draw-
bridge of Hitler's fortress. And since the fortress has no roof, the whole
of the German heartland lay exposed to constant attack." Meanwhile,
my father attacked my grandmother's letters analyzing the current
geopolitical shift in power:

VPI Blacksburg, Va.   The 23rd of September 1943
My Dears,

Thanks for your letter today, that is for the one dated Sept. 20th.
M. Le Curé has his head in the clouds if he thinks the war will be over
by Christmas. He seems like a good chap but not too knowledgeable
about politics—despite the contacts he appears to have. . . . It's very

nice of M. Le Curé to believe they're preparing me for a post in DC, or to "teach French soldiers." For your information, the course Military French is for <u>all</u> the language students in the STAR Units as well as many civilian students at many universities. . . . He should use his imagination less. Keep him close—but don't court him too much. He could become <u>very</u> useful when I've finished my studies. To that end, be good friends—but don't let it become an obsession.

I have the impression that a good number of influential people (not in the Army or the Marines, etc.!) entertain the most idiotic notions about the length of this war. Mrs. Rosenthal says that La Guardia and Morris have similar illusions. There will really be some disappointed people at Christmas! It's true that we can see an end now—it's not the way that it was a year ago—but please consider the facts: the Boches forces are still quite formidable, and their leaders are fighting on with nothing to lose. As we know all the characteristics of the square heads[2] there is little reason to wait for a popular uprising.

The victory over Italy—who wouldn't fight for the Boches, as is demonstrated by the fact that they're fighting them now— isn't a good barometer. Remember the fierce battle that the enemy waged in a very small corner of Tunisia. I have at least the impression that something completely unexpected is brewing, and that the European war will go on until the summer of 1944. As far as Japan is concerned, there's no point in discussing your point, chère Mamo. Come on! A little more reason, and a little less wish fulfillment! I'm writing you in this way because your financial actions shouldn't be influenced by this kind of nonsense. . . .

As it is almost 23h, "Bonsoir, Mesdames et Messieurs, bonsoir mes Demoiselles." I have to go wash my pen. It's stopped up and has started to leak all of a sudden.

Kisses,
Walter

* * * *

Days sped by and rumors flew. My father and his friends hoped that, wherever they were sent, it would be as luxurious as the VPI campus. Finally, as September came to a close, he got his wish.

VPI, VIRGINIA   September 28th, 1943
My Dears,

Thank you for the two packages that we're in the midst of enjoying, and for the letter.

I learned from the Times that Rosh Hashanah began this evening. I had the impression that the holiday started later. And so, my apologies and Happy New Year!

Chère Mamo, you say I like to eat while studying. You seem to have the impression that I'm studying. I do practically nothing—I go to classes (this morning I forgot a few), I read, sleep, or write letters—sometimes I listen. No homework, no exams. This morning the Military French prof left, and a Franco-American and I took charge of the class; it was fun for a change. It was about terms having to do with the maneuvers of an armored tank division.

My friend told me that he has seen my name on a list for Yale (1 ½ h. from NY). We don't yet know when it will be published, but we will leave on Monday. That would be ideal. It seems that I won't get a furlough; I'm really mad about it, because there was ample time for one and I haven't had my furlough. To show our contempt, a group of us are growing mustaches.

I just saw another of my friends, and he said he had definitely seen my name on the list. I have moxie!

I've already bought my PFC chevron: we call them Praying For Corporal.

To eliminate any possible misunderstanding: Michigan is no longer in the running. The telegram was sent before this letter. I have to go to bed now.

Good night, and again, my best wishes for the new year.

Yours,

Walter

*   *   *   *

Seemingly overnight, the Yale campus filled to capacity with soldiers pouring through its wrought-iron gates. The monochromatic tone of the uniformed men struck an unfamiliar chord with the undergrads, who now made up the minority. They had no choice but to stand by and watch as a parade of soldiers carrying cardboard suitcases at their sides marched past and into the dormitories, which caused some friction. In their minds, perhaps, a degree from Yale would be devalued by the less-educated swarm, hovering around three thousand soldiers, that had invaded campus. Universities such as Yale had a strong history of anti-Semitism and had "Jewish quotas." They were much less likely to admit students or give tenure to faculty with Jewish backgrounds. This changed during the years after the war, but through the ASTP program the school had no choice but to welcome the soldiers, Jew and Gentile alike. By year's end, there were between six and seven thousand soldiers in training on campus, the largest student population in the university's history. My father's letters give us only part of the picture of Yale in 1943.

A few men stood by scratching their chins as 250 men lined up for the second time that day and waited for role call before "Old Shit And Guts" let his men go with an "Aaaat Eeeease!" The 1st military platoon, made up of all those over six feet tall, and the 4th academic platoon fell out of line and relaxed their posture.

"Well, banzai! This is loony," my father said to no one in particular.

He and the other soldiers marched in formation across campus toward their classes. The sandbags stacked against every building on the Yale campus was an ever-present reminder of what could happen. The sandbags offered the ivy-clad buildings some protection from bombs dropped during an air raid, unless of course there was a direct hit. From the top of campus' tallest buildings, soldiers manned lookout stations equipped with telephones and would report any damage or fires.

As he was marching, my father spotted a familiar face. As he drew closer, he recognized Alfred Whitney Griswold, the future president of Yale. My father was now mapping the path that would take him back to Europe. He aimed forward with one eye to the past and the other steadily focused toward the future. The autumnal New England weather, the crisp, cool air after a long hot summer, reminded him of a fall day in St. Moritz. When it rained, the overcast skies darkening the heavy buildings was a reminder of Brussels. He politely stopped the approaching man, who recognized him as well. Professor Griswold was the head of the ASTP program at Yale. They shook hands and exchanged niceties.

"There isn't anything that I can do about it, Private Wolff. I presented your case to the colonel, but in view of the fact that you are a language specialist, the Army is of the opinion that you should have no difficulty with a hard language such as Japanese."

"Well, thank you ever so much for your efforts and good day," said my father as they continued on their respective ways. How the head of the special training programs in languages and civil affairs at Yale and this private first class were first introduced isn't clear, but my grandparents were friendly with Professor Griswold as well. Fortunately or unfortunately, my father had passed his written and oral exams in French, German, Italian, and Spanish. The brief encounter assured him of his standing in the specialized training program, but he had other ideas.

Later that weekend, after a rushed and grumpy departure from Grand Central Station in New York, my father hastily bid his parents and Ellen goodbye and ran into his Swiss friend, Brandeis, on the train back to New Haven. They talked all the way back to Yale. Brandeis told my father, "I'm convinced they'll deploy only the crème de la crème for a tour in Japan."

"Well, I think that by staying average, neither too high nor too low, there's very little possibility of getting assigned there based on my studies." Translation: Do as little as possible, stay slightly above the fray but not too far in the lead, and he won't be their first choice for the Pacific Theater.

When the conductor called over the loudspeaker, "Next stop, Nuuew Haaven!" the two refugee soldiers gathered their things and stood by the doors as the train pulled to a slow stop, lining up with the platform. Before walking back to campus, my father stopped at the newsstand and bought a newspaper and *Time* magazine. He would have to ask his parents to pick up a copy of *France-Amérique* and send it along with his rubber-soled tennis shoes and shorts for calisthenics. The paper had been founded months earlier by French exiles. It was the voice of the Resistance and a forum for Charles de Gaulle, the exiled leader of Free France, with articles by impassioned journalists and first-hand accounts of Occupied France and war news. Unlike its American counterparts, *France-Amérique* published articles that came from the country's heart and soul that fueled my father's outrage.

One, entitled the "Extermination of French Jews," made *my* hair stand on end, so I can only imagine what it did to him. When I read it in the offices of *France-Amérique*, I could almost hear my father saying, "Now you see, Ninotchka, you understand what we were up against. I couldn't tell you before. You had to find out on your own."

Between the July 16 and August 18, 1942, 28,000 "Isrealites" were arrested in the occupied zone and interned in concentration camps of the Vélodrome d'Hiver and Parc du Princes. Over the course of the first weeks of October 1942, 35,000 Jewish families were brutally separated and exterminated. In September of 1942, the number of Jews deported from the "unoccupied" zone grew to 1,300.

There currently exists in France almost fifty concentration camps for the Jews. Women and children are usually sent to Beaune-la-Rolande. Then the women and children ages thirteen and older are transported to Poland and the Ukraine, where we completely lose track of them.

Children two to thirteen years of age remain, without any supervision, at the Pithiviers camp where a severe epidemic of Diphtheria is raging and where they are dying by the hundreds.

Much later I would learn that one of those fifty concentration camps was located in the furniture warehouse belonging to my mother's cousin, in the center of Paris.

Another article described in vivid detail what happened when one prisoner at a concentration camp fainted one morning and fell to the ground just as he lifted the handles of his wheelbarrow. He was taken away by the Germans. The next morning before reporting to work, the prisoners were forced to stand at attention, heads held high as the unfortunate man from the day before knelt on the ground in front of them, looking utterly gray, his temples bloodied. He had been beaten so violently about the head that one eye hung out of its orbit, suspended only by the attached nerve.

Yale marched to a different beat during World War II. Glenn Miller and his Army Air Force Band rehearsed and jammed for music-hungry servicemen in the dining halls before taking their uniquely American style to the troops abroad. Music was the greatest morale booster in the European Theater, carrying listeners through the war with the sounds of Swing, until Miller's plane went down and he was lost in the icy waters of the English Channel in December 1944 on his way to Paris to join the band as they toured France.

Before sitting down to his studies, my father "peeled off" another letter to his parents and slipped in a book of matches from Camp Pickett and an article from *Time* magazine. He was always fond of taking little mementos. He wouldn't be going home this weekend. With two upcoming exams and 165 pages of history to read after having received his books a short two days earlier, there was no time. Japanese was becoming easier as the weeks progressed; he was up to about 250 phrases. My father was determined to stay in the program, so visits home would have to be sacrificed to study. If my grandmother couldn't see him, she would inundate him with more packages from home. Pralines arrived along with a pullover sweater and pair of striped pajamas so big they were better suited to fit the oversized frame of his Uncle Fred, my grandfather's brother, who was in Marseille during the period before their escape. In the package, my father also found that week's issue of *France-Amérique* and a stock certificate from my grandfather. He was becoming a capitalist!

He finished his letter with the sentence, "Kyòo oua koré de yamamashiòo" (Let's stop for today). After mailing the letter, he returned to his studies. After more reflection, he decided he would do better to excel in history and his other classes but just glide by in Japanese. We have very different ideas about gliding by. My father took hundreds of pages of notes in Japanese class alone. The margins have been written in, words are underlined, and accents are drawn, all to aid in memorization and pronunciation. He had made much more than the slight effort that he led everyone to believe. He was only pretending to do poorly. If he had to prove himself, then he would do so at a moment's notice.

Along came more letters and packages. This time they contained shirts, gym shorts, heavy wool long johns, orange juice, and fruit. He gently threatened my grandmother that she would soon be receiving a large package of returned items from the store that she apparently thought she was helping him open. With a certain adolescent charm, he ended the letter by saying he would be coming for Sunday lunch at his favorite restaurant on 79th Street: Chez Mamo. He rather enjoyed the little trip to New York; it was fun. He'd call on his best friend, Monroe, still too young to be drafted. Since failing out of ASTP was not to his advantage, he settled in and decorated his room at Yale. He hung up maps and his sister Ellen's whimsical watercolors of Central Park, giving the little space charm and warmth, and lit the room with six different lamps he had collected.

An obvious awareness of design was flourishing. At this point, my father had no idea that one day he would become New York's king of lamps, accessories, and what I used to refer to as "Ready-to-Wear Furniture." Items purchased at his stores could be picked up or delivered, assembled or not, depending on the customer's choice. Advertisements for Bon Marché were a fixture on the pages of the *New York Times* for close to forty years. He was a trendsetter, a master at transforming Bauhaus designs into affordable pieces of furniture for a bargain-savvy consumer who insisted on great design. In the 1990s, the Bon Marché building was bought by the New School and renamed Henry Arnhold Hall—another bizarre coincidence, since they were childhood friends at Belmunt in Switzerland as well as fellow Ritchie Boys.

By November, phone calls and trips home became less frequent, while, paradoxically, paranoia about his well-being and temper seemed to be running high as he stayed in Connecticut on a more regular basis. He was not all that unhappy with the workload or the routine as it was. Quite to the contrary, he was dating a girl whom he took to see Noel Coward's madcap comedy *Blithe Spirit* at New Haven's Schubert Theater one evening after he finished sentinel duty. There were fewer letters home, and on the occasions when he did write he explained at length how much less time he had and that his parents and Ellen should lower their expectations. One night when he returned to his room to find numerous telephone messages from Ellen, who was worried that he had fallen ill, he had a fit. To keep up with the family's demand, he spent the long hours of class time writing letters instead of listening to lectures on military history, etc. He figured he was being more productive than the third of the company who took their siesta, while a third studied Japanese and the last third bore holes into the classroom walls by staring at the same spot for hours. Soon, an outbreak of flu brought Yale to its knees and almost sent my father to a sanitarium.

What follows is the funniest moment of my father's experience at Yale, before final exams and his transfer to Camp Grant in Rockford, Illinois:

December 20th, 1943

My Dears,

Thanks for the big package. I have enough stuff now to open a large store—I do not have the intention of doing so. I'll send back the underwear, and I hope you won't continue sending me things I really have no need for.

It was a pretty exciting weekend for me. I think, as you can tell from my previous reports, there has never been a CQ (Charge of Quarters) in our company with more to do. It started when I began my service at 17:45. A man from my company came in like a hurricane and told me his buddy had a temperature of 102.7 F. I put another guy in my place and went up to see for myself. I took his pulse: 100/min! I wrapped him up in some covers and went back down to the office. I tried to get hold of the Sgt., the Capt., HQ-ASTP, HQ Air Force, Navy Infirmary. Finally, I decided to take responsibility. I telephoned the hospital, asked them for an emergency ambulance—which arrived after an hour.

Afterward, we found out that 5 soldiers on guard duty (the commander included) had left camp and 25 men who weren't allowed to leave had also left. Telephone calls every 3 minutes for the soldiers: HQ, Provost Marshall, and 3 other companies wanted to know this or that on top of all the routine work that needed to be done. At midnight, I was relieved until noon on Sunday—12 hours, which I spent sleeping. After that, I had to keep tabs on each man who went to eat.

After that, a man whose father had died that morning asked for an emergency furlough; 10 phone calls to find our captain. I had to convince the guy not to leave camp without permission—despite the circumstances. Another 10 calls. Another guy from Philly called to extend his pass. It was getting crazy. Furthermore, the captain was in a bad mood because he didn't have his weekend, so he was quibbling and in general just hassling annoying me. After 1745 they relieved me for good, but at roll call part of my squad (I'm the acting squad leader [2 stripes]) wasn't there; [and] that had to [have been planned ahead]—anyway, it was interesting to manage a company. Because of the absence of the commander and the Sgt. I was absolutely the boss. I was automatically saying, "Co F, Charge of Quarters speaking!" The telephone operator said to me, "You are kind of busy today, aren't you?"

Well, I have to study for an exam the day after tomorrow. See you Thursday evening!

Yours,

Walter

*   *   *   *

In January 1944, my father was transferred from the ASTP program at Yale to Camp Grant, a facility built during World War I in Rockford, Illinois. The camp was so large that it served not only as a medical training center but also as a detention center for German POWs. During the three months my father spent there, he met refugee soldiers from all over Europe, including his friend Joe Poser's brother from boarding school in Switzerland, as well as others he knew from New York. In March he became an American citizen.

Two friends, corporals Baymiller and Gallenbeck, accompanied him as he marched up the grand marble steps into the Circuit Court of Winnebago County in Rockford. They stood as his witnesses when he became the first American in his family, raising his right hand to swear allegiance[3] and fidelity to the United States of America, along with the forty-eight other people who took the oath that day, promising to defend and protect the homeland against all enemies, foreign or domestic. My father was now free. No longer the stateless refugee, he would never be forced to wear politics or religion on his sleeve. He would never have to look over his shoulder ever again.

When the clerk examined his certificate of arrival, he looked up at my father and remarked, "S.S. *Navemar*, September of forty-one? Pheew, you're a lucky young man, you know that, dontcha?!"

"It's a miracle I'm alive, sir," my father said in response.

With his two buddies at his side to serve as witnesses, he said, "I do" so many times in the two minutes it took to become an American that he felt as though he was getting married. After they signed all the

necessary papers with my father's new fountain pen, the men walked
out of the courthouse, passing the statue of the Civil War soldier, and
went to the bar at the old Nelson Hotel for a toast. My father couldn't
help but notice that the weather was like Saint Moritz in May. The
azure skies melted the snow and wet the streets. He loved it when the
sun shone on a cold crisp day, often remarking that it was "Swiss-ish."
He didn't officially become an American for another forty-eight hours,
but over a fine vintage Coca-Cola they raised their glasses and, on
March 1, 1944, they celebrated Walter C. Wolff as he became Citizen
Wolff. The middle initial C was added in the army because Americans
usually have middle names. The C stood for nothing, but I know my

Camp Grant, spring 1944.

father and I know he chose it as a joke. WC, meaning "water closet," is on every sign on every bathroom door in every public place in Europe.

At Camp Grant, he couldn't get enough of the roast beef sandwiches and pineapple juice. Having never tasted such an exotic juice, he wondered where it came from. The innocence of some of his discoveries is funny. The things we're so accustomed to and take for granted were new to him even two years after living in America.

After lunch he returned to the barracks to find that someone must have stuffed the pipes again. It was so hot that the windows had fogged and condensation was dripping onto the sills, while sweat was rolling off the soldiers' brows. They were not supposed to open the windows because of the convoluted air conditioning system—one pipe pushed fresh air into the room while the other sucked out the used air. The communal radio played what my father called Kentucky hillbilly music in competition with his short-wave radio, which was tuned in tandem with the corporal's to WQXR in New York City. For better reception, my father used his helmet as an antenna to boost the explosive, rhythmic sounds of Tchaikovsky. The corporal, a violinist with the Minneapolis Symphony Orchestra in civilian life, raised the volume on his four-dial Emerson radio at key moments during the symphony. As soon as the trumpets blew into the string section, they upped the ante and blasted the hillbilly music. Tchaikovsky's crashing chords reverberated throughout the barracks, and the bluegrass fell away. Suddenly, the cacophony of sound was interrupted by the news: "Leaving trails of steaming vapor in their wake, United States bombers bound for Berlin destroy armament industries in and around the Nazi war capital. Their first daylight mission over the heart of Hitler's fortress, American bombers combined with British forces are pounding Germany with raids around the clock."

The low *ba-ta-ta-tam*, *ba-ta-ta-tam*, *ba-ta-ta-tam* of artillery could be heard in the background of the reporter's broadcast.

In all, sixty-eight American planes failed to return. But the next day and the next, American bombers returned in follow-up raids. Today, squadrons like these in ever-increasing numbers are taking the war home to Germany itself. In other news, Ralph Heinzen, a Paris correspondent, reports, "Back from her fourth wartime journey of mercy, the Swedish exchange ship *Gripsholm* arrives in New York harbor. Aboard are 663 Americans, home from Nazi internment and prison camps. Wounded soldiers, war correspondents, and diplomats are among her passenger list. They bring firsthand news of conditions in Nazi-occupied countries. Douglas MacArthur, nephew of General MacArthur, was attached to the American embassy at Vichy. 'We're very glad to get home. We've been thirteen months interned in Germany, and thirteen bad months for the Germans as well as for ourselves. Because in those thirteen months, Germany has lost the war. They know they're whipped, but they're wondering how they're going to get out of it. Last year, Hitler has lost tremendously his prestige, particularly as a military leader. All through Europe, there is a very fierce underground warfare going on against Germany. In every occupied country of Europe but particularly in France, there is this mighty organization of courageous patriots who are waging a war day and night against the forces of occupation.'"[4]

Cheers could be heard erupting around radios all over camp, as this barracks' battle for the airwaves ended and news of the real war poured through. For the rest of the afternoon, my father made himself comfortable. With his pipe hanging from his mouth, he leaned over his stationery and wrote letters:

> Cher Papo, My best wishes for your birthday. I hope you have a good year of health and prosperity, and I really regret not being able to be with you for your birthday. Well, c'est la guerre! . . . I hope the gloves are large enough. If they aren't, then you can send them back to me, and I can easily exchange them. If they get dirty, you can wash them with bath soap.
>
> The news from Europe is excellent. The situation is certainly much better than a year ago—at least an end is in sight, though I'm not expecting an immediate end. . . .
>
> Again, my best wishes,
> kisses . . .

When he was done, he folded the letter and enclosed it with the gloves for my grandfather. This lovely gesture would turn into an interstate comedy, with the gloves taking center stage as questions about size became part of several letters, ending with my father imploring my grandfather to bring them with him to Chicago when they came for a visit. When he couldn't find a smaller pair of gloves after my grandfather gave them back, he wrote, "Shall I send them to you anyway? It's better than nothing! . . . Cher Papo, do you want the gloves (the same pair you had), or what? It seems soldiers have larger hands than civilians—there are no smaller ones. Frankly, I don't know what to do."

Leaning back against the metal frame of his bunk, Dad settled in to read through his new issue of *France-Amérique*. It established, as he said, "contact with the old world, my old world, and the present." Every once in a while, despite his usual lack of emotion, the pathos comes through with sparkling clarity, and, from extraordinary details about the war's progress, its effects on him also seep through. He could have been called to battle at any point, and the letters would have changed dramatically, as they do later.

For now, they flowed home almost daily. During the two months that he was stationed at Camp Grant, my father sent home more than sixty pages of letters and telegrams. I wonder how much correspondence I would have inherited if he too had saved everything he received. In the immense amount of discussion and quarreling that filtered through the postal system, my grandmother's and aunt's passionate disdain for one another was a constant thread that wove through the fabric of the letters, the words between them corrosive for the rest of their lives.

At one point, my grandmother thought the letters had been censored and got nervous. My father had to explain that within the territorial limits of the US there was no censorship unless the military took a special interest in a person, but he clearly wasn't one of them. My grandmother also had the idea she could influence on his behalf anyone she encountered who had a connection to the army. He grew very concerned that she and her friend Junot were hindering his progress, and he wrote to make sure that only he was in charge of his "business." While acknowledging their good intentions, he told her there was really no point in trying, without access to the appropriate offices where decisions were made. Recommendations could be made, but only the War Department confirmed them, not West 79th Street. "Every soldier can be sent wherever the government wants, to New York, Texas, the moon, Mars, Europe, or Africa. . . . Read your newspapers. Do as you wish, but leave me and my affairs out of it!"

Omi also suggested that he get a room in town so he could bathe and take care of himself. My father had to assure her that the barracks did indeed have outlets for electric razors above every mirror, the shower room was entirely covered with aluminum plaques so there was an opportunity to shave everywhere, and every washroom had a footbath. This was the US Army, not the German army, but even with that rejoinder a steady stream of letters and care packages kept arriving.

Most of the guys my father met during the months he was at Camp Grant were ex-ASTP friends he made while at Yale and soldiers of the same caliber from other technical schools, like the private who studied Japanese at the University of Michigan. They hated studying Japanese so much that one night, while exchanging stories about the various language programs, they joked about forming the "Society Against the Propagation of the Japanese Language." He eased into comfortable familiarity with them, dropping some of his reserve. He soon discovered that his company was made up of platoons separated into groups of intelligentsia, illiterates, and professional athletes. The community of refugee soldiers was just contained enough that, if he wasn't running into friends he had made along the way in the army, he found old friends and acquaintances from Europe, including the brother of a friend from boarding school in St. Moritz.

Although he never encountered any anti-Semitic behavior among the men at Grant, a portion of the camp housed German prisoners behind guarded barbed-wire fences. That was when, for a brief moment, he contemplated a position as an MP. On several occasions, my father was used as an interpreter and, perhaps for the first time, did come face to face with the enemy POWs. He spoke to them in his best Prussian accent. Many of them had arrived on the *Queen Mary*, docking in New York after passing the Statue of Liberty, a far cry from my family's passage on the *Navemar*. The POWs came to Chicago in Pullman cars sitting on upholstered seats—all very civilized in comparison to Germany, where captives traveled by boxcar.

The prisoners at Camp Grant had surrendered in North Africa. After spotting the American army, they gambled for safe and humane treatment under the Geneva Convention and won. The United States adhered to the Geneva Convention rules to such a degree that prisoners were not only treated humanely but were paid a stipend commensurate with the rank of a US army private and lived in accommodations that far surpassed any in the German army. They were given army uniforms printed boldly with PW on the backs and every amenity to keep themselves clean; they had showers and toilet paper, and wanted for nothing other than their freedom. They ate better than they would have in Europe at the time and far better than if they had been caught by the Russian army, where rations likely would have to be supplemented by rodents they captured. German POWs in the United States eventually numbered in the hundreds of thousands, and very few tried to escape. In fact, while my father wandered the streets of Chicago with friends, some of the POWs were on work duty cleaning the streets. The thought behind their treatment was that if we followed the Geneva Convention rules, the Germans might do as well with their American POWs. They were eventually repatriated after the war, and some emigrated legally to the United States, making permanent homes here during the postwar years.

In my father's interview with the Shoah Foundation, he looks down while he speaks about this. He clearly sees their faces on the screen behind his eyes. When he is done with the recollection, the camera catches him again as he rubs his chin after admitting, "Each one of them I would have gladly killed with my own hands, but"—he hesitates for a moment and looks up—"I am not a killing person."

The slightest stumble or bad luck in my father's escape could have sent him north over the Polish border to Auschwitz. There he would have stared through a barbed-wire fence and lived on starvation rations, drinking green water for as long as he survived. The constant reminder that he could never take any portion of his freedom for granted is at the heart of my father's story. What an incredible sense of satisfaction he must have felt when he left camp for court as a stateless refugee and returned later in the day as an American. On his petition for naturalization, when asked his "present nationality," he wrote, "None." But when he looked across the fence or shouted orders to the POWs, his talent for compartmentalization took over.

Ten months in the army and my father still had not been placed in any kind of serious position. Camp Grant was disorganized enough for him to continue his practice of avoiding any of the army's grunt training and get away with it. Until he was able to transfer, he was up to his old tricks. Any time he had KP duty or anything requiring him to sully his hands, he would ask for a medical checkup, get new glasses, have his teeth examined, or even volunteer to wash windows at the clinic. His only complaint was that the camp was so small that it took less time to be seen for an appointment, forcing his return to whatever he was trying to avoid in the first place. Without much to do, he would often sneak an afternoon siesta. One day, he was startled awake when he heard footsteps. He jumped up and out of bed, standing to attention so fast that the sergeant looked at him and yelled, "Jesus Christ, Private Wolff, you must have a bad conscience. Get back to sleep!"

American citizenship, no longer being an "enemy alien" in the training ground of America's defenders, meant that he could now apply for reclassification to positions that his refugee status had formerly closed to him. A lot of permanent posts were open at three general hospitals being formed abroad. He thought about applying to one of those first, since they were located in safe zones in Casablanca or Southern Australia as opposed to the Pacific Theater where he was very adamant that he did not want to go.

In the meantime, he spent a lot of time in Rockford, which in 1944 was a two-hour drive from Chicago. It had a population of about 80,000, not the small village my father had imagined. There were buses, trolley cars, and all sorts of restaurants, shops, movie theaters, drugstores, and department stores just like he found in the East: Shulte, Walgreens, Liggets, Woolworth, Kress, and the list went on. It also had the USO, the likes of which he had never seen before. Housed in one building, there were two ballrooms, a swimming pool, a music room, enormous game rooms, a snack bar, half a dozen luxurious lounges with rugs and couches, and even a tailor. One day my father sat on a plush velvet armchair sewing his military rank patch onto his new coat. He could hear a near perfect rendition of Chopin's "La Polonaise" coming from a piano somewhere down the hall. While taking a moment to listen to the music, he happened to notice the magnificent quality of the fabric as he rubbed the cloth between his fingers: it was lighter, with longer wool fibers than usual. A lieutenant appeared from behind him and observed quietly as he struggled to stitch the patch on. He let him continue for a moment longer before he said, "Hello."

My father made a move to stand to attention, but the lieutenant stopped him. "At ease, Private. May I show you how it's supposed to be done?"

Faster than he could utter a response, the superior officer took the coat from his hands and began to sew the chevrons on for him. As the lieutenant finished his handiwork, a pretty young lady came into the room and brought my father a sandwich and a cup of coffee. My father looked at the lieutenant and back at the girl, incredulous. He stole an appraising view of the volunteer's derriere as it disappeared from sight, and reported in a letter: "Only in the US Army. Life is grand. The best USO in the world, excellent food and a chorus of pretty blond Swedes to serve me.... Only in the army. Rockford spends serious money on us, and lucky for me Grant is situated in the midst of a great crop of immigrants stemming from Nordic ancestry.... Uummf, pas mal!"

Several weeks after arriving at Camp Grant, my father became the personal tutor for a soldier who was originally from Portugal. He spoke no English but was multilingual and able to speak French, Spanish, Russian, and Polish. Dad was given a new uniform and relieved of busy work. Waldman had almost completed a medical degree at the University of Lisbon before he fled to the US. They communicated mostly in French, and following the same method as was used for the Japanese classes at Yale, my father began teaching his pupil. It turned out that Private Waldman left Portugal for political reasons. While he was in school, he was an active member of the Revisionist Party and a student leader of the Anti-Fascist movement against the Portuguese equivalent of the Hitler Youth group that was called Mocidade Portuguesa, a compulsory paramilitary group.

Camp Grant was turning out to be a lot of fun. He was having a great time with the other guys in his barracks and was becoming father confessor, general counsel, and wise man to all. Beginning to feel like their guru, he was glad to oblige. One private even consulted him about his upcoming marriage. His superiors became so dependent upon his language skills that they transferred him out of his platoon and into what he referred to as "Waldman's Illiterate Platoon," so that he could be closer to his charge. He didn't entirely trust this bunch, until he returned to his barracks shortly after moving in and found that they had put away his things, sent off his laundry, and made his bed in a gesture of appreciation. Just what the prince ordered—an entire platoon of soldiers who would now serve as his personal valets. To top it off, they gave him the one spot in the barracks in a corner area. After a while, he realized that they weren't all as dumb as he originally thought, when he learned that one soldier in his new quarters was an ex-editor of a democratic paper in Madrid, one was a Harvard graduate, and another who worked in Classification spoke French.

Not the type to sit for long without some ambition to push forward, my father was getting restless. His assignment as live-in interpreter made him feel more like a nanny. Although he was given a variety of other assignments throughout his stay, they were really just busy work. Very often he slept late and spent at least part of the day reading anything he could get his hands on to keep himself intellectually sated. Since magazines and newspapers were not enough, he bought himself a copy of *U.S. Foreign Policy: Shield of the Republic* by Walter Lippmann, the renowned journalist and author.

Tutoring and nights out with Waldman were fun, but he was disgusted with his student's lack of progress because he took no initiative to learn the language and my father couldn't tolerate anyone who wouldn't at least make an effort. He needed to find a way to get into the G-2 Intelligence Training Program, but as long as he was stuck at Camp Grant, he might as well make the best of it. He decided that the best way to teach Waldman to speak English was to go out socially with him. This way he might be forced into speaking English even if it was only to pick up girls. He was sadly mistaken.

One night they went into Rockford and saw the new Jean Gabin film, *The Impostor,* before going to the service club for a dance hosted by the B'nai B'rith Foundation. He wrote in his letter, dated February 17, 1944:

> I pitied my poor student who just stood there, unable to com-
> municate, I politely introduced him to my [dance] partner. He

smiled angelically and in the most pleasing voice started to swear like a truck driver in Portuguese, calling her everything under the sun. My friend from Yale, who speaks P[ortuguese], and I almost burst out laughing. I cannot imitate for you what he called her but it wasn't pretty. My little friend asked what he was saying, and I answered that he said that she was charming and that he really would like to speak to her, but he spoke so little English.

I tried to stop him to no avail. She asked me again what he was saying. I said he thought she had a "million $ smile." All of that in the sweetest voice with an engaging smile—he did the same thing with the lt. the other day—and he told me that he has already done it with a colonel once. If he does that again I'm going to break his head. We have so much fun with that guy!

As if Waldman's antics on the dance floor weren't enough, having caught sight of a photograph of Aunt Ellen he was smitten. Don Juan started a wartime letter writing campaign in Spanish in hopes of gaining a new pen pal in Ellen. Dad's letters were right behind his, cautioning big sister to watch out for wolves, because he was already engaged.

When he was off duty my father spent as much time as he was allowed in Rockford or Chicago sightseeing by himself or at one point with the young Swede he'd met. While in Chicago, my father ran into several more friends, one of whom was a decorated "Franco-Boche" (German-French) who had formerly served in the French army. He had earned two medals, including the Croix de Guerre, for acts of heroism. He was now in G-2, military intelligence, earned a good salary, and was certain to be commissioned shortly. He was doing extremely interesting work with prisoners but couldn't elaborate on the details. The mystery alone struck my father, and he felt even more ambivalent about joining the Medical Corps. With a new law sending soldiers overseas after one year of military service, my father could never be "an essential man" with the medical department because his post was provisional, and his friend was sure the army would never have 100 percent confidence in any German-born national. He would never be chosen for more "delicate" work. On the other hand, because he was not, as my father put it, "a first-class physical specimen," his chances for a more interesting post were far better than the others. In any case, even provisional positions such as an instructor were on notice that, as soon as orders came through, they could be shipped out from one day to the next.

After running into his friend in Chicago, he went to his commander and spoke to him about applying for a position in G-2. He found out he was eligible to enter General Intelligence, and he knew an officer at headquarters who would facilitate the process. His excitement was met with yet another wall of paranoia from his mother. He responded with exasperation, enumerating every reason why, specifically because "his physical value was second rate," he would be the perfect candidate for intelligence, because he could handle himself anywhere and, speaking as many languages as he did, he could always make himself indispensable.

Unsure of where his next posting would be but absolutely certain the army had something special in store for him, he wrote: "As our mayor Fiorello says, 'PATIENCE AND FORTITUDE' —The army directs, I follow . . . (after determining the direction)."

CHAPTER 7

The Ritchie Boy Takes On
the Pentagon

Somewhere on a troop train in Pennsylvania, the train sergeant opened the door to a car and, leaning a heavy hand on the seat, said, "May I have your attention men? Soldier, turn down that music, will ya? There's gonna be three men in each section for sleepin' tonight. Two on the lowa' berths, an' one on the uppah'."

"How do we know where we go?"

"You'll find out tonight boys, so at ease. Oh, and anyone caught smokin' in the berths will get KP and peel petatas for the resta' the trip. Is that clear?"

"Yes, Sarge," called out a chorus of men. The sergeant walked through to the next car. The men resumed their former adolescent contortions of relaxation, splaying out over the seats in every direction. Some of the guys sat with shoes off, lounging awkwardly on their seats, while others crouched in the corridors and played cards and dice. A couple of the fellas were reading comic books they had traded for. Before going into the train's lavatory, one guy who was leaning out of the train window pulled his head back in, dog tags clinking against the glass, and spoke over his shoulder to the black porter.

"Hey boy, you know where we're goin'?"

The porter answered politely, "Oh, no suh, that's one thing ahhhm not allowed to tell." The porter had been asked that same question many times before and sat back down on the hard wooden seat next to the lavatory. From another car came the faint sounds of a kazoo band playing "Auld Lang Syne." My father turned his radio back up and continued writing the letter he had just started.

April 7, 1944

My Dears,

   Praise the Lord—Hallelujah! The train is rolling east, southeast to be exact. We have just left Pittsburgh and our destination is X. But, as a good algebraist, I found a solution to the equation X + DC. We left Camp Grant at 4h (16h). It was an immense convoy. . . . . I was a little scared that they had changed our orders. But when they divided us into groups—and when my group was full of students—and when they put us on the two Pullman wagons at the end of the train, I was reassured. We had a Pullman with little compartments for 3, a restaurant wagon, service and all of the comforts. It's almost a dream. I'm with a really nice gang.

   My TSF is playing dance music—there is a cocktail on the table . . . from my destination X, I will telegraph or telephone you. I hope that my handwriting is excused. I am hoping that I will have a pass this weekend, but I don't know yet. I will come to Lakewood.

   Kisses

   Walter

   The Transportation Corps of the US Army directed the largest military mobilization in history from its nerve center in Washington, DC. Gigantic lit boards showed the direction and destination of every troop train and its location across the nation. WWII was a war of movement, and America's war machine was being dispersed all over the world. Army ground forces moved 30 million soldiers, troops, and machinery across the continental United States. By the end of the war, 7 million soldiers and 126 million tons of tanks, guns, and machinery had been directed to battlefronts all across the globe.

   The next morning, the soldiers heard: "Attention men, we're stopping at the next station. Be ready to get off."

*   *   *   *

April 7, 1944, my grandparents and Ellen were at the Laurel-in-the-Pines Hotel in Lakewood, New Jersey, celebrating Passover. My father had just arrived at Washington, DC's Walter Reed Medical Center to

continue with his basic training. The *New York Times* was awash with articles about the symbolism of Easter and Passover falling so close together.
A year after the Warsaw Uprising, the paper had taken a decidedly more
sympathetic tone as news of Hitlerite atrocities filled its pages. With no
assurance that freedom would prevail, Passover 1944 was a poignant
reminder that without a lengthy and difficult struggle, the world would
continue to confront the oppression of the Nazis. With millions held
as slaves in concentration camps and ghettos across the globe, people of
all faiths were urged not to give up the fight. A *New York Times* article
that same date asserted that the true definition of religious freedom
was creative freedom. As the most precious gift of our civilization, it is
what allows for rebirth and reconstruction after prejudice, tyranny, and
the devastation of war. Rabbis urged Americans at home and on the
battlefronts of every theater of war to prepare for the decisive blow that
would bring about the largest celebration of freedom the world had
ever seen. Provisions that included 7,000 gallons of sacramental wine
and thousands of boxes of Matzoh were made for all Jewish soldiers to
be served a Passover meal wherever they were stationed. Lieutenant
General Mark W. Clark, commander of the United States Fifth Army,
addressed a thousand of them at a seder near the Italian front in Naples:

"Tonight you are eating unleavened bread just as your forebears ate
unleavened bread. Because the Exodus came so quickly, the dough had
no time to rise. There was a time of unleavened bread in this war. The
time when it looked as though we might not have time to rise—time
to raise an army and equip it, time to stop the onrush of a Germany that
has already risen. But the bread has begun to rise. It started at Alamein.
It was rising higher when the Fifth Army invaded Italy. It is reaching the
top of the pan and soon the time will come when it will spread out . . .
and the victory will be ours."

Flowers and trees were in full bloom, accenting red brick buildings
and their black roofs. Walter Reed was impressive. My father could not
get over how each barracks was outfitted with a very small armoire for
every man, ice water on every floor, tiled bathrooms, chrome fixtures,
and shiny floors. There were automats for cigarettes, candy, chewing
gum, and nuts. The PX was a veritable department store. There were
restaurants and even a "bar," as well as a grocery store, cinema, recre-
ation rooms, barber, tailor, shoe repair, laundry, dry cleaner, and post

office. Mess halls were open for a full hour and soldiers could come and go as they pleased. Since passes to New York were given out only once a month, my father was perfectly happy to stay in town that first weekend and do some sightseeing on his own during his time off. He walked for hours. The cherry trees were magnificent, their flowers swayed in the warm breeze, blanketing the ground below them with a lush carpet of pink petals. He eventually stopped for dinner. As he entered the restaurant, he overheard a heated argument between a US fighter pilot and a waiter. Watching for a moment as they traded impatient gestures accompanying what was obviously a language problem, he approached. Spying the patch sewn to the soldier's shoulder that read "France," my father immediately understood how he could help. He walked closer and offered, "Pardon, est-ce que je pourrais peut-être vous aider?"

The pilot was rather surprised but nonetheless pleased to have been spoken to in French. He explained that there was a little "mistake" on his bill. The waiter had come to the conclusion that if the man couldn't speak English, maybe he couldn't add either. Grateful for the timely interruption, he introduced himself as Sergeant Pierre Bartella, from Paris. He and my father became fast friends and spent a good deal of time together over the next two months, going to as many night-spots as they could fit in to their schedules. During one evening out, they went on a double date with two girls they met at the Press Club, taking them to the smorgasbord at the Occidental around the corner from the White House. The two men made quite an impression, with their dashing uniforms and foreign accents. Hoping to spend the night in town, my father had arranged for a room with Mme. Aron, a family friend. Washington was going to be another pleasant sojourn. He was free from four in the afternoon until eleven at night; they got a pass once a month, and KP duty was mandatory only one Sunday the first month. More than enough time to enjoy the nation's capitol.

The family had not been together since the end of March. Omi's unrelenting efforts to control her son may have been soothing to her anxiety, but they were driving my father crazy. Yet, as clever as my father was, I'm beginning to think he enabled my grandmother's paranoia. If one knows someone will come undone at the slightest mishap, why on earth would the condition of one's feet become topic for discussion, as it was in more than one letter in April 1944? Was there really so little to talk about, or was there more to this?

Sunday came and with it his assignment for CQ (Charge of Quarters). He situated himself at the desk with his short-wave radio nearby. The phone rang. Tempted by the deliciously soft voice at the other end, my father responded flirtatiously with, "Oh, I'm sorry, he's not here right now. May I have your name and a number where I, uhh … I mean, you can be reached, and I'll take a message?"

My father leaned back in his chair and fondled the bowl of his silky briar wood pipe as he listened to the flirtatious voice at the other end. He blew out some smoke and with an equally flirtatious tone commented, "Eh, you have brown hair, how lovely."

Taking a chance he asked, "Do you have a couple of friends for two of my buddies, we could all go out together. It'll be a great evening, I can promise you that."

"Tant pis," he thought after he hung up. "First come, first serve. If she's as cute in person as she sounds over the phone, well then."

He cocked his head to one side, relit his pipe, and considered what a windfall it was to be back in Washington again. He had not been since his first week at Walter Reed in April. There was no time to waste. The first month had been relatively demanding, but not so much that he couldn't plan his advancement. The first thing he did was make an appointment for an interview at Reclassification. He wore a sharply tailored khaki uniform instead of the standard-issue green one. He paid close attention to every detail of his image by mirroring his civilian elegance and emulating that of his superiors. The interviewing lieutenant had listened carefully to my father and offered to assign him to the Medical Department of the Allied Military Government. Thinking on his feet, he countered the offer with every cogent reason he could think of for not receiving that assignment, until the lieutenant responded that he would take everything into consideration and that my father should make another appointment with him as soon as he was finished training at Walter Reed in May.

Feeling encouraged by the interview, he left the office thinking about who he could ask to write letters of recommendation on his behalf. When the time came to submit his application, he would be prepared. He scribbled a list of names, and next to each he wrote their position:

Joseph A. Beisler, Assistant Trust Officer, Manufacturers Trust
    Company
Professor Otto P. Peterson, Officer of the French Academy, Paris,
    France
E. F. Khun, Assistant Manager, Foreign Department of
    Manufacturer's Hanover Trust
Colonel F. A. Commandant William F. Howe, Army Services
    Forces, Yale University
Lee L. Rosenthal, The City Center of Music and Drama
    (Monroe's mother)
Robert L. Oppenheimer, French Embassy

When his list was finished, he put it away for later. On his way to dinner, he stopped at a drugstore. Spotting a major from the Adjutant General's Office (AGO) in one of the aisles, he casually walked over and started a conversation about the weather. They spoke for a little while until, satisfied that he had made a suitable impression, he excused himself and walked to the mess hall. Within moments, a colonel sat down next to him. With courteous reserve, my father nonchalantly asked about the medical service of the Department of Civil Affairs (AMGICA). He was told that assignments for soldiers outside the medical department were rare. My father explained his ambitions further, telling the colonel as he had the major that in fact he did not want to leave. Quite to the contrary, he was considering being an attaché to the medical or health service of the Department of Civil Affairs. When the colonel finished with his dinner, he excused himself and left the table. Between the lieutenant at the Reclassification office, the major, and the colonel, he had gathered some very useful intelligence about how to advance his position. He loved Washington.

Most importantly, he found out during his conversation at Reclassification that he would be interviewed at the Pentagon. There really was no time to waste. He had to capitalize on these chance encounters. As soon as time allowed, he would casually drop by the French embassy and pay a little visit to Robert L. Oppenheimer to thank him personally for his kindness at Fort Dix. While he had the man's attention, he would ask him if he might elaborate upon the French government's plans for the administration of the freed territories—and of course, in what capacity he could be the most useful. Then, if the visit had gone well, he would ask for a letter of recommendation before leaving. The others he would write to.

Within weeks of his visit with Oppenheimer, he received all of his letters of recommendation. Reading each carefully and noting how complimentary they were, he stacked them neatly with his application for Warrant Officer in a manila file and placed it in his metal capitol file:

Robert L. Oppehheimer: ". . . was in touch with him at the time he was stationed at Fort Dix . . . I can certify that he has a perfect knowledge of the French language . . . favorably impressed as to his character and abilities."

Professor Otto P. Peterson: "A most conscientious, reliable, and industrious young man . . . possessed of excellent character. He speaks and writes French, German and English fluently, and can also converse in Spanish . . . has travelled extensively in Europe . . . his travels have deepened his understanding of the languages he mastered."

Joseph A. Beisler: "Walter Wolff . . . requested the consideration of his application for Warrant Officer in the Army of the United States . . . known him personally for several years . . . known his family for even a longer period . . . he is an intelligent and honest individual . . . possessed of many capabilities . . . will be of use to the Army in the rank of Warrant Officer . . . fine character . . . applies himself to a job . . . successful conclusion . . . Recommend . . . serious consideration of . . . Application . . . he can be of great service to the Army and his country."

Not long after his interview and the chance encounters with some of Washington's military elite, my father boldly walked into the Pentagon and found his way to the office of the colonel whom Mr. Kresser had recommended he meet about becoming an intelligence officer. Some of Kresser's former colleagues had now risen to high positions there. As he crossed the threshold, my father made note of the surprised look on the officer's face as he pointedly finished what he was doing before looking up to ask, "How did you get in here?"

"Sir, I simply told the guard that I had to see you and that I could not possibly tell him what I had to tell you, and he let me through."

My father paused for effect, holding the colonel's eyes just long enough before he could no longer resist and a wry smile broke across his face.

The man looked back at him with equal candor and a slight downturn to his mouth contrasting his raised eyebrows. As he took in a breath, placing both hands on his desk, he said, "You got into the War Department? We can use you."

This was one of the few stories that, if pressed, my father would tell about his army days and one of the few that is not recounted in his letters. He submitted his application for a posting to intelligence training and waited for a response following what would be a thorough investigation of the former stateless citizen and resident alien whose last legal passport had been Belgian. In the meantime, the program at Walter Reed was interesting enough. He was placed in Thoracic Surgery—preparing for operations and recovery. The nurses and WACs were very competent, the work was not hard, but it was engaging: he made beds, took patient temperatures, pulses, and monitored breathing, distributed pineapple juice (drank his share as well), and observed surgery. By the end of June, with his twentieth birthday fast approaching, he arranged for my grandparents and Ellen to come for a visit. Should his orders come through, he might be unable to see them for a while. He booked rooms for them at the Hotel Hamilton. They arrived Friday, the 30th of June, and stayed the weekend. Almost as soon as their visit ended on July 2, my father was off again.

His company left their barracks at ten o'clock. After a massive delay caused by a derailment farther south, they finally boarded the Pullman at four a.m. Around midnight, Captain Haden had pulled my father aside and confirmed that his orders had arrived; the Secretary of War, Henry L. Stimson, had approved his application and he would be transferred to Camp Ritchie, the intelligence training center at Cascade, Maryland, but it was too late to annul his travel orders. Unbelievably, they were sending him back to Camp Grant in Illinois! No matter, he was on army time. They reached Rockford by midnight the following night. As soon as they arrived, they were given bivouac orders and were to be in the field for three days. Out of shape and out of practice from months of inactivity, they were back to the barracks by Wednesday, in time to receive a furlough on Thursday and for him to spend his twentieth birthday in Chicago.

Hotel Knickerbocker
Chicago, Illinois

July 9th, 1944

My Dears,

Well, I still have not begun my voyage east, but I did spend the weekend in Chicago. I spent over an hour looking for a room at all sorts of hotels . . . on the recommendations of taxi drivers whom I thought were well informed—until an official procured one here, at the Officer's Club. I had to share the room with a Captain/dentist; don't look a gift horse in the mouth! I have yet to see a soldier here. I spent the morning strolling around and above all sleeping, reading the newspaper etc.

After that I ate a delicious dinner at Jacques, a place a little like L'Escargot—with a "Ung bong verre de veng." . . . I don't know exactly when I will leave Camp Grant, but it's either Monday or Tuesday. If possible, I will pass through N.Y. and I will let you know how and when. I suppose that I will be traveling alone which will be quite pleasant. The whole business developed quickly.

Hasta la vista!

Walter

On the way back to camp my father ran into the WAC he had dated during his time in Rockford. They chatted for a long time, and when their conversation dulled into a comfortable silence, his eyes wandered to the next aisle. In the corner someone had left a newspaper folded between the seat and the window.

"Do you mind?" asked my father as he leaned across and reached for the paper. It read: *The Evening Independent*, St. Petersburg, Florida. July 7, 1944. He turned twenty the next day.

He lost himself in the paper for a couple of minutes, flipping through the first few pages until he stopped to read an article about a French farmer who was a distant cousin of Edmond Rostand, the author of *Cyrano de Bergerac*. His château in Flamanville was an hour or so from Noyelles-sur-Mer on the Normandy coast, not far from where they had been hiding during the summer of 1940. Unlike the owners of the château in Noyelles, Rostand had insisted on remaining to keep an eye on his land. The article goes on to describe what it was like to live under the same roof as the enemy. "When the officers were drunk, which happened fairly often, they went mad." My father was all too familiar with their behavior. He thumbed through until he found the continuation of the article from the front page about de Gaulle's visit to Washington and remarked to the WAC, "De Gaulle visited General Pershing at Walter Reed the other day. Look at them," and he pointed to the photograph. "I would have loved to have seen that hard-headed general."

With the change of season since he was last here, Camp Grant was much prettier. There were trees, bushes, flowers, and little gardens everywhere. His "elevated" status amused him. With thirteen or fourteen months of service behind them while the majority of the new recruits at Grant had only been in the army for about seventeen weeks, his troop was considered veterans. They doled out advice and exchanged stories with the "blues." A few days later, my father boarded a train heading east, bypassing New York on his way south. Looking out of the train window, he thought how wonderful it was to be alone if only for a little while. He could finally look ahead. If he was going to get shot at or killed, he believed it should be against the Germans rather than by any other army. They were his enemy. He would train at Camp Ritchie for close to a year.

UNITED STATES ARMY
CAMP RITCHIE
MARYLAND
[official stationery]

July 12TH, 1944

LOOSE LIPS SINK SHIPS!
My Dears,
I got here at 3 o'clock this afternoon. Since the train did not pass through N.Y., I couldn't stop to see you. For the next week I'll be confined to the post. After that, we shall see.

I repeat that from now on all information concerning my activities that you may have are not to be a subject of discussion for the family or anyone else. On my arrival here, I learned that it's not impossible, once I have my qualifications, that a commission of lieutenant will be awarded to me on completion of my training. *Qui vivra verra.*

The camp is situated in the wooded hills of Maryland—it's really nice. There is a little lake where we can swim. The quality of the men is excellent. The food is abundant and 1st class. The barracks are really good. Classes don't start until the 21st, and I will spend the rest of the days being interviewed and doing minor jobs—and a lot of KP. I saw some staff sergeants [my father included a sketch] repairing the pavement this afternoon—and sergeants first class [sketch] doing laundry. I don't care, and it's only for a few days and if I get the job I want I won't have that much work.

The training will be hard and rigorous, especially mentally, without excessive discipline (everything is very informal)—but if after 8 weeks I'll be a lieutenant [sketch] or a master sergeant [sketch] it'll be worth it. If I can earn my commission here, I won't have to spend three months of misery in officer's school. I won't have a "perm[anent]." Only at the end of training. What a pity.

Kisses,

Walter

I'm really happy to be here!

P.S. Please send me two (not more) uniform shirts, and my laundry along with the uniform. (Not more.) W.C.W.

After a year and a half of moving about in a no-man's-land of young recruits and army indecision, finally my father was at a place where he could hone his skills. During World War II, over 19,600 soldiers were trained at Camp Ritchie. These men became known as the Ritchie Boys and were sent overseas in the capacity as intelligence officers and experts in a new kind of psychological warfare. Troops were transferred to Camp Ritchie under classified orders and arrived alone or in small groups. Once there, they were ordered not to discuss their posting with anyone. The barracks at the camp were filled with young refugees who had escaped from all over Europe.

Many had been born in Germany, like my father. Some had escaped concentration camps. Many had lost their entire family. They were chosen to be part of this new program because they, better than anyone else in the army, could infiltrate the psyche of their prisoners precisely because they were their cultural equals. They understood the mentality of the enemy intimately, unlike their American-born comrades; they were raised in a world at war or fraught with the tensions of the build-up to war. Now assembled at one camp, they moved together easily and with a genial familiarity they had thought lost in the wake of their private battles to survive. Because most of these young men had left loved ones behind and knew nothing of their fate, a profound and unifying bond was created, which made them a very powerful and cohesive unit of soldiers.

Days at Ritchie were spent in intensive training in the classroom and on the field in interrogation and counter-intelligence techniques. Here mental acuity was valued more than the conditioning of one's body. Classes were hard, very thorough, and interesting; much more intensive than the ASTP program at Yale. My father felt in his element. He was studying mathematics in connection with cartography as well as communications and radio intelligence, where he learned how to transmit and intercept information. Ritchie Boys were also trained in sabotage, photo intelligence, and intelligence record keeping, but by far the most important aspect of the IPW (Interrogation Prisoner of War) course was to impart a thorough knowledge of the German army, its organization and tactics, its maps and map symbols, and its documents and records of every description. Even though most of the officers and men at Camp Ritchie were being trained as IPWs, they were required to take a course in the organization of the American army, the British army, the French army, and the Italian army.

Most of the men in my father's barracks were French. He ran into old friends, a Belgian fellow from the Victor Hugo Circle in Paris and some buddies he hadn't seen since Camp Pickett; a cook, a Greek, and another soldier named Wolff. My father and the other Wolff found each other at headquarters when their dossiers got mixed up. A man named Henry Arnhold would find me in Washington, DC, sixty-eight years after he ran into my father in the mess hall at Camp Ritchie. He recognized my name on the program when I was there to give the keynote speech at an event commemorating the seventieth anniversary of the founding of Camp Ritchie. I was so moved when he stopped me that tears just rolled down my face. It was my fiftieth birthday and his memories of my family were the perfect gift.

> July 23rd
> My Dears,
>   Before I go to sleep, a little note … Ellen, imagine who I ran into today: HaHa (Henry Arnhold). He has been here for a year—he was on KP and put my chicken on my plate when I looked at him—and he looked at me—we recognized each other at the same time … Good Night,
>   Walter

The air had cooled some with the coming change of season, but the classroom remained close. Yet, even with the open windows, nothing would distract my father, not the lake outside, not the backdrop of the Blue Ridge Mountains. None of that was more alluring than the promise of what he held in his hands. After being shuttled around the camp for the first couple of weeks from one specialty to another, he wound up in Order of Battle class to train as an expert in the details of the enemy army. This class gave "Ritchie Boys" the tools needed to recognize which role each German soldier played, so that during interrogation they could sort through a POW's lies and evasions to get to the truth. The knowledge of one small fact from this book could potentially force a POW during an interrogation to release a vast quantity of information.

Hope of that lay within the sheets of a five-by-seven, six-hundred-page manual called the *Order of Battle of the German Army*. Its cover warns: "RESTRICTED THIS DOCUMENT MUST NOT FALL INTO ENEMY HANDS" in bold letters. My father carefully unstapled the pages and punched holes in each one to fit them in a black three-ring binder he had bought. The manual provided a detailed explanation of the organization of the German army, with the name of every commanding officer and their position to date. Two of these manuals survive intact; they are dated February 1944 and March 1945: before D-Day and after. These manuals were updated, revised, and redistributed as soon as information changed.

The 1944 issue shows the details of every uniform in the Wehrmacht, whose forces many of my father's comrades would face on the beaches of Normandy in June. His notes are scribbled in the margins and across the pages, indicating where units have been disbanded. Names are crossed out and their replacements penciled in. Leafing through the fragile pages, I remember a detail from his testimony for the Shoah Foundation. My father said, "A namesake of mine, General of the SS Wolff, was a prisoner at my camp for a while until we sent him to Nuremberg. That was sort of . . . almost funny. I have his visiting card if you want to see it. You know, if you become a high-ranking general in the SS, you can imagine you earned your stripes."

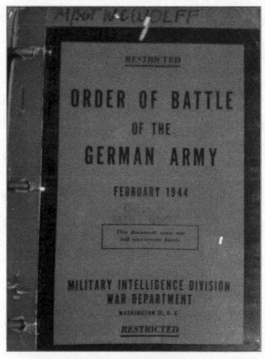

Order of Battle, German army.

I opened the book and carefully thumbed through to the list at the back, until I found his name. The namesake had become a prisoner of war. For the first time since I began to reconstruct my father's story, hunter had been captured and the hunted saw the tide change. Faced with the magnitude of their crimes, my father chose a memory laced with humor to override his rage. Two men with the same last name, Jew and murderous anti-Semite face to face. One was sent to Nuremberg, the other helped to ensure his prosecution.

SS-Obergruppenführer and General of the Waffen SS Karl Wolff NSDP 695 131, SS number 14 235, was responsible for the mass killings of more than 300,000 Jews throughout occupied Europe, for the forces that carried out the murders had to report directly back to him. He was subordinate only to Hitler and Himmler. Considered Himmler's right-hand man and closest confidant for at least a decade, he was such an intimate that Himmler called him Wolffie. Wolff was the top-ranking Nazi in northern Italy from 1943 to 1945. He claimed to have foiled a plot to kidnap Pope Pius XII. He understood that the Italians were a nation of deeply pious Catholics who would not trust their faith to anyone except their pope and the Vatican, so he claimed to have taken the initiative to foil the kidnap attempt in order to further the interests of the Nazi Party in Italy. My father remembered: "He was Himmler's right hand and number three out of all of them until he fell out of his favor. That's when Hitler sent him to supervise Il Duce. Never one to waste talent! That one I sent straight to Nuremberg. It's kind of, almost funny."

Calling card of SS-Obergruppenführer and General of the Waffen SS Karl Wolff.

With August came the liberation of Paris, which proved almost more than my father could bear. The following excerpts from his letters point to his loss of patience as summer closed in on the autumn of the war itself.

August 24th, 1944

My Dears,

Thank you for your letter, chère Mamo.

Yesterday we learned of the liberation of Paris. I would have given a lot to see the citizens throw the Boches out after 4 years of the most profound humiliation.

It is beautiful here now—a splendid blue sky and nice and cool at the same time.

Kisses,

Walter

*   *   *   *

August 25th, 1944

My Dears,

It's horrible—with the current events I can no longer study—I have no more patience and I don't see the reason—even though I have very difficult exams ahead of me. Our troops are in Reims tonight, they will be in Metz and Lille tomorrow—in Brussels soon, if we can continue our push without giving respite to our enemies—without giving them the time to organize the Somme and the Marne fronts. In truth I would like to be there when we give them the "coup de grâce."

I would like to be a part of their debacle, just as I had to witness the tragedy of the civilized countries—I would like to terrorize them like they terrorized ours. Other than that, nothing new. I would have already called you—but I am not sure exactly where you are right now . . .

The weather is beautiful here—but already cold at night. That's how I like it.

Well, that's all for today.

Yours,

Walter

On the second of September, Dad wrote home noting the significance of that date in 1939, when the Germans had invaded Holland and Austria. Almost immediately afterward, my father and Ellen were escorted from their boarding school in St. Moritz back to Brussels for their final months at home, before the impending German attack forced their long journey through the battle zones of Belgium, France, and Spain.

He wrote home much less often over the months to come, and perhaps because I had fewer to choose from, the tone of the letters became more desperate and anxious as the dream of returning to Europe became a reality.

UNITED STATES ARMY
CAMP RITCHIE
MARYLAND

22 Sept 44

My Dears,

I have not written to you in a while, but from my telephone calls you know I'm alive.

Thank you for the shirt and the belt—it was very prompt. Also, for the 3 last letters, chère Mamo.

If I haven't written, it's that I have an awful lot to do. The day before yesterday I was notified that I am qualified, among 7 others in my class, to take the exam to obtain the lieutenant's certificate (directly, without going through OCS [Officers Candidate School]). I accepted immediately. Yesterday I took the exam—it was pretty hard but, compared to the others, I didn't finish badly.

Since this morning I have been waiting to go before a board, or officer's commission. If I pass that, I will still have 2 obstacles: the medical exam and the interview with the Commanding General. If I pass everything (frankly, I strongly doubt it), I will be Lt. at the end of next week. But I say again—in view of my age, it could very well be that, being perfectly qualified, I still won't get my certificate, anyhow . . . ?

It's like a father waiting for a baby and who would like to know if it is a boy or a girl. I have been waiting since 8 o'clock this morning—that is to say, I have come back for the 3rd time. Qui vivra verra.

Well, it was brief—but longer than most of the interviews. Now, I have to go before the medical board.

Goodbye—have little hope that I will get the position and be promoted to Master Sergeant right away.

Walter

French control sec.

Friday October 13th, 1944

My Dears,

What "a job" I have for the next eleven days! It's really good. I play a civilian 2 times a day and I get interrogated. For this afternoon, I was assigned the role of the owner of a whore house who wants to make an arrangement with the American army. Boy, will we have fun!

Other than that, nothing new to report from my front. Ah yes, I have a new friend—the 1st Sgt. of the WAC dept. here. She's good—no kidding—about 21 years old.

You should see me dressed as a civilian—I am wearing gray pants, a black jacket—with the Legion of Honor—(after all, it is an honorable profession) and a big handkerchief that sticks out of my pocket. With that, a hat, and gloves. And for 4 hours of this they pay me $138—a month.

Well, goodbye

Kisses,

Your

Walter

P.S. On my return I found the package. Thanks a lot—but I don't want any more for the moment, film either. W.C.W.

My father anxiously followed the course of the Allied campaign for the next couple of months. In December, the German army launched an offensive against the advancing Allied army in the Ardennes that became known as the Battle of the Bulge. My father had predicted the Allied riposte in a telephone conversation with his parents, and wrote them on December 29: "My Dears, Under the heading of 'I told you so,' what I predicted happened; the Boche offensive was stopped and our counter attack started within 5 days of my 'prediction.'"

The letters from Camp Ritchie can easily be misinterpreted as mundane, but, reading between the lines, my father's frustration emerges from the banality. What he chooses not to convey serves to sharpen the larger picture of events unfolding around him, beyond his reach, as history comes into focus. My father yearned to be part of that history. During his year and a half of boredom in the army, he propelled his own advancement, as much as circumstances would allow. By December he had graduated to the rank of master sergeant.

Camp Ritchie card with my father's rank, signed April 10, 1945.

In April, with the war coming to a close and the Allies achieving unprecedented success, my father felt he had to take action if he was ever going to get back to Europe, so he committed a deliberate act of insubordination. He walked into the personnel office at Camp Ritchie, which was headed by a female colonel, sat down nonchalantly on the edge of her desk, and said,

"Come on now, do something for me. Get me a job."

"Job? A job? I could court-martial you for this. Now, Master Sergeant Wolff, if you please . . . "

One week later my father was on a plane, and this young man's dream of giving the enemy the "coup de grâce" seemed finally within his grasp. The boy plagued with memories of having to witness civilized countries overtaken by barbarity yearned to "terrorize those who terrorized our own." He was not only going to witness the enemy's debacle firsthand but take part in securing their permanent defeat. But days before he left, the nation suffered another blow. Just as an artist painting his portrait put a daub of red to the canvas, President Roosevelt pinched his forehead with his left hand and complained that he had a terrible headache. A few hours later news spread among Americans that their much loved and revered leader was dead from a brain hemorrhage. In a rare display of heartfelt emotion and fear, he wrote to his thirteen-year-old cousin, Pierre, the day that President Roosevelt died, just two weeks before he would leave for Europe via North Africa:

UNITED STATES ARMY

Thursday, April 12, 1945

Dear Pierre,

Thanks a lot for your letters.

Tonight a great man is no longer. We have lost, as the whole world has, a great leader with great experience, with ability and moral integrity.

I am sad and horrified at the same time. Sad for our loss—and horrified because of the possible consequences for the nation and our cause. It is true that the victorious end of the war is assured, but the peace that we hope to establish has lost the support of a great force.

I do not know when I will be leaving. I hope that it will be one of these days. Goodbye and I hope to see you again!

Cordially,

Your

Walter

P.S. Please give my apologies to your parents, especially your father whom I have not seen since my last stay in N.Y., for not having telephoned before my departure. W.C.W.

PART THREE

Return from Exile

CHAPTER 8

Coup de Grâce: Vetting War Criminals from Mussolini's Masses

Ritter, a war correspondent from WLW, "The Nation's Station," in Cincinnati, looked like an *Esquire* magazine cut-out of a colonel.

"I regret that I cannot tell you, sir," said my father in an even but determined tone.

The reporter was a very dignified man with white hair. My father rather enjoyed this little power play and was intrigued by his opponent's manner and elegance. He was sure that he knew how to have a good time now and then and probably had good taste in food and fun. As Ritter began his line of questioning again, my father turned to his unit to check on his men, who were being weighed and processed. As he did so, another passenger, a civilian, started to argue with him while trying to cut to the front of the line.

"I'm gonna miss my plane, if your boys don't get a move on it! I paid eight hundred dollars for my ticket!"

Not one to raise his voice, my father countered the yelling by answering in an authoritative, yet courteous tone. It was how he spoke to us, and when he did, whatever behavior was being displayed was silenced. Immediately. He turned back to the man and said in a voice as crisp as his new, perfectly tailored uniform, "Pardon me, sir, but this group of men that you wish so badly to get in front of are ahead of you, and until each one is weighed and processed, you will not move forward." Without blinking an eye, my father added, "Eight hundred dollars or not."

It had been a long day of medical exams, injections, paperwork, and all the red tape it took to get the soldiers out of the Air Transport

Command building and onto an airplane. They had been told they'd
be leaving three days later, but their orders were moved up to 4:30 that
morning. Because military intelligence was full of such surprises, as my
father pointed out, he and his group stayed up all night to prepare for
their new departure time. By three a.m. they had packed everything
required, including their personal belongings.

The ATC building was as enormous and complicated as the
Pentagon, my father wrote, but as usual he found someone to help him
along in the form of a pretty young secretary, who served as his guardian
angel all day. With her at his side, he got his unit all of their uniforms
and new equipment for their as-yet-undisclosed destination. They were
allowed to take sixty-five pounds total, excluding clothing but including overcoat, belt, canteen, and bayonet. Never one to travel lightly, my
father had a time packing it all, so he redistributed his short-wave radio
and other items he couldn't do without to the less encumbered. Before
their departure, the soldiers were paid and told they were allowed to
carry only fifty dollars. Of course, with what my father already had
stashed in his pocket, he had too much. Nice boy that he was, he immediately converted seventy-five dollars into travelers checks, leaving him
with fifty American dollars. The exact sum authorized.

The sun lowered its weary head to the horizon as the wheels of
the C54 lifted off the tarmac and the hum of the silver, four-propeller
plane echoed throughout the cabin. At ten after eight that evening the
captain made an announcement. Having always looked up at the sky, my
father now found himself in the novel position of looking down from
22,000 feet above the earth's surface. Unable to find traditional writing
paper, he unwrapped his official dossier and ripped the brown paper
into sheets, fished around, and found a dull pencil with which he wrote:

Extracts From My Travel Journal

2015 EWT. The plane has just taken off from the military airport
in Washington, D.C. It was 2010 at departure to be exact. I have a
magnificent view. The monuments at the capital are still just within
sight behind us, lit by a subtle rose-colored light from the last rays
of the setting sun. Because, there, on the ground down below,
it's almost night—The rose is disappearing fast and yielding to

gray—which has already become blacker and more impenetrable. In places, lights pierce the evening. Here, above the earth, it's still day. A golden light enters through the little round windows of our cabin in the sky. . . . If only you could see the celestial scene unfolding before my eyes.

28 April 1945—2150 On Board an A.T.C Plane.

Above Philadelphia. After Our Departure From Washington D.C. At 2010—The surrender of the Boches was announced. The pilots announced the good news. What a shame that President Roosevelt couldn't have seen that!

2215—At the moment we're over New York. Shame that we're flying over Manhattan at this angle, since the plane is covering up some of the view, but I think I could make out the 59th Street Bridge, Central Park, and Hayden Planetarium. . . .

The plane is as luxurious as the rest of the installations at the ATC in D.C. It's magnificent, a C54 with four engines. The cabin is even pressurized. The seats are velvet and become a lounge chair if you press a button. I've never had a more comfortable seat on any form of transportation that I've ever taken! Above each seat there is an air vent and a lamp—The steward just came by to serve us coffee, sandwiches, oranges, and cake. The steward is a sergeant, who seems like a fathead but actually is quite nice and makes good coffee.

Oh yes, the itinerary. By the time you read this story, it will be ancient history. Due to that fact, I hope Mr. Censor won't object if I tell you that from Newfoundland we'll fly over the Azores to Casablanca, where we'll stay for two days, and then stop over in Tunis before heading toward Italy for the rest of the voyage. We'll spend two days in Naples and then on to Florence. I knew it! Unofficially, and from a few simple deductions made during the preparations for our departure, I knew prima that unfortunately it wouldn't be France, segundo that we'd be going by plane. . . . I have a team of fifteen men with me, several of whom are friends of mine. George Villiers is sitting next to me. He's Parisian—and as disgusted as I am that we're not on our way to Paris like our other friend, Merman, who left yesterday with another team. To quote the perfect expression, c'est la guerre! Anyway, we wouldn't have stayed in France long because the front is in Germany—and if I had the choice between the Boches and the Italians, I would again choose the Italians!

Oh, you should have seen New York and the surrounding metropolitan area. It's gigantic! It's an enormous lake of lights—even seen from the air. What a city! What a beautiful view it must be during peacetime, without the partial blackout. But even so, it is unparalleled. Streets, [and] avenues invisible, just an enormous mass—cut only by the Hudson and the East Rivers.

Everyone is asleep now, with the exception of the war correspondent, who is reading. The lamps are designed so the light hits only the person using it. I suppose you're asking why I'm not asleep. Simple, really, I can't—I want to write—I need to communicate my impressions to someone! . . .

It seems we're above Hudson Bay right now. At 0230 EWT, 29 April, we'll arrive in Newfoundland. The plane is flying so gently, it seems incredible that we're going 350 km an hour. On a train one could never write like this. And what a beautiful night! Below us, occasionally, is a lake of light that appears then disappears in the distance lost to darkness. In front of us, but still quite far away, one can see clouds.

Tonight, for the first time, I understand with all my soul what the abstract in mathematical terms—in terms such as Eternity or Infinity—represents. I was forced to understand them intellectually but, truthfully, they were just dead words in my mind! Suddenly, I understand their reality, their sense, and their unity. Eternity, Infinity—they are the same in this nothingness, time and space, space and time.

Above, the vaulted sky is resplendent . . . a full moon that reflects off the aluminum wing just like in a Hollywood film. Now we're flying through some clouds, so beautiful. Like little cotton balls floating in the atmosphere. . . .

29 April 0007 Eastern War Time: Now I'll stop writing for a moment and, after using the absolutely charming toilet at rear of the cabin, complete with all imaginable comforts, your personal war correspondent will sleep a little.

0255 EWT:

Approaching Newfoundland. The airport. We land, and by bus they take us to a refectory for lunch. Excellent. I discover:

1. the KP don't seem as miserable as in the US.

2. the little Newfoundlanders aren't lacking in charm. The little waitress was nice. She told me that all New Yorkers seem a little nutty.

That's Andy of Newfoundland. The name of the base is Harmon Field. Also, we found out that the armistice is just a story. If it doesn't happen today, it will happen tomorrow. We left Newfoundland at 0415. Below us, I believe, is Nova Scotia. I see snow, ice. We see the Atlantic and, beyond that, air. We switched aircraft; now it's for sixteen men.

Still a smooth flight, practically no movement; it has less vibration than a bus, more like a 1942 Packard.

I gained access to my baggage, and henceforth I will write on white paper. It must be pretty cold outside, but here in the cabin it's too hot, and I've turned the fan on above me to cool my head. The guy next to me is a Tech. Sgt. in the Air Force—born in Frankfurt, 38 years old, intelligent, pleasant. He's from Boston. Also in our group, two buddies who've been with me since November 1944. In front of me is a Parisian of Russian parents. He's a very nice boy. I am so pleased to have someone I can speak French with. He's a student at Columbia (School of Music). He isn't yet 19 years old, which makes him the Benjamin of the group. He's the only one younger than me. The rest are of mediocre caliber and not important. They do what I tell them, at least for now, and everything's fine.

(That's it for now; I see nothing but clouds.)

Flying over an iceberg. A pal woke me up to show me. What a magnificent view! The blue sky is radiant. I would have liked to see the sun rise. It must have been a beautiful sight. I'm going back to sleep. 0800: We eat again. Sandwich, coffee, doughnut, pineapple juice etc. . . . We're really hungry.

We're flying over the Atlantic at 7,000 feet, above the clouds. From time to time the wings cut through the clouds. They seem like a sea of bubble bath. It would be a good advertisement for Supersuds.

The poor colonel is so bored. I lent him my Encore magazine. He's really nice and quite young.

The war correspondent/ex army officer is such a funny combination of Colonel Blimp and the little man with a red face and white mustache with a blonde on one knee and a cocktail on the other.

There is some turbulence now, but it's practically nothing. From my writing you can see, it practically nothing. God, would I like a cigarette! We aren't allowed to smoke aboard, so everyone is chewing. It reminds me of the subway to Flatbush. They're like cows chewing cud—cows that make Carnation Instant Milk. Before boarding the plane, speaking of dairy products, I gorged myself on ice cream.

If I think back to the way I came to the United States—if I compare it with my deluxe plane—and the troop transport on which I escaped—I can only say that I must have had some nerve.

We're approaching the Azores. They're not yet within view. Quite wonderful, though. Blue sky above, a few scattered white clouds below. Below the clouds—the sea is as blue as the sky. If the plane were upside down one would never know which end was up except for the sensation in the stomach. I'll ask for permission to take photographs.

Arrival in Terser. At 1315 EWT, we leave the island. . . . In Tercera it was already 1800. Picturesque island, beautiful view from above. Looks like a mosaic. Bought some Portuguese cigarettes with absolutely black tobacco, like cigars. I engaged the native "mess boys" in conversation and it went really well. I also became a member of the Short Snorters Club, made up of those of us crossing the Atlantic by plane. Important!

When I left the plane, I also left my magazines. When I returned, they'd been stolen—the rest of my stuff wasn't touched—minor tragedy.

Approaching the African continent. We'll be in Casablanca soon. I hope we stay for an hour or two. Qui vivra verra! You know, the plane is perfect for crossing the big pond. We're crossing to the African side.

30th of April—In Casablanca, it's exactly 0040 now. . . . We left
D.C. 24 hours ago. With the five-hour time difference, we've been
on the road for 29 hours.

That's it for now.

Until the next edition, good-bye

Walter

*   *   *   *

The last days of the war. Of all days to fly to Europe, he leaves on the
28th of April. On that day Mussolini along with his lover Clara Petacci
was executed and hung from steel girders at a gas station in Piazzale
Loreto in the center of Milan. On that day, Dachau was liberated. And
finally, on that day the British news services reported that Himmler
had sought negotiations with the Allies, offering to surrender the
German armies to Eisenhower, which led the BBC to make an erroneous and premature announcement heard all over the world. Between
what Hitler considered a supreme act of betrayal by his most trusted
ally and the death of Mussolini, he drafted his final political testament
before poisoning Eva Braun and taking his own life. He wrote: "I have
decided . . . to remain in Berlin and there, of my own free will, to
choose death at the moment when I believe the position of the Führer
and chancellor itself can no longer be held. . . . I myself, as founder and
creator of this movement, have preferred death to cowardly abdication
or even capitulation."

During the five days that it took my father and his unit to reach
southern Italy from Washington, DC, the war came to a final and definite conclusion. As they touched down successively in Newfoundland,
the Azores, Casablanca, Oran, and finally Tunis, the Germans surrendered to General Mark W. Clark in Caserta, ending the spring offensive.
Hitler and Eva Braun were dead, Mussolini's battered body was buried,
and Nazi propaganda minister Joseph Goebbels and his wife took the
lives of their six young children by injecting them with morphine and
then placing a cyanide tablet in each of their innocent mouths before
taking their own lives in Hitler's bunker. The children were found
neatly prone in their nightclothes, with their hair combed just so.

Night stole the remains of the African day, plunging the northern coast into darkness. The troop plane flew across the Tyrrhenian Sea toward the southern Italian coast. The only color in the velvety blackness was the flashing light at the tip of each wing. The sleepy lieutenant from Lorraine who had been chatting with my father was telling him how she had been promoted to lieutenant in the French army before she began to yawn and slowly leaned into his uniform, gently letting her head fall upon his shoulder, where it remained for the rest of the flight. He glanced over at his friend George, who was sitting behind an RAF lieutenant and an American sailor. Scarcely moving a muscle so as not to disturb the lieutenant from Lorraine, he mouthed with his chin protruded and his lips pursed toward the Red Cross volunteer: "Toi aussi?"

"Eh oui," whispered George. The Parisian held the girl in his arms until he too fell into a deep sleep. When the girl woke up, she unhinged herself and went off to play pinochle with the pilot.

Opening his eyes a short while later, George said, "L'avion vole tout seul . . . autopilote!" (The plane is flying all by itself. Autopilot!) After he heard the door to the cockpit close, he glanced around, looking to fill his now-vacant arms.

The early morning light highlighted the coastline as the plane flew over the Mars-like terrain of the volcanic Phlegraean Fields outside of Naples, still bubbling and steaming with seismic activity. Now and again my father could make out the Roman and Greek ruins, some of which were hidden beneath the crisp azure blue of the sea. Cloud cover masked the damage to the towns and villages below. Moments later, in what felt like an instant, the wheels skidded against the tarmac.

*   *   *   *

I read the next letters a hundred times before I recognized his omissions. On the surface they are simple and wonderful, but they never tell the whole story. Now that I have a better foundation, I have more questions. The problem was phrasing the questions to provide for the correct answers. At first they came haltingly, and, since the questions were unclear, the answers were always wrong. But by studying the wrong answers, I found the vocabulary for the next question, and the next, until, as in a chase in a good book, I began sleuthing like an obsessed gumshoe.

1550 May 3rd, 1945

On an airplane above Southern Italy:

I haven't written you since Casablanca . . . on May 1st, also by air. It's from there that I'm continuing my story, and I'll write you about Casa and Africa later. . . .

We arrived at our destination in Southern Italy without incident. There, apparently no one had heard of us. Finally, after three hours of going between the cafeteria and the PX, I succeeded in securing our transport with the baggage. Ah, the good old telephone! When we arrived at our HQ, our commander received us very cordially. It was in a very nice town. We had great quarters in an annex of an immense royal castle. The officer's mess was located in the main area, and the cooks prepared the food in the basement . . . European cuisine. Upon arrival, the commander gave me my choice of jobs. I chose (and then you can tell everyone else because that will be my address). I chose Quartermaster of the 5th Army Regiments. I could have had a job as Quartermaster of the entire Army Regiments—of the Mediterranean, but I chose this for good reason. You see, there is so much damage in the South, to have a pleasant life I prefer the North. The war is over anyway, and my placement would be the same in both cases. Anyhow, I don't like the climate there. Last night I went to Naples. They say one should see this city and then die. As far as I'm concerned, one should die first. It's an ugly place, and so very Italian. I'll discuss it again at the end of this letter or in the next. Before the end of the day, I will have passed through Florence. Fast life I'm leading here!

I hope you received my 20-page letter sent from Casablanca by airmail. That letter was written aboard an airplane and gave you all the details about our crossing that the censor would allow. . . .

At the moment we're circling the Italian coastline and approaching Rome. My buddy says we've already passed over it. No, it's not Rome. From the other side we see the island of Elba. We have a group of USO entertainers with us on this flight, some of them famous, and the young women are extremely beautiful. . . . I would love to take pictures of every one of them. They're all wearing uniforms. Now we're passing through a small storm, and the girls have woken up and we've taken the opportunity to get their autographs.

I'm here at my temporary destination. I also visited Florence, a beautiful city, slightly damaged. Tomorrow we push on. It's better here in the North—everything is more civilized. And I understand their Italian perfectly, whereas in the south I had a hard time understanding. This evening when I arrived at airport Y, I couldn't get transport—until I saw a poilu [French soldier] with a jeep who promptly took us where we needed to go. I'm so glad I brought my TSF. It's a treasure, and it works everywhere. We were really welcomed here as well, by the GIs and the Tommys both.

All of my letters are for everyone. I have no time to repeat myself . . . I'm doing the work of a correspondent—speaking to dozens of people. Please send your letters by AIRMAIL.

Having read to this point, I had a general idea of where my father was but couldn't figure out the details. If he was flying over Southern Italy, where exactly was this "immense royal castle" he wrote about? By digging, I found out that they were taken to Reggia Caserta, the seat of the Allied Command Headquarters of General Mark W. Clark, after landing at Marcianise Airfield north-northwest of Naples. Caserta is Italy's version of Versailles. It is a twelve-hundred-room castle built in the 1700s for the Duke of Bourbon. When architect Luigi Vanvitelli designed Reggia Caserta, I doubt he had any idea that Allied soldiers would use it as their headquarters any more than he thought he should engineer the grand staircase to support the load from 5th Army Regiment's jeeps as they drove up and down them, with the soldiers who were in too much of a hurry to walk.

The letter, dated May 3rd, was still confusing, because he was flying north and arrived at a temporary destination. One morning, at my favorite Italian café in New York, I started a conversation with my friend Lorenzo, the maître d'. He was a history buff and a voracious reader, originally from Salò, on Lake Garda in Lombardy. He listened to my queries carefully, and within a minute my months of exasperation evaporated when he said that my father must have gone to Salò. Later that day, I called him after I'd had the chance to do some more research about the events that unfolded in the days and hours before and after Mussolini's death. With my new understanding, the answer was obvious. Salò had been the seat of the former Fascist government, and that's where my father must have flown. Before fleeing toward the Swiss border, Mussolini and his convoy had packed at least one truck with documents and another with boxes of files, which, if I'm not mistaken, remain at the bottom of Lake Como to this day. Over the course of the next two days my father made his way back to Southern Italy and the castle in Caserta, where he became one of the first postmortem translators of Mussolini's documents.

May 5th, 1945

Evening

My Dears,

After having read and classified the documents of the ex-Duce B. Mussolini during the past two days, and after having translated one part of the orders of the Allied Forces to the Nazis in Northern Italy for unconditional surrender, I'm very happy to be writing in French. Ah, what a pleasure it is to take an active part in the humiliation of these arrogant murderers, what a pleasure to write their defeat and our victory.

You have certainly read the history of the surrender of General Vietinghoff and the SS General Wolff (whom everyone teasingly calls "my cousin"). Well, that surrender occurred about 100 feet from the building where I work.

Yes, I am, for the moment at least, in the headquarters of General Mark Clark as the address shows. I had so much to do with Benito's paperwork that I had no time to see anything. It was so interesting to follow the minute details of the history of Fascism, of all the participants in this tragedy without a happy ending. The bastard KEPT everything, but everything. We had 42 postal bags in all—and that represents only a part of his personal documents. There is so much that I understand now. There were complete dossiers on his collaboration with Hitler, from 1931 on. Italy's part in the Spanish Civil War, the defeat of the Macaronis at Guadalajara, dossiers on the scandal in which his sons were implicated, on his daughter, Edda Ciano, who wasn't the most religious of people, etc. . . . etc. . . . He was as conniving as a Boche, the bastard.

I visited Florence, a beautiful city with heavy damage in some parts, but in general everything is normal. The stores aren't empty here, we find a little of everything, including some luxury items. The people are very friendly, not like in the South.

The reason? Because the South was already poor before our attack and the German defense, which caused terrible damage, whereas here the Boches are responsible. The murderers mined entire neighborhoods, especially on the Arno, near the bridges they blew up before their departure. You should have seen the neighborhoods bordering the river: they looked like Abbeville.

With all of this Italian paperwork I've been reading, my Italian is coming back very quickly; and so I can speak to people. In the main, I've noticed that the common people, those who are influenced by propaganda directed at the masses, admit that for them fascism represents order and education. They blame us for their misery, which admittedly is great; because in peacetime and before our arrival, they ate better. They forget that it is to Hitler and the idiocy of Muss. that they owe their misery. The North suffered a lot during the [German] occupation. Our arrival was their liberation.

Still, here, as in the South, I see far too many people wearing one or the other of the Fascist uniforms with the symbols removed, sometimes replaced by the star of the partisans, or the insignia of the new police and army.

The wine isn't bad and as ever not very expensive, but I refuse to drink anything stronger, because the bastards put rubbing alcohol in the Cognac, vermouth, etc. That practice is forbidden with wine, though they sometimes cut it with water. That at least isn't harmful and is easily noticed.

Everyone is trying to buy my TSF because no one has one. There aren't any cigarettes for the civilians. Our ration is the same as we had at Ritchie—and I have too many. If I sold them, I could make a fortune, but I'm not interested. 1 lire is equal to one penny—nothing. However, we can buy everything at the PX. What you can send me is my flashlight. And I don't want that square thing you bought, Chère Mamo; I would really like the one with the long neck and the ring I attached. Also, in limited quantities I would accept chocolate, not the pralines or other sticky candy, but ordinary Hershey etc. . . . And nothing else for the moment. If I need anything else, I'll write to you. I hope to find the time tomorrow to write again. Please note: my address is G2 sec. HQ 15th Army group A PO 777. Halt. Let me revise that. Instead, write me at 2680 HQ co M.I.S APO 512. You could reach me there even if I were transferred.

Kisses,

Walter

Mt. Vesuvius loomed in the background as they headed north through the fertile plains of Campania. Sometimes, come nightfall, rising gases from the volcano would streak the night sky, creating an eerie incandescence. My father's first few days in Italy were the beginning of what he would call his Cook's tour of Europe, leading him north from the heel and south again to a room where the treasure trove of Mussolini's vital documents waited for him to sift through. Despite the richness of what my father left me from his years in the army, there is one missing piece that has yet to turn up. From one of those forty-two postal bags, my father, shall we say, purloined a letter that was part of a correspondence between Mussolini and his son-in-law, Count Galeazzo Ciano, which my father discusses in a letter dated June 26, 1945:

As far as the Ciano affair is concerned, I'm in possession of a very interesting document. I'm sure, dear Ellen, your Italian is sufficient to understand the letter. I want you to make some cash with it. Go to the *New York Times* or the *Post* or *PM*—but not to the Fascist Hearst-McCormack press. DO NOT give them the letter, but have them make photocopies. I'm certain someone will find it of interest. The envelope is very important, because it authenticates the letter inside. If it is published, I'd like to see the article; after all, an international prostitute should have a little publicity. <u>Do not give out your address or mine, nor my name or yours.</u> *Capice*? If you're asked where you got it, you can say someone sent it from Italy. It will make a good supplement to Ciano's personal journal if it's published in the *Times*! And get paid for this, it has value!!

The whereabouts of the letter remain a mystery.

* * * *

Even with all the devastation, there was no question that my father was happy to be back in Europe after four years. The Continent was his life force and would lend him strength until blood stopped flowing to his heart and he took his last breath. I am sure that, from the moment he landed and caught sight of the bright Italian sun as it lit the marble walls of Italy's Versailles, he decided he would never again countenance such a long absence. As he traveled, he observed the debris left in the wake of the tidal wave of war. He was consumed by what he saw and struggled to understand how this much devastation was possible. He wanted to reassure his readers of the will and hope of those who were not as lucky.

VE Day Headquarters 5th Army Regiment—Somewhere in Italy.
                                                          May 7th 1945
My Dears,
         ... Many, in fact most, of the towns north of Florence are badly damaged. Entire villas completely razed. Sometimes the whole villa was destroyed except for one room left intact, other times it's only half destroyed. The people: stoic, happy it's over.
         Politically, the Communists are the best organized party, the most vociferous. On the roads, the partisans are returning home. Tired, weighted down with their equipment, on foot, on military trucks, by cart, by bicycle, and by car. We also see refugees return-ing—to what, I don't know. We passed by recent battlefields where the land mines had scarcely been removed (but they have been, Chère Mamo). On the roads, there are hundreds of trucks filled with troops from the US, England, Sikhs, Canadians, Italians, Poles, and the Israelite legion, etc. ... etc. ... There are also trucks with prisoners repatriated from camps in Northern Italy and Austria. Again this morning, I took some really interesting photographs in Modena, of a column of trucks filled with Russians, Greeks, New Zealanders, Mongolians (Russians that the Boches forced into their army).
         I noticed a young girl by the side of the road seated next to one of the drivers. I wondered where she could be from. I approached

and asked, "Russki? Popolski? Italiano? Deutsch? Française?" When I said, "Française?" she responded, "Moi, Belge!"

You should have seen her face when I said to her, in French, that I had once lived in Brussels. She was from Gand [Ghent] and had been forced to work for the Boches. She told me I was the first to speak to her in her own language. Then I told her she was free—which she didn't seem to know—and that from now on she had no reason to worry. If I were a war correspondent, I could really write some stories. Inflation is less noticeable here than in the South. Wine, for example, costs 100 lira ($1 in Naples, 70 lira (70 cents). In Florence and Modena, 1 liter costs 30–35 lira.

Have just listened to the news from London via the 5th Army [Mobile Expeditionary] Radio, and also from Paris, from (Sottens) Switzerland, from Germany (that was funny!) on my little radio. Paris was reporting how New York was celebrating the victory— On the one hand, I would have loved to have been there, but I still like living these historic moments here, where I feel part of this victorious machine. The fight must have been hard here. You should see the hills, the winding roads, and the trenches.

As far as my personal situation is concerned, I'm in the royal castle at Z. I'm getting used to this royal lifestyle. We find castles in all the cities here. This one is not as big as the last but is gigantic all the same. I sleep on the ground floor, with a band of Ritchissois. Our offices are in the room next door. I now have a sleeping bag and a folding cot. I'm telling you, it's luxurious. We eat in a large room that has certainly seen better days—and we eat well. The Italians serve the food, and because I speak to them, I'm always well taken care of. But I don't think we'll remain here. We'll move and go to another part of Italy, that I know for sure. More on Modena: The Boches left only two weeks ago. In the stores, we find everything. It's not like during peacetime, but it's okay. There are a fair number of houses that have been destroyed. All the military instillations have been razed, they tell me. Very picturesque little town. The people seem happy to see us. They're nice, and basically we're well regarded. They suffered, but they're proud and civilized; that's because their men contributed to their liberation. Not like in the South, where their morale and self-esteem are low. It's a better race here. Those Neapolitans are not worth two cents. Already in Florence the people are very pleasant.

Kisses,

Walter

That's it for now. It's midnight. (We get up at 8 o'clock here, no kidding, not like in the US.)

P.S. My letters are for everyone, but keep them for me—it's my war journal.

*   *   *   *

Via Emilia at Portale Via Del Carmine in Modena, Italy, June 1945.

Now that my father had returned to Europe, he added a rich visual dialogue of snapshots and postcards to illustrate his letters. I wish I could walk within their confines. There are so many of them. Some are faded, or blurry, but they reveal life as my father saw it and not necessarily as moviegoers saw it portrayed in newsreels. There are a few hundred photographs. The raw expression caught in the lens is what intrigues me. Perhaps it's the expression in someone's eyes or a dog roaming the background of a picture with a striking composition, or maybe it's just that life goes on at the familiar pace of peacetime.

Yet people appear to be in a hurry: they have to rebuild. The war is over. They have to replace the fallen stones. Architecture that stood for centuries now lies crumbled, in ruined piles in every hamlet, village, and city. In the foreground, people continue on their way.

One photo fascinates me. I'm completely captivated by a man riding his bike down Via Emilia past the Portale Via Del Carmine in Modena. He's wearing a beret, passing crumbled buildings. Business is as usual. Just like in the movie *The Bicycle Thief*, the man's clothing reveals that he's a laborer. His livelihood surely depends on his bike. Only days into what would become a devastating postwar depression in Italy, he stands out from the rest because he's not dressed in a suit. He moves across the landscape of the photograph. In my mind, he has already moved off, leaving me to search beyond him to reconstruct time and place, the way the city was.

In another photo, displaced people wait in neat rows. A soldier appears to be walking the line. People reach as far back as the eye can see. A man stands tall, shouldering his life on his back: he carries a duffel bag so large it threatens to topple him. He's wearing a hat—all the men are—and he's holding what appears to be a newspaper. The people all look middle-aged. War did that. They wait patiently; they need to be repatriated. Where are the children? One man is looking straight at my father while he takes the photograph. He appears to be asking himself what the American soldier is doing. The women in the foreground stand uncomplaining, heads tilted down, their faces stern. Theirs is a veneer of passivity from years of accumulated stress while they ran for their lives. They seem to evince a hopelessness about their fate, a numbness, in contrast to the furtive ambulation of the people in the photo with the cyclist.

It had been my father's good fortune to arrive after the battles ended, to witness for himself a metamorphosis of the people as they made their transition from the roles they played during the war. He saw from every vantage point what his life would have been like had he not escaped, and had he managed to survive the war. Return had its advantages, destruction and all. Truth be told, his life was far more interesting in Europe than the one he led back in New York. My father's letters tell in rich detail what he did and where he went. There is no need to tailor his words, dressed as they were with the excitement of just being present in the moment. It had been exactly five years since

Displaced Persons—refugees returning home.

their nightmare began on May 10, 1940, when the Germans invaded Holland and Belgium and their destiny unfolded as they dodged bombs falling from the springtime sky. Now the invaders were prisoners.

The week after VE Day he left Southern Italy behind for good. From Caserta he made his way north up the boot to Verona and Ghedi Air Base, southeast and southwest of Lake Garda, respectively. He would shuttle between the two locations until July. His unit was attached to, but not part of, the 5th Army. Once he reached Verona, he took in the breadth of destruction from the spring offensive along the river Po, which had occurred during his last weeks of training at Camp Ritchie in April. The aftermath of battle was visible everywhere. In the ditches at the roadsides lay the carcasses of overturned vehicles. As they approached the Po, he and his comrades came upon an uninterrupted chain of vehicles of every sort: burned, mangled, intact but overturned. There were carts, cars, buses, motorcycles, and tanks that reminded my father of the ones he had seen in 1940 before their escape.

Where vehicles had been concealed behind a house, the entire house had been set on fire and destroyed. Mantova, situated on the river's edge, was terribly damaged, with hundreds, possibly thousands of burned-out vehicles lining the roads. Every bridge and the approaches to them were completely destroyed. It had been two weeks since the German army pulled out, but he could still see the enormous contribution the US Air Force made to defeat the Boches.

In Verona he and his men occupied what was then considered an ultramodern apartment house. He casually mentions that the 5th Army's predecessors had been the SS. They led a luxurious life. My father not only took their place without any hesitation but put to good use anything they'd left behind. In fact, in a nearby garage he found a stock of enemy blankets covered in DDT, a poisonous insecticide. He shook the DDT powder off the blankets and used them as mattress covers.

But where were the dead? My father makes no reference to them, and there are no signs of them in his photographs until much later when he visits a liberated concentration camp in Germany. I remember the lingering smell after 9/11. It took five months to dissipate before the air smelled fresh again. I wonder how long it took to bury the bodies, shoulder to shoulder in mass graves. I wonder about the rest of the people, the mourners who marched behind the coffins of their loved ones, accompanied by the sounds of footsteps, ringing bells, and their echoing cries of "Jesu Christo, Madonna" lingering in the fragrant fog of incense.

At Ghedi and at the POW camp in Verona, as well as the nearby POW camp at Modena, his job was to carry out the provisions of the unconditional surrender by administering, supervising, and initiating the registration and screening of almost 100,000 German POWs with a team of six men. They weren't responsible for the complete administration of all of these men—the remnant of the German army's Heeresgruppe 14 [14th Army Group] and the many other units attached to it were doing a lot of the work under his watchful eyes.

My father noted that he was becoming an expert on concentration camps, but his team's mission was made more difficult by the chief of the Allied military staff who commanded the camp and with whom he was in constant tug of war. The camp commander insisted on maintaining the organization and the discipline of the Wehrmacht and leaving the

German generals at the Ghedi POW camp, Italy, June 1945.

administration of orders in the hands of the Germans themselves, or as my father so eloquently put it, "those bastards." Of course, it wasn't in my father's nature to oppose any approach that would lessen his workload or that of the Allied soldiers, but the commander's policy was making matters more complicated in some ways. No matter this difference of opinion, the goal my father and his men pursued was to cut off the arms and legs of Heeresgruppe 14, with the support of the Supreme High Commander of the Allied Expeditionary Force, Dwight D. Eisenhower.

My father's job entailed giving direct orders to the Boches and ensuring they were followed—a powerful position for such a young man. He had no regard whatsoever for rank, no matter whether the prisoner was a colonel or a commander. He wasn't afraid. His routine was as follows: every morning, he went to the German major general and told him what he wanted from him and his men. The Germans were very cooperative and happy to follow his directives, but they insisted on saluting. He described in his letters how he never returned the courtesy, no matter what—unless a superior Allied officer saluted at the same time, and then it was inevitable. This was the only way to treat them; and it was fun to terrorize the Boches, to the extent permitted by law.

His goal was to find the recalcitrants: those who should spend a lengthy amount of time in prison. He and his team required the

(Top left) My father December 1945, Paris. His pipes (one is shown in the frontispiece photograph) were so much a part of his essence that we chose to bury him with one stuck to his hip the way he always carried them.

(Top right) My father and me at about age ten in northern Italy. I loved when he held my face that way.

(Bottom) My father holding Jacob when he was about eleven months old. Their features were similar even at that point.

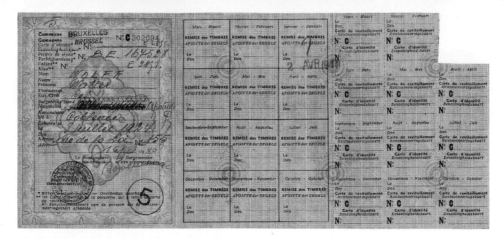

Food ration card issued in Brussels showing my father's place of birth as Koblenz and his birth date.

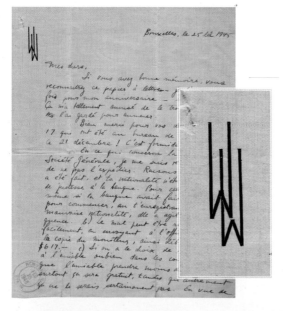

(Above) Identity card showing that my father was in Marseille, France on May 14, 1941, before heading across the border to Spain.

(Left) Recovered bar mitzvah stationery with WW initials, Brussels, December 1945.

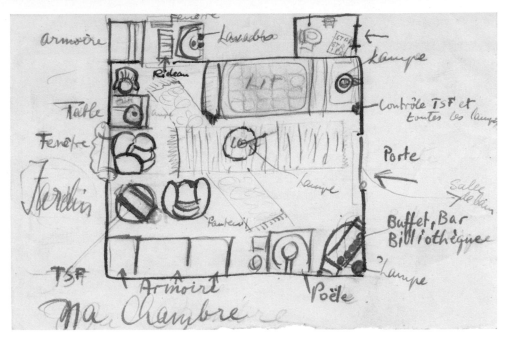

Floor plan sketch of my father's room in Linz, Austria. 1945.

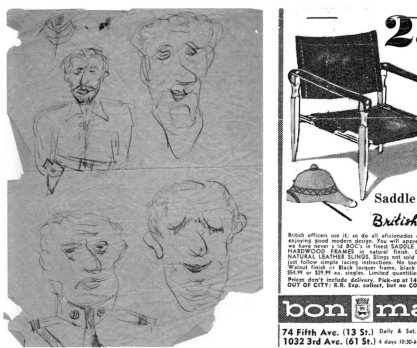

(Left) Sketches of soldiers, 1945.

(Right) Bon Marché advertisement from the *New York Times*. Notice the logo placed between the words "Bon" and "Marché" and the similarity to the Reich stationery on the following page.

Nationalsozialistische ☭ Deutsche Arbeiterpartei

Gauleitung Oberdonau

Schnellbrief

Unser Zeichen: Ihr Zeichen: Linz a. D., den le 9 Septembre 45
                                                        Landhaus, Fernruf 55-60, 60-70

Betrifft:

Mes chers,

Pour commencer, merci de ta lettre , chère Mamo,
datée du 28 août-- de cette année.

Je viens de finir mon 'midnight snack'qui consistait
de: bouillon, jambon juif, pain autrichien, et de vin allemand--
-américain
combinaison extraordinaire, mais, je l!admets, excellente. La
viande , d'ailleurs, m'était fournie de mon me ami, le cuistot
Français- en échange de quelques cigarettes Slovaques-- que je
ne fume pas, mais que j'emploie pour le 'biseness'. Ah oui---
The Columbia Broadcasting System is furnishing the South-American
music with it.

Je n'ai rien foutu de sérieux depuis vendredi après-
midi, mon ½ jour libre. Vendredi soir, "le coveth Roche- Hachanah
on avait une grande party, danse, etc. On avait un orchestre
américain de 16 pièces. Samedi matin je suis partis en compagnie
d'un copain , pour passer mesdeux jours libre dans la campagne.
J'avais arrangé d'avance avec notre commandant (il est devenu
commandant il ya 3 jours) qu'onm aura une voiture. Nous allâmes
à Attersee, un petit village au bord du lac qui porte ce même
nom. On nous donna une chambre dans un hôtel confisqué par nos
troupes.

Q 0178 — 578 41

Nazi Party stationery and a letter home September 9, 1945,
wishing the family a happy Rosh Hashanah.

walter wolff associates, inc. • 26 east 14th street, new york 3, n. y.

ch 3-6035

manufacturers   of·   ·modern   furniture

Walter Wolff Associates. Early stationery using "Reich red."

Among the photos and stationery my father kept
from the Nazi papers were the following ones. Here,
Heinrich Himmler inspects some Hitler Youth.

Hitler at the theater (undated).

Linz an der Donau,
Adolf Hitler Platz,
1940.

Herman Goering.

SS soldier conversing
with Heinrich
Himmler.

Children following
SS parade.

SS inspection,
October 10, 1938.

Inspection.

prisoners to fill out bogus registration forms in order to ferret out the real criminals—the Nazis—and in this the forms were helpful but not completely effective. Skillful questioning was sometimes required as well. Since my father was responsible for the "well-being" of several hundred of those murderers, regretfully, he had to be selective. His preference was that they all be incarcerated and never have a moment of freedom ever again. Whether he sat across a desk from a prisoner during an interrogation or watched the interned soldiers divested of their former selves and vying for shade under the hot, dusty summer sun, he took pride in his task. He was getting even. One of his favorite games was to conceal his identity and call himself Robert Anderson, so that, at least to begin with, the POW wouldn't surmise he was Jewish. This disguise sometimes carried over into later life, when a customer asked who the furniture designer was at Bon Marché. If my father was on the sales floor, he would reply that Robert Anderson was the designer, even though it was actually he himself.

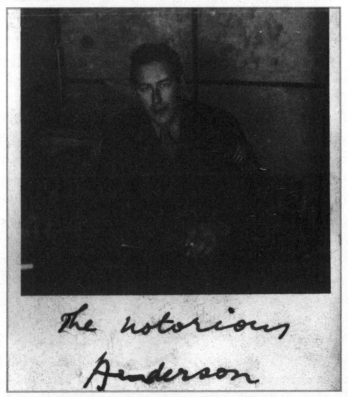

My father's alter ego, the notorious Mr. Anderson.

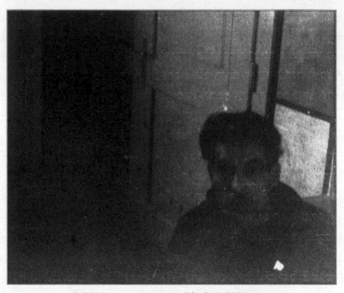

POW interrogation at Ghedi POW camp.

At nine o'clock one morning he was still in bed under his cool rayon sheets when the phone rang. He dressed quickly in a uniform that he had sent to be pressed the day before—crisper clothes were more comfortable in the heat. He arrived at headquarters not ten minutes later, sporting his new eight-shot pistol in a leather holster at his hip. He liked to hide his expressive eyes behind his aviator sunglasses so he could mask any emotion that might escape. With his starched uniform and shoes polished to a sheen so bright they reflected the sun, he always felt like a director manipulating his cast—among whom were some of World War II's most notorious criminals. He arrived at headquarters too late to translate the order of the day, which was for the colonel to stand in for the general, whom he thought a first class idiot anyway. Unfortunately, my father doesn't always disclose the name of every military figure he encountered, but in this letter he does describe how he arrived just in time to see the infamous General von Senger Etterlin standing in formation at the head of the line.

Frido von Senger und Etterlin was a corps commander known as one of "Hitler's Generals." He was the famous defender at Monte Cassino who nevertheless opposed Nazism in principle; as well, he was the chief negotiator who engineered the surrender of German forces to General Mark Clark on behalf of General Vietinghoff. He had been ordered to act as Vietinghoff's representative when Vietinghoff wouldn't give a definitive answer as to whether he would accept the terms of surrender. Appointed by telephone by generals Joachim Lemelsen and Traugott Herr, von Senger Etterlin flew to Florence where, on May 4, during a ceremony at the 15th Army Group headquarters, his surrender of the remaining Axis forces in Italy ended World War II in the Mediterranean. Afterward, von Senger Etterlin was held at several POW camps in Italy and later in Great Britain. After his release and repatriation in 1948, he wrote his now famous memoir, *Neither Fear Nor Hope: The Wartime Memoirs of the German Defender of Cassino.*

As my father approached the formation, he could hear the Allied colonel say to von Senger Etterlin in German with the aid of his interpreter: "Hundert Prozent Kooperation oder anderes! Genug mit der Nazi-Propaganda und dem passiven Widerstand, nun sind es FOLGEN ohne Ausnahme und ohne Unterschied zwischen den Reihen!" (One hundred percent cooperation or else! Enough with the Nazi propaganda and the passive resistance. Henceforth it's OBEY without exception, and without any distinction between the ranks!)

My father observed the scene before him and thought, "There is a new wind blowing. Those arrogant brutes, look at them: dirty, tired, miserable—beaten. There are thousands upon thousands of them, almost completely docile ... Swine!!"

A little later he watched as a bunch of SS carried out his orders to clean latrines for two hours, and then during a free moment he wrote:

May 13th, 1945

My Dears,

My job right now is to oversee the ... German prisoners—today is the last day. When that's finished, we will have completed it in three days. We work 6 hours a day with 2 breaks ...The camp is in an open field ringed by barbed wire, outside the city. . . .

Our system is the following: We take a hundred or so from Kompanie Schreiber, we sit them down, we explain what we want, and then they do the work under our supervision. Ah, what a pleasure it is to scream at those officers—colonels, Kommandants, captains, lieutenants who were once so full of arrogance! You should have seen them jump at my command. I say something once, and the second time I scream! I caught one of the bastards giving the Nazi salute, so I told him if I saw that one more time he would stand at attention for an hour in the hot sun and go for two days without eating. I can do that if I wish.

We take their name, rank, serial number, address, and civilian and military occupation. We tell them it's so we can notify their families, but it's because we're looking for criminals of war. After the officers, there were the rest of the Germans, and after that, there were the foreigners.

The camp is organized as follows: it is divided in three sections, I, II, III, etc., etc. Each one is divided into thirty companies, at 100 men in each Lager [section]. Each Lager has one "Lager Führer" [section commander], and each company has a "Kompanie Führer" [company captain] that we selected. Our idea is to let the Boches work for themselves (and take advantage of their love of discipline), under our strict surveillance. For the most part, my time is taken up with our "INT" [International] section, which contains; 10–1,500 Russians, Poles, Yugoslavs, Bulgarians, Greeks, Dutch, French, Fascists, Alsatians and Lorrains, German Armed Forces, French civilians contracted to work for the Germans, Indochinese, and Belgians— all the nations of the globe, Turks included. These people all come here for some reason or another and have to be cleared or locked up. I have a hell of a time talking to these people—but usually find some direct or indirect means of communication with them. We separate them by nationality. Suddenly, they all want to be Czechs, Austrian, or French; others proudly tell us they're 1/4 Jewish, a feat they should have kept hidden for another month. We found one 100% Jew (caught by mistake with the partisans). His name is Wolff; he left Germany in '35, found refuge in Italy, and was in hiding until his capture. The poor guy was imprisoned with all these Boches. We immediately liberated him, and this evening he's a free man.

Then we had most of the battalion that guarded Pétain. I personally oversaw and organized their registration. They're afraid to return to France, which I can well understand. I told them that what I was writing down was for the Red Cross, and then I marked each paper with "French Fascist." There was one Gaullist among them (he spoke to me later), and I told him to keep on observing them in order to provide the French government with information. It seems there are some among them who'd like to go back to France and organize uprisings. I'll fix them! I also had a group of Indochinese who spoke only a few words of French. Luckily, I found a Belgian from Schaerbeek who speaks a little Annamite [a region in Indochina that was taken over by the French during the nineteenth century]. I also had a few Russians who fought alongside the partisans, I spoke Italian to them. The Russians are not a problem—a Russian commission took charge of them. Then there was the Italian Fascist division. Oh, what a circus! Some of them asked to join our army. I replied that it was too late to change sides.

You should see this camp. No barracks, just makeshift tents for those who've managed to secure one. The rest are out in the open under the hot sun and the twilight sky! (It's hot.) Too bad it's not raining! Naturally, they complain—"Why are you complaining?" I ask. "You're only tasting a small part of the medicine you used to dole out to others. To which they respond, "Dast ist ja wieder Anderes, eine andere Sache!" (That is a whole other matter!) To which I reply, "MERDE!"

Sun and dust at the POW camp in Modena, May 1945.

I personally have no problem dealing with them, since I know you have to give the Germans an order without saying "please." I always speak with a light American accent, and I'm known to the Major General as Sergeant Anderson. Sometimes, for special occasions, especially for the SS, I become Stabsfeldwebel Kohn [Warrant Officer Kohn]. The other day, we had a good time. We had a group of those pigs to transport out of the camp. One of our sergeants, whose face is like a map of Palestine, made them repeat by heart: "Wir sind die Henker Europas gewesen. Das war doch ein Witz, meine Herren—Jetzt lachen, eins zwei drei." (We have been Europe's executioners. That was a joke, gentlemen, now laugh, one two three.)

Their laugh wasn't loud enough by far, but we were laughing uproariously. These men were none too happy after having to repeat: "Jawohl!" (Yes!) after each sentence. Funny, no? . . . It's difficult to describe this scene, but tomorrow I'll ask for permission to photograph it. We also have 600 Stabshelferinnen [secretaries]. We call them "BLITZMAEDELS or FLINTENWEIBER" [Fast Girls or Flinterweiber, a play on the derogatory Nazi term for gun-toting women in the Soviet army]. We have thirty who do our secretarial work. We have a dozen or so trustees, German anti-Fascists, who help us. They've been with us for nine months. The Italian carabinieri who guard us just called me. There was an Italian sailor from the anti-Fascist Italian marines who wanted me to provide transport to take the Fascist sailors to prison in Milan. That's only one example of the problems I have to solve. Whether it's the electrician who wants a flashlight or a young girl who tells me through tears that her father was wounded by the "Americani" or a woman looking for her brother who was deported to Germany—the carabinieri bring them to me, since I'm one of the two sergeants who speak Italian. And yet my Italian isn't great. And I'm not forgetting about Spanish, either. This afternoon I tried to speak Spanish to a Turkish internee, and I assure you, that was hard.

There are so many interesting things I'd like to tell you, but although censorship has been abolished, security has to be observed.

Kisses,

Walter

* * * *

After Ghedi, my father left for the camp near Verona, where another 80,000 POWs had to be registered and painstakingly sorted through to ferret out the SS and war criminals.

After a long day, my dad lay in bed puffing on his final cigarette of the day and took a last sip from his three-bottle ration of Cognac as he reread a letter he'd written on stationery left behind by Major General Reinhard Jäeckel. Why waste perfectly good paper? As he drifted off, his thoughts ran the gamut. Not one to express his deepest feelings, he had no choice but to let his emotions raise their voice while he slept. Dreams of soldiers and generals mixed with the red of the cherries he had eaten just hours before, forming a lattice of black and white with splatters of red. Juice ran or blood flowed, he could no longer tell. He watched as the men built the barbed-wire fences, only this time his dream allowed him to exact the revenge he so carefully contained during wakefulness. While the SS man who slept in his bed before him probably dreamed of Jews to torture and kill, my father could finally face what he truly felt from the safety of his unconscious. The red of revenge would come every tomorrow as he continued to interrogate the seemingly endless parade of prisoners. There were thousands of scores to settle, as he balanced their lack of morality with his code of ethics. He thought back to the methods of interrogation he learned at Ritchie. Instill fear in the prisoners through depravity, and a false sense of good will to unearth the truth. The promise of just half a cigarette was enough to elicit information, to coerce the answer to a question. The soldiers were tired, they wanted to go home, or to jail, but most just wanted to stop fighting. The war had been long and they had been defeated.

As part of an effort to draw out the most useful and talented of their prisoners, one of the first things they did was to identify the cooks, many of whom had worked at the finest hotels before the war. With 80,000 prisoners, surely there were some that could put together a good meal? They chose the best and, as my father would forever refer to them, the rest of "the Krauts" were sent off to do manual labor. They were put to work finishing the barbed-wire fences that enclosed their fate, with the major general ordered to do more of the labor than the others. Once a large airfield, the camp was a bevy of activity, with

columns of trucks and all-terrain vehicles arriving day and night. The
defeated soldiers wandered around barefoot and in boxer shorts, as
the early summer sun heated the parched land. Among them were
some who had taken sadistic pride in their job torturing human beings
in their charge. Tents rose above the flat ground; waves of heat blurred
the sharp edges of things. Here the rules set by the Geneva Convention
were followed, and while the only shelter was basic, there existed the
promise of life. Although the heat felt like an oven, they would never
be gassed and burned whole like their victims. Up to and including
the last frenzied moments of the war, the Nazis threw the bodies of as
many people as they could exterminate onto their tiered oven racks.
Finish the job, tally the count, be efficient to the end.

My father's office was located in a half-finished building once
used for administrative purposes. After he learned they would be there
for at least another week, he had phones and lights installed. Unlike at
Ghedi, where they had authority and their orders were carried out to
the letter, here they were no longer allowed to impose their own rules
and the process slowed. From the delay, something amazing occurred.
Hidden in plain sight were thirty souls, a group of French and Belgian
civilians, who had been falsely interned by the partisans. After they'd
been carefully interrogated, authorization was granted to liberate
them. One older Frenchman had been a prisoner of the Germans
for five years before he escaped. Desperate to show my father his
gratitude but with nothing to give him, he had another thought.

"La prochaine fois que vous êtes à Paris, venez nous chercher."
"The next time you're in Paris, look us up," he implored. His wife
owned a glove shop, and he wanted to give my father a pair of gloves
as a gift for my grandmother. He wrote the address down on a scrap of
paper and handed it to my father.

Moments like this are rendered in the letters with such simplicity that
it's not until sometime later that my emotions surface. This leads me back
to the photograph of the POW camp to take a closer look. How, among
this mass of humanity who arrived at a rate of a thousand men per hour
during the first weeks after the unconditional surrender, did my father find
a handful whom he could return to their loved ones, who by then might
have given up hope? In this group was also a Belgian man whom my father
helped reunite with his wife after they'd been separated by the partisans.

A partisan in Modena, Italy.

For now at least, my father was content with this stop on his Cook's tour and was looking forward to the next location, which he guessed would be farther north. Whenever he rode through the surrounding towns, whether he was on army time or during his time off, he noted how rubble concealed the former lives of its inhabitants. He remembered things as they had been during peacetime when he vacationed in Italy with his family. My grandparents had picked up my father and Aunt Ellen from boarding school in St. Moritz and driven down the steep, winding roads out of the mountains to Lake Como. Later, we used to make the same drive year after year, and only once, in Bergamo, did my father mention his wartime past in Italy. Maybe he found a sense of control in recapturing the happiness and freedom that was robbed from his youth.

By now, Dad had been back and forth between Ghedi and Verona several times during his first month in Europe, as well as Modena. He loved his assignment, but what he couldn't get accustomed to was the overwhelming gratitude of those he set free. He was embarrassed by their effusive joy, and if he lingered even a moment too long with them he might reveal a part of himself that he couldn't allow to show. Certainly not to a group of strangers whose sudden, intense happiness was like a field of sunflowers craning their fragile necks toward the sky after the rains have ended.

*   *   *   *

At this point my father had been away from his family for two years. The void he left at home was filled for Omi and Ellen by continuing their barrage of letters and care packages. They seemed to persist in the erroneous belief that he must be living on tight rations, which brought back memories of their escape. He explained to them that he fed his army rations to the dogs—to be exact, the German police dogs taken from the Nazis who were now being cared for as pets by the other soldiers. He chose not to have one himself, because, after all, the canines weren't bilingual and he thought better of chasing after a bunch of dogs shouting commands in German.

Among the men he worked with, his lieutenant and two guys from Hanover and Franconia were, as he put it, "*chic*" (good guys). They understood one another well. But the others, he said, were better classified as a bunch of "*miese Jieden.*"* Many of them had been overseas for two and a half years without a break. They were battle-worn, yet still hadn't received the required six stripes to achieve his rank of master sergeant and often resented that fact. They had three (sergeant), four (staff sergeant), or five (sergeant first class), or sometimes none at all. He on the other hand had earned his stripes in fairly rapid succession, in part due to his talent for the languages he spoke not only fluently but flawlessly, without any other country's accent infringing on the one he chose to speak at that very moment. The only language he spoke with any discernible accent at that time was English, and even that was evolving daily into a more American patois. This made him somewhat of a chameleon, a quality that, as I said, may have saved his life at the château in 1940. The only thing that held him back seemed

---

* Yiddish for "miserable Jews."

to be his age. He wasn't even twenty-one yet, and most of the other soldiers who held the same rank were older.

At Ghedi he had been second in command and had performed his work with ease. Unlike some of the other officers, he had no fear of assuming the responsibilities assigned him. For one example, some Austrian deserters from the German army were fighting with Italian patriots who had been brought to the camp by accident. Against my father's orders, the Italians had been mixed in with the Nazis. Naturally, things didn't go well. One poor fellow who was brought to his office arrived looking completely frazzled. When my father questioned him, the Italian slowly ran his thumb across his neck and said the Nazis had promised to slit his throat during the night.

Upon hearing that, my father immediately asked his lieutenant for full authority. That given, he motioned to the man to follow him and they went straight to camp. Remember, it was a former airfield. It was immense; the length end to end was several kilometers. When they arrived he said, "Andare prendere le altri, e tutti i bagagli e rincontra mi di nuovo qui," telling the Italian to get the others in his group and have all seventeen of them meet him back there with all of their baggage.

"Va be," said the Italian, in an unidentifiable accent, and he went off to get the others. After waiting about an hour, my father lost patience and began patrolling the camp in the Mercedes Benz he had acquired complete with a WH license plate. When he came upon a crowd, he quickly pulled to stop and, as the motor fell silent, he heard the angry mob yelling, "TÖTEN!!!" (KILL 'EM!!!)

My father screamed out, "ZERSTREUEN SOFORT UND SCHNELL!" (DISPERSE IMMEDIATELY, AND DO IT FAST!)

His order was ignored, so he gestured toward his revolver and repeated, "ZERSTREUEN SOFORT UND SCHNELL!"

An immediate result. At the sight of his hand reaching for the gun at his hip, about three hundred men just stopped dead in their tracks. All they needed was to see a show of force. When things calmed down, my father learned that one of the men in the group had already been taken away and beaten. He ordered one of the Boche commanders to drive him around until he found the man. With no hesitation whatsoever, my father walked into a tent where an *Armeefeldrichter* (a German army field judge) had been realigning the now more prominent features of the Italian's swollen face, grabbed the injured man, and took him out of danger. Within an hour of the incident all of the men were en route to a reception center for refugees. We never find out what happened to the Armeefeldrichter or the others involved in the incident, since my father was more concerned about the refugees.

Within days of that incident, my father was informed that he would no longer be retained in his section. He was a member of company 2680 HQ MIS, which was attached to, but not part of, the 5th Army. It seems that someone had protested his captain's "tour de force" in having placed him in the 5th Army's interrogation center in the first place, without having done the proper paperwork. As my father explained in his letter, he was "legally" part of the Documents section, so for him the announcement just meant that he would move on to a more interesting position in another location, a further stop on his Cook's tour.

There is an interesting misdated letter that must be from around this time, which is in response to one that my father wrote to someone named Jimmy, who held a military position in Washington. Jimmy was an old comrade of Mr. Kresser, the family friend who had saved their lives. He wrote back, offering to help my father attain a position with the Allied Control Commission for Germany led by General Lucius Dubignon Clay, who was General Eisenhower's deputy in Germany in 1945 and who, during Eisenhower's presidency, would become his emissary. Presumably because of this intervention, my father's next stop in the tour was set. He would leave the following day with his captain for an overnight in Salzburg, after which he would return to Verona for two more weeks of interrogating high-ranking prisoners and grilling them on the prevailing economic conditions of the Reich. Then he would be responsible for taking his men to Vienna, where one of the perks of the new position was to have airplanes at their disposal. Nice.

With his last weeks of work in Verona came *dolce far niente*, in other words, time off, and with that an account of life in early postwar Italy as seen through my father's eyes. These extracts are taken from a three-week period in June 1945 before he left for Austria.

Having finished the main work, our Lt. has made two groups of our detachment of 9 to take off for two days each. We left Ghedi the night before last in our jeep at about 1900 Hrs. We decided to go to Como and then onto Milan. . . .

At 9 o'clock, after a magnificent trip on the Autostrada (with compliments to the house of Mussolini) we had gotten close to Como, to Canzo. Since we spotted a good restaurant, we decided to eat again, which we did with gusto. A guy who worked in the black market, very nice by the way, had recommended the restaurant—which was also clean and modern. And, just to prove there was nowhere better, he came with us. On the way we picked up one of his friends, a comedian. We laughed so hard during our little banquet. Later, the owner joined us. By midnight we'd consumed several different wines, all of the finest quality, and four different types of liqueur. [When we were in the area once as a family, walking up an enormous outdoor staircase, my father pointed up and said he remembered having a little too much to drink one night in the army and he drove his jeep straight to the top.]

The country here in the North is so rich that the Boches' pillaging had little effect. The bill came to 4000 lira—for an 8-person banquet. That's $5.00 a head. I guarantee that you would have paid at least $15.00 for the same thing. . . We slept in a really clean hotel.

At about eleven we left for Milan—where we arrived just in time to eat again. We brought Marini, our friend from the night before, with us and he led us to a café for another meal. On the way, we stopped for an aperitif and to eat a delicious cake—the kind that one finds only at Hanselmann in St. Moritz.

After dinner we went somewhere where we were introduced to an enormous man with a stomach of fantastic proportions, Antonio. He seemed to be the head of the local black market. We had yet another drink. I then bought two dozen pairs of silk stockings at a ridiculous price. They offered me 100 dozen—it's not for lack of money, but how to send them to America?

As far as money is concerned, I have yet to touch my salary or my special fund. I'll send the stockings as soon as possible. Too bad I couldn't by 100 or 200 dozen. Then we ran a few other errands with our friends and I bought all sorts of things. We find everything here with the exception of coffee, which we have anyway. We confiscated it from the SS (a good source!). If you hear there's nothing to be had in Northern Italy, it's not true. Compared to my training in Vichy, Marseille, Lyon, etc. . . . Then I had a haircut and a shave, a rub down, and a manicure etc., etc. for 80 lira ($0.80). . . . Gold on the black market is at 1000 lira a gram. . . .

After a few more stops at cafés we went . . . Yes, to eat again! At one of the cafés, I came across an Italian Jew on his way back from Switzerland, where he had flee to be an intern [sic]. He told me that everything can be had in Switzerland. Currency hasn't been affected by inflation; the franc is still good. Yes, the prices are a bit higher than normal, but not from inflation. One centime is still one centime, and it retains its value. This is important, because one Italian centesimo has disappeared—it doesn't exist anymore. A radio that should have cost 440.00 or more in America when we could buy them goes for 12500 lira, $125.00. One thing there is hardly any of is cigarettes.

The town [Milan] didn't suffer much from the war. Here and there one finds houses destroyed; a road half-destroyed. The Communists are extremely active, as everywhere, but Milan is redder than ever. The big Antonio is a leader of the Communist party. After dinner we went dancing at a private apartment on the roof of a very modern house. It lasted until three o'clock in the morning, after which we went to sleep. We got up at 9, and after breakfast we went into town once again to run some errands. After another meal in the style previously described, we left for Cano. There is a little lake there before the mountains begin, near Como. It is 1800 hours now. I swam and took a sunbath. After another feast we'll return to Milan, where we have some more business, then we go back to Ghedi. My Italian has come back, and I speak better than ever, though not yet as one should. The Boches are detested everywhere. They acted like pigs here, which is exactly what they are. The Fascists are finished as well.

I also bought a tie for you, dear Papa, a genuine silk tie for $4.00. Yesterday, I was in Verona. Here is a list of things I brought back in my car—all a supplement to my three meals a day that we receive in the mess for special troops: One case of rations (to pay our "rent" on the farm and for the dogs—we don't eat that!). One case of pineapple, in one-pound boxes (I'm in the middle of having one right now), a case of V-8 Cocktail, one kilo of coffee, one kilo of butter (because we can't find any on a farm with thirty cows!), a kilo and a half of soap, Portuguese sardines supplied by the SS as well as the highest quality salamis. And above all, please don't send me a watch if you haven't already done so. I'll be sending one myself to cousin Pierre when I can find the time. I think I also mentioned not to send any handkerchiefs etc. . . . I've bought dozens more here in addition to the ones I left with.

Friday morning two friends and I left for yet another little three-and-a-half day excursion. A new one. You see, the Captain never knew anything about our last excursion, and the Lt. suggested they give us a few days off. The Captain was so happy with all our "hard" work that he agreed. So, this time it will be completely offi-cial. Ah, what a hard life I lead! This morning someone came by at 9 o'clock and we were still in bed. . . . I don't really care! (It was a 2nd Lieutenant Rothschild who speaks with a certain "accent"—and I've yelled at him many times because he doesn't do his work.)

We took a lot of photos yesterday, of our dogs, the farm, our-selves, and also our dinner last night. Every night we have dinner about 7 Km. away from here in a tiny village at a very rustic inn. Last night it consisted of: salami (top quality), butter, bread, chicken bouillon with egg and croutons, white and red wine, roasted chicken, eggplant, spaghetti with cheese sauce, cherries, peaches, coffee (half the "national" brand, the other half the coffee that we gave them for our private consumption). Anything and as much as we want.

We went to the opera in Brescia, The Merry Widow. We had such a good time. It was a comic opera but the actors and actresses took themselves so seriously and we had the royal box seats. After the first act, we went out and bought flowers. We wanted to have a little fun, and we sent them to the prima donna, the widow, with the compliments of two adoring "American" fans. . . .

I went to the movies to see I Married a Witch a second time. Very amusing. At the same time they showed the film about Buchenwald. Excellent results: a number of the women cried and the men were horrified. We should force every German, European, and American to see this film. The movie house is modern and air-conditioned—I'll go back. Afterwards, I felt like drinking something, and it was after last call and the MP wouldn't let me in. So I invited him to have one on me, which he immediately accepted, and he let me in. Simple, huh?

We have all the comforts of home now. Barber, TSF repair, film developing, mimeograph service, ice cream parlor, garage, tailor, laundry, etc. . . . Other than that, we have a Boche dog expert, which is of the utmost necessity, with all of our dogs and one little cat. Our PX rations are distributed twice a month. As far as I'm concerned, I've refused my entire ration with the exception of beer, fruit juice, and cigarettes. It's true that I have four cartons in reserve (on this note, please no more cigarettes). I bought a beautiful camera, with a telephoto lens. They tell me it's a "Mezie." I also have two revolvers now. On my night table there is a really nice office lamp, which is also mine. . . . I've also sent off a package for you with souvenirs. . . .

In a few days I'll be in a new country. I still have lira; I think I'll start a soldier's account, because, in spite of it all, I can't spend everything. I have my strategic reserve, which I won't touch. If it interests you 1) in Germany, one Swiss franc sells for 500 marks. 2) Near the Austrian border 1 mark sells for 3 lira despite the official rate of 10 lira for 1 mark—the beautiful little spiral, it will be a perfect end for the episode that was the Third Reich. The French franc is rising. . . .

We can ask for a furlough. I'll request France and Belgium in order to take care of my finances. In my request I'll include the powers of attorney that you've given me. After all, I have to put the bank account . . . in order and see to our homes in Brussels [they had several apartments at their former building at 155 Rue de la Loi]. If I receive the furlough—and this is doubtful—I'll try to sneak off to Nice, Marseille, Lyon, [and] Paris, where I'll stay for several days. From there I'd like to proceed by car or plane to Brussels. Perhaps I'll go to Paris directly and will pass through the other cities on the way back. All of this, however, is hypothetical.

Also, I've learned that we'll be going to Austria . . . and that we'll probably get a hotel on the Wolfgangsee [a lake in the Salzburg region]. We'll be attached to the Control Commission— which is what I wanted.

CHAPTER 9

It Is Your Moral Duty: DPs Among the Ruins in Austria and Germany

Finito, my father's puppy.

While my father was en route to Austria, Harry Truman, the former justice of the peace who was now a leader of the Western world, was preparing for his first journey overseas as president. This was also his first Atlantic crossing since soldiering during World War I. He was going to meet Stalin and Churchill in Berlin at the Potsdam Conference to discuss the terms that would end World War II and lay the groundwork for Germany's postwar government.

The leaders were supposed to design a new future for Germany to grow a stable postwar economy. However, the division of the country into four separate and distinct zones of Allied occupation by the United States, Great Britain, the Soviet Union, and France, as well as the revision of the German-Polish-Soviet border, became major points of contention, with the three superpowers unintentionally ushering in the Cold War that lasted until the fall of the Berlin Wall and the first steps toward German reunification in 1989. Had some of the broad strokes of the plans at Potsdam been laid out differently, tensions and divisiveness might not have risen to such high levels and the Cold War might have been averted.

While traveling abroad, my father wasn't the only one writing home to his mother and sister, of course. So was President Truman. In 1955, *Life* magazine published excerpts from the president's then-forthcoming memoir. In what is now one of his most famous "Dear Mamma" letters, he addressed his mother and sister Mary from the Potsdam Conference in July 1945. He must have penned it after a long and frustrating day with Stalin and Churchill. He wrote, "Dear Mamma and Mary, . . . You never saw such a pig-headed people as the Russians. I hope I never have to hold another conference with them—but, of course I will." Whether a young soldier addresses his mother as "Chère Mamo," as my father did, or a president writes "Dear Mamma," I guess the common thread that exists among us all is that, no matter what one's rank or stature, mother is always mamma.

On the fourth of July, my father and his captain left San Michele near Verona after he was transferred to the 15th Army Group. They loaded their little truck with all their belongings and piled into the front seat with one extra passenger, the smallest of war orphans, a little brown dog of undetermined variety they had named Finito. Judging by the photographs of people posing with both my father and said mutt, this tiny fellow wreaked havoc with all of the women they met along the way.

They passed through Riveretto, where they stopped to eat, then Trento, Bolzano, and Brenner, crossing the border well past nightfall. Temperatures fell as they climbed through the mountains toward the Brenner Pass. My father layered his uniform with his Eisenhower jacket and winter field coat against the crisp alpine air. Once they arrived in Innsbruck, they stopped at one of the city's largest hotels and stayed for a day and a half before moving on. In his opinion, the city wasn't heavily damaged, but a reader looking at the photograph he took while walking down Wilhelm-Greil-Strasse might have another opinion, for it clearly shows the damage as people and pets go about their lives.

While there, he ran into a lot of friends and former traveling companions, a harbinger of things to come. The locals tried to be friendly, none more than the young fräuleins, whose advances were met with disinterest at best.

Wilhelm-Greil-Strasse, Innsbruck, Austria, July 5, 1945.

"Pull over for a moment," said my father to the captain, who was taking his turn at the wheel. They were leaving Innsbruck, making their way to Salzburg. He adjusted his gun holster and got out of the truck. Ever since he had crossed into enemy territory, he wore his revolver at all times. He trusted no one. One never knew, he thought, the occasion might arise when he'd have to use it—at least that was the hope. He now had three guns in his collection, two Beretta 7/65 and his weighty army-issue .45. A short time later, my father emerged from the shop, smiling from behind his army-issue Ray-Bans, holding a case of wine and a bottle of thirty-year-old Cognac, which he would open during a quiet moment on his birthday. Ray Ban Aviator glasses were the rage since General MacArthur was photographed wearing them after landing in the Philippines, and my father loved the look.

"There's still too much of everything on the shelves here. Sausages at the butchers, bread in the bakeries . . . I wish we were still in Italy. I bought us a case of wine. The bastard didn't want to sell it to me, but in the end," said my father, with his pipe dangling from the side of his mouth, "he sold me as much as I wanted, and for only forty-five cents a bottle. Kraut bastard, I hate these Austro-Boches. Do you see how they look at us with such curiosity? They have a mortal fear of the USSR and France."

"Bad conscience," said Captain Lafon, as he started the engine.

Minutes before midnight, my father settled in with his thirty-year-old Cognac. After having spent the evening at the movies and a show with friends, he ushered in his twenty-first birthday during a quiet, more solitary moment. I always wondered why we celebrated birthdays the night before in my family, and I guess this occasion was no exception.

He had a room in a private house in Salzburg, located on a street confiscated by the Allied Occupying Forces. The civilians had been thrown out the door. He tuned his TSF until he came to a program in progress from New York and then turned his attention to a letter he'd started earlier in the day, which began remarkably, "I'm writing you from the office at the Gestapo building."

The former Gestapo headquarters in Salzburg has a unique history. During the Anschluss, the annexation of Austria by Germany in March 1938, the Gestapo moved into a five-hundred-year-old monastery of Franciscan brothers near Mozartplatz. They threw out the monks and used the building as both their headquarters and a prison, complete with interrogation and torture rooms. Right after liberation, the US Army requisitioned thousands of properties to house their troops and supply activities in their occupation zones. Wehrmacht installations and Nazi Party buildings were high on their list of properties to requisition. Salzburg was in the American Zone, and the former Gestapo headquarters was temporarily requisitioned by the army. Later, the first free Austrian radio station started broadcasting from this building. Austria became an independent country again in 1956, but it wasn't until the late seventies that the Franciscan monks moved back into the complex. It has been a monastery ever since. In less than a generation, this building went from heaven to hell and back.

*   *   *   *

Below them, Salzburg looked like a miniature replica of itself in a toy store display. With each curve, they reached an ever-higher altitude, gaining on their destination. At this distance, the familiar shapes of buildings and houses were obscured into anonymity, the crimes committed within their walls all but lost to consciousness. My father surrendered to the scenery. Its irresistible beauty tugged at his senses. As the car pulled against every hairpin curve, they warned of their approach with loud honks of the horn. The narrow roads were finally dry. The gray of the previous days of rain now gave way to an azure-blue sky, made more spectacular by the backdrop of sparkling snow-capped peaks and emerald-green forests. No day was more appreciated by my father than one spent driving along a scenic route, high in the mountains in crisp, sunny weather. The winding roads above Salzburg are some of the most beautiful in all of Europe, playground to the wealthy, with panoramas so exquisite that any writer would dream of calling such a serene place home to goad their muse into creativity. Hitler did. He rented a small cottage called Haus Wachenfeld after his release from prison in 1924 to finish *Mein Kampf*. In 1933, he used the proceeds from the 4.5 million copies sold to buy the cottage, and then, acting as his own architect, he renovated it, expanded it, and renamed it Berghof. It was such a marvel of design and décor that his little home-improvement project was featured in the November 1938 issue of *Homes and Garden* magazine. Later, the entire area became the vacation destination for the Nazi elite and political guests of the regime. On the occasion of the Führer's fiftieth birthday, Martin Gorman had the Eagle's Nest, the teahouse perched on the mountain's summit, constructed as a gift to him on behalf of the Nazi Party. On July 8, my father's twenty-first birthday, he walked gaily among its ruins.

My father at Hitler's retreat, the Eagle's Nest, on his twenty-first birthday,
July 8, 1945.

NATIONAL SOCIALISTICHE DEUTCHE
ARBEITERPARTEI

Guleitung, Salzburg

den Mozartplatz 8-10

My new address:

HQ 15th A.G. (USOFA)

6695 MIS Co (Austria) Salzburg, July 9th, 1945APO 777

Heil New Order!

Yesterday I visited Berchtesgaden and Obersalzburg. Our Air
Force did a good job! Beautifully decorated, a sublime view—
ruins. I took three rolls of film. After we visited the Eagle's Nest,
another few hundred meters above was another palace. That one
was not destroyed except for a door I was forced to destroy. You
see, I had decided that Schickelgruber's[5] house was a perfect place
to urinate. So, while I was in the middle of doing my business, a
young woman from the Diplomatic Corps came in through the
open door, open because someone had taken the two doorknobs
as souvenirs—and, terribly embarrassed, closed the door.

I should have used my revolver to destroy the lock, but as
everyone was army, a gunshot might have been misinterpreted.

With two good kicks, the door was open. I left a souvenir of my visit. As to the young woman, I can only say that someone not with the DC would have understood that it was indeed a WC. Nobody could believe my version of the story, and today everyone is telling me that if you chase a woman and she enters a certain place, one has to abandon the chase. It should have been my initials [WC] that did that. Today I found a swastika-emblazoned brassard in the house. That gives me carte blanche; this evening I liberated several crystal liqueur glasses and a pretty linen tablecloth of the highest quality, just what I'll need for my apartment in Vienna.

I see in the papers that the "Missouri justice of the peace" likes to travel. He's en route to Europe this evening. How thrilling. He'll most likely give his views on agriculture to Misters Churchill and Stalin. I suppose we'll still have a few ministerial remnants— there are still a few people left in government with an above high-school education. What a scandal.

Well, good night. I have to go see Salzburg's cretin of a mayor tomorrow. Wednesday, I'll probably go to Munich. They say it's not very interesting—more putsch, more beer, more Munich. My heart bleeds.

Heil to me! (Or: Mit Yiddischem Gruss!)

Yours,

Walter

*   *   *   *

My father's letters say little about his mission with Captain Lafon, to whom he was "lend-leased" for a period of about four weeks, but it is highly likely that he and Lafon, along with the men with whom my father worked, spent the rest of their service in the war going to some of the hundreds of camps throughout Austria and Germany that were being used as temporary shelters and processing centers for Displaced Persons, or DPs. DPs were the vast numbers of people who had been released from Hitler's concentration, forced labor, and prisoner-of-war camps by Germany's defeat. Many were Eastern Europeans, and many were Jews. Many of them couldn't simply be repatriated because they feared religious and political persecution if they were to return home.

Repatriation was further complicated by the fact that many countries were slow to commit to accepting refugees from other countries. It seems likely that, among other assignments, my father continued his work to root out likely war criminals during visits to the DP camps, perhaps by eliciting information about their imprisonment or abuse as slave laborers or perhaps by seeking out former military personnel or collaborators who might be hiding among them.

From Salzburg, he and Lafon soon traveled to Munich. Though not mentioned in his letters, there happened to be several DP camps in the area. He wrote instead about war damage, and the state of society as witnessed on both sides of the torn landscape, within the limits of the DP camps and outside them. What he saw and felt would drive him to take a more active role in the compassionate welfare of those with whom he came into contact.

The movement of the jeep made the camera sway, and the leather strap was pulling at his neck. Every time he pressed the silver button, the shutter closed around an image. The sound it made was an audible marker; every click framed devastation left in the wake of seventy-one Allied bombings. The ancient capital of Bavaria was on its knees but hadn't begun to ask the world for forgiveness. Not yet; it was too soon. My father was certain of one thing: thus far in his life he had been very

Munich, July 13, 1945.

Main railroad station, Munich, July 13, 1945.

privileged and fortunate, but at that moment he felt no compassion for the blight and penury that stemmed from the Third Reich. In ruined Munich, only two hotels and about a quarter of the houses were still standing. The city center was demolished. Her population was diminished by half. Inhabitants wandered aimlessly about, shell-shocked and defeated. Though some streets gave an illusion of normalcy, upon closer inspection only the buildings' façades stood behind the lush summer foliage. Lives once conducted within the privacy of homes were left exposed and vulnerable in the gaping remains of entire neighborhoods. Some streets sustained close to no damage, but they were among the few. In other areas, burnt-out buildings extended as far as the eye could see. Hanging from blown-out windows were white flags, begging for peace. Children climbed to previously unreachable treetops on hills of debris. While the light of evening was still strong enough, my father continued to record what he saw, shooting roll after roll of film as they neared Maximilianstrasse.

Then, as if by some reflex, he lapsed momentarily into his mother tongue and said under his breath, "Summa Summarem . . . es ist ein Vergnügen zu Besuch die Haupstadt der Bewegung. Nicht wert zu rekonstruieren."

"What are you saying?" asked Lafon.

"Huh? Oh . . . nothing. I was thinking out loud. I said, 'In sum total, it's a pleasure to visit the capital of the movement. Not worth reconstructing. . . .'" He trailed off again.

The Hotel Vier Jahreszeiten, Munich's most opulent, had been a wellspring of Nazi activity. Not only did it play host to some of Hitler's earliest supporters—members of a German occultist group called the Thule Society, whose logo was an abstracted swastika, the Sanskrit symbol of fertility, and whose unyielding goal of Aryan purity catapulted his career—but he and an entire cast of high-ranking Nazis had been its frequent guests. The bedrooms and banquet halls of the hotel had served the top echelon of the Reich and their lovers. In August 1939, Hitler addressed the Wehrmacht from one of its many meeting rooms. In March of 1944, most of the hotel was destroyed during an Allied bombing run, leaving only the part leading to Maximilianstrasse intact. On May 1, one week before the end of the war, it was requisitioned by the US Army.

The hotel is located only two blocks away from where the remains of the Ohel-Jakob-Synagogue, wrecked on Kristallnacht, still lay on Herzog-Rudolf-Strasse. The synagogue had been burned to the ground on that infamous November night in 1938 when hundreds of synagogues were torched in Germany and Austria, tens of thousands of Jews were arrested, and thirty-six were killed as violent retribution for the murder of the low-level secretary, Ernst Vom Rath, of the German embassy in Paris, by a German Jew named Herschel Grynszpan who had been sent to live with relatives in Paris because of the Nazi laws against Jews. The seventeen-year-old was outraged to hear what had happened to his family several weeks earlier, when the Nazis deported thousands of Polish Jews living in Germany by piling them into boxcars and sending them back to Poland. In a bold act of would-be resistance, Grynszpan acquired a gun and, intending to kill the ambassador, Count Von Welczeck, instead shot and killed the lowly secretary sent to find out what the boy wanted.

So much happened under its roof, but the Vier Jahreszeiten remains the keeper of its Nazi secrets. Who knows what my father may have heard about the hotel's past, but it does give me pause to think that he laid his head to rest where Hitler had slept too, and perhaps on the same down pillow or bed linen. The persecuted returned to one of the pantheons of the movement in its birthplace, and slept soundly in bed.

During their two days in Munich, and in between official business, my father and Lafon spent their free time eating, drinking, and sourcing inventory for a little export business. If they were on the road and there was work to be done, my father would stop people in the street, perform an informal investigation, and offer cigarettes for information. Standard operating procedure. He had accumulated sixty packs of cigarettes, including his rations, and tobacco was fair trade. The mark (or Reichsmark, RM) still had value: a good bottle of wine went for 4.50 marks (about 45 cents), an illustrated postcard for 20 RM (two cents), and a horrible-tasting glass of something masquerading as beer for 30 pfennigs. While they ate at a small bistro, he bought thirty bottles of fine liqueur to bring back to Austria in addition to another forty or so that he would acquire when their journey to the Rhineland continued over the next few days. The plan was to sell the bottles at a good profit and render a service at the same time. Good liqueur was difficult to obtain in Austria.

In the next few days, traveling on from Munich, my father had no choice but to remember and confront childhood memories as flashbacks paraded across his mind's eye, as he drove along the flag-lined streets that formed his path to Landau.

Heidelberg, July 16th, 1945
Evening

My Dears,

Yesterday morning we left Munich for Stuttgart on the Autobahn. The Autobahn is in good shape, except for a few bridges. We passed by Ulm—a city completely RAZED except the shell of the cathedral and the surroundings.

I took pictures there too. Stuttgart WAS a city. The center is no longer in existence, but I had a nice room because of the MIS* after my name at one of the two hotels that partially still exist. I shared it with a diplomatic courier from Yugoslavia, who travels between Paris and Rome. He, being Yugoslav, tells me that Tito's regime, for which he works, is not Communist but pure and simple anarchy.

---

*Military Intelligence Service.

ULM, Germany

15 July 1945

The cathedral in Ulm, Germany.

He says that the political view of "willst Du Nicht Bruder, so schlag'
ich Dir den Schaedel ein" (If you don't agree, brother, I'll smash your
head in!) is the order of the day for the intellectuals, and if they don't
agree with that they'll be assassinated (and not by the Fascists). He
tells me that France, which is truly far to the left, condemns Tito.
He also tells me—we speak in French all the time—that the French
have instituted a reign of terror in their zone—in short, they behave
like the Germans did in France. They empty the cellars, they take the
cars—EVERYTHING—I do my best to imitate them—to act like a
savage. When I want something, I give them the choice of either selling it to me or I requisition it. If there's any discussion, I take it. I have

a new acquisition, a small pocket revolver, smaller than my hand—it's just what I needed, 6.25 caliber, and it's not a toy. At least, I know I can <u>always</u> carry that, because it's no trouble and not a bother.

I was in Bretten at about noon. The first building had a red flag with Stalin's image on it. It was a swimming pool requisitioned by the Russian ex-prisoners. Unfortunately, most of the little villages show little destruction. I also passed through Bruchsal, pretty damaged. Heidelberg is in fine shape, no damage—except for two bridges. One finds a lot of things and great meals as well. All of the stores are open. I'm writing to you from an ultra-chic house—three houses occupied by the Special Forces.

I had a strange adventure this afternoon passing through the center of town. Suddenly, I came upon a scene that, for several reasons, seemed very familiar. Then, all of a sudden, I saw a store where I had a little accident many years before. I never imagined I'd remember the place and could never have described what it looked like, but suddenly even seeing the place made me remember the incident. Tomorrow we'll pass through Landau en route to Wiesbaden, where we have things to do.

If I have enough time and the house is still standing, I'll empty it of its "contents." I don't want the Boches to empty it. In all likelihood, I'll ask a few French officers (it's their occupied zone) to occupy the house. If I can find them, I'll go into the other houses and empty them as well.

Qui vivra verra!

Please send me a pair of sunglasses, aviators. Well, tomorrow will be a long day.

Good Night.

Yours,

Walter

*   *   *   *

The countryside had changed almost beyond recognition, except for the Rhine River, whose magnificent waters wrapped the torn landscape in a silk ribbon. By late evening, my father and Lafon stopped for supper somewhere on the road, then drove the rest of the way to Landau. Turning into the first road that led toward the city center, they came upon an alley of red, white, and blue flags whose imagery was so striking that even in the darkness it was reminiscent of Monet's lush painting, *Rue St. Denis*. The last time he had encountered such a welcome was after my family crossed the border at Moulin and arrived to Vichy in June 1940, with "USA" painted on their car in big white letters and Omi's flag made of red, white, and blue rags blowing from the antenna. He could still hear the applause of the bystanders when they thought the Americans had finally arrived. This, on the other hand, was a street full of flags, the colors dancing and swaying like a celebration in the evening breeze.

Moments later, their dusty green jeep pulled around to Industriestrasse 13 and my father said to Lafon, "Slow down. Here it is, number 13a. Let me out. This is a moment these people won't soon forget." From working and traveling together for a month now, Lafon and my father had developed a shorthand, bypassing the usual formality that separates rank.

The route the two men had taken from Heidelberg earlier that afternoon had been stained by blood from centuries of conflict, dating back as far as the Crusaders. For centuries, Jews had a strong presence all along the southern Palatinate of the Rhineland. Time and again, enough survived massacres in the region to regain their foothold and reorganize their communities. Many of them became wine merchants like my family. The gold ring I inherited bears the insignia of a wolf with the letter W sitting in a shield under a crown. This insignia has been in my family for generations and was the logo for the Wolff family "Hauswein."

Every so often along the road, a shard of glass pointing up from the ruins of a synagogue took aim with the blinding white light from the mid-July sun. All over Germany, once-unique and beautiful pieces of architecture dotting towns and cities now lay in small hills of dusty red brick, twisted metal, and broken glass. The men and their puppy, Finito, passed through Mannheim, Ludwigshafen, Mainz, Wiesbaden, Rudesheim, and Speyer on their way to Landau, where my grandmother's family once lived. Mannheim no longer existed. Its ruins were marked with graffiti that read: "Wir werden siegen—Und Jetzt Gerade—Fuehrer befhel—wir folgen—Sieg um Jeden Preis—

Nieh mehr 9 November, 1918—etc. . . . etc. . . ." (We will win—now a straight line—Führer commands us—we will follow—victory at any price—no more November 9th, 1918 . . .).

Destroyed buildings in Mainz, Germany.

The underlying meaning of these words is eerie and grotesque. November 9 had been a signal date again and again throughout recent German history. In 1918 Kaiser Wilhelm abdicated his throne, fleeing to Holland and ushering in the German Revolution that ultimately gave birth to the Weimar Republic. In 1923 Hitler staged his Beer Hall Putsch in a failed attempt to take over the new government in Berlin. With the support of three thousand Nazis, he staged a march that was stopped by the police and ended with the death of sixteen of his supporters. Lastly, in 1938 Goebbels took advantage of the significance of the date to organize Kristallnacht, ordering the destruction of Jewish stores and property and then sending thousands of Jews to concentration camps, permanently marking it in history as the official start of the Shoah.

Excluding the city of Frankenthal, which still had one American unit stationed there, this part of Germany was now a French zone extending to Mainz. Traveling through the French zone posed a new sort of difficulty for my father. Wherever he stopped to ask for directions, the French were shocked and confused by what appeared to be a countryman wearing an American uniform, and he was forced to explain the circumstances under which he came to be in the American army.

Kühn home at Industriestrasse 13, Landau, Germany. Photo taken after my father took back the house from its occupiers, July 1945.

During the earlier part of the day, my father and Lafon had stopped in Wiesbaden for several hours. At the end of the war, the Twelfth Army Group had transformed the town into one of two major collection points for evidence and looted artwork and as a base for the OSS—a secret intelligence branch whose many activities required German-Jewish translators and interrogators. Those who were actively involved in sorting through the masses of plundered art were aptly named the Monuments Men. An old champagne factory that included an inventory of four thousand bottles of sparkling wine and several other buildings were requisitioned and turned into document and interrogation centers, where my father helped a very understaffed Twelfth Army Group vet war criminals for prosecution at Nuremberg and Dachau, where the less notorious were sent. When they finally found the house on Industriestrasse, it was about 10:30 that night. I'll let my father's letter describe the rest of this most remarkable moment on his journey back from exile:

Under New Management!
National Party of the Third Reich
~~Gauletung Salzburg~~ רשכה (Kosher)
Salzburg July 21st, 1945
. . . To get to Landau we had to pass through Speyer and all the small villages you must have been familiar with. . . . Finally, after having asked a soldier and three civilians, I at last found the house. It's true, it really is a beautiful house. Not damaged at all except for the windows. When I rang the bell, all the lights were turned off. I screamed, "Ich gebe Ihnen genau zwei Minuten zum Aufmachen, dann schiesse ich die Tür nieder!" (I will give you exactly two minutes, and then I will shoot the door down!)

It took them exactly 30 seconds to open it. A man, trembling, opened it and asked me what I wanted. I told him I was the legal owner of the house, actually his nephew. He told me that the house belonged to a Mrs. Kopf.

Losing patience, I told him that was really interesting, but he should open the gate immediately so I could enter with my car. During which time the families Kopf and Maatz (or Martz) were taken away. I declared that I wanted two beds with linen on the first floor. But I was assured that the apartment on the first floor was poorly furnished, and

I went downstairs to the cellar with the captain, where I took the Kopf daughter's room. She was married to a young Nazi, Jaeger.

Naturally, all the Boches wanted an explanation of who I was, which left all of them with their mouths open. The older Kopf told me that Aunt Meti had ceded the house and that she was the legal owner—to which I responded that, if she would allow me to see the signed contract, I would believe her. I then said that I would consult with the French Military Government tomorrow. "Ich werde Sie dann benchrichtigen lassen über die Entscheidung die ich treffen werde." (I will then advise you of the decision that has been made.)

She then showed me the signed contract, which had been signed at the Polizei Praesidium between her and the Nazis and mentioned the laws of expropriation etc. . . . She paid 65,000 Mk. for the house, on which I gave her a little lecture about the morality of not buying stolen goods, etc. . . . etc. . . . all the while playing with my revolver.

After that I sent everyone off to bed, telling them I wanted 6 eggs with breakfast at 9 o'clock tomorrow. I'm sorry you weren't there. It was very amusing. We were in the second room to the right of the entry, and we took the smaller living room, which was the third one down. The furniture was in good shape, but on the doors we could see cracked glass, etc., and we could see that it was a good house. A few panes were broken.

Breakfast was served by the younger Jaeger, who had just come back from the army. Then I went to see the other tenants, asking them to pay (an average of) RM 95 a month. Everyone remembered Aunt Meti. One very elderly lady named Mme. Hertel was there. Her Jewish daughter-in-law was in Poland, and her son lost his life as a consequence. I told them, "Poland—dead."

Then I went into their office, told them I wanted 40 bottles of wine, this, that, and the other thing. I took the car then, drove to the center, and found the governing military body—on Paradeplatz to be exact. A street called Gerberstrasse is 75% destroyed, as is almost the entire town center. We had to clear the debris [so that we could pass through]. Paradeplatz is OK. A French WAC introduced me to the governor. I told him the story and asked that the house be emptied except for the elderly lady and French people put in it. He said they would empty it, but because Landau isn't important, there are hardly any troops and it would be hard to place some in the house. I told him that was all right and gave him Aunt Meti's address.

After that, I visited the addresses of Aunt Erna, Aunt Hedvige, and Mai. All three homes were hardly damaged, but I had no time to go inside. I would have had them emptied too, but I didn't know if they had been sold. I had a hard time finding those places because the Boche cops are so ignorant and give terrible directions. Then I took copious photographs of the houses from every side. Before leaving for Neustadt, I informed the dear family Kopf that the military government would communicate my decision to them. . . .

There are seven rolls of film to illustrate this edition.

Kisses, Yours,

Walter

The next week, after his return to Salzburg, my father penned a letter to Aunt Meti* that included the rough draft of the letter he later sent to the governing body in Landau concerning the disposition of the house:

Salzburg, 27 July '45

Dear Aunt Meti,

Enclosed you will find the rough draft of the letter I sent to the French military government of Landau, after I had visited them in person. I made some changes, but essentially that's the text.

I imagine you read my lengthy "report" on the matter at 79th Street, and I do hope you were satisfied with my action. I just resent the idea of these swine living in the house you own—especially Kopf Co. I wish you had been there when I had the whole gang out of bed till midnight, listening to my little speech about morality and the decadent Jew's return—in uniform. I was very sorry to have had

---

*My aunt's formal name was Meta. Meti must have been a nickname.

only a little time. I would have liked to evict the bastards personally. But I believe the French commander will keep on his promise.

I hope you don't work too hard—I'm not. I'm enjoying a "Cook's tour." Well, so long and thanks for the birthday card.

Love,

Walter

P.S. You can tell my mother to continue sending me avalanches of packages—it will save her the trouble of having to read my letters. I'm opening a food and tobacco store shortly.

By this time my father was furious with my grandmother, for he had arrived in Salzburg to find an entire mailbag filled to overflowing with packages and letters. No amount of reassurance could ever pacify her worry, and he was embarrassed by the constant windfall. The other soldiers were making fun of him. He stopped sending her letters for two weeks and threatened that if he received any more packages during that time, he wouldn't write for three weeks.

During his two weeks of silence, my father sent the finished version of the following letter to the French commander in Landau, written on Third Reich stationery:

Rough Draft

Salzburg 27 July '45
Military Government
French Military Government
City of Landau (Palatinate, Germany)

Mon Commandant,

At the time of our meeting on the morning of the 18th of July, 1945, I discussed with you the subject of the house at Industriestrasse 13a, belonging to my aunt, Mrs. Meta Bach etc. Bklyn, New York. I declared to you then that Mrs. Bach has given me full power regarding the disposition of all the property belonging to her in Europe. I could, if necessary, send a copy of said document.

Here, however, in brief is the history of the house. It was built by Bernard Kuhn. After his unexpected death in Manheim in '41, the house became the property of my aunt, Meta Bach. Before her departure for the USA, the Nazis tried by force to obtain my aunt's signature, ceding all the rights in the house to the Nazi state. My aunt refused to give her signature. Naturally, this was not a great obstacle to the Nazis, who, without losing any time, "sold" the house, for 65,000 RM. to Ida Kopf of Landau.

However, in the "sales contract" that is in the hands of Frau Kopf, we can clearly see that the "legality" of this sale is based solely upon a supposed law confiscating property from people of the Jewish religion and putting it into the account of the Third Reich. Obviously, the greatest civilized nations like France and the United States do not recognize such exercises in extortion and expropriation. The civil and moral laws of our civilization do not sanction the sale of stolen goods. Yet Frau Kopf admits that she knew very well that it was not Mrs. Bach who sold her the house!

Consequently, being responsible for the house, by virtue of my full powers, one more time, I beg of you to empty this property of the Boches, except for the elderly Mrs. Hertel and her sick son, whose wife was murdered by the enemy.

If the house could serve for the comfort of the French troops, you are naturally welcome to make good use of it. Please confirm the receipt of this letter.

Thank you for your kindness and attention to this matter, my Commander.

Best Regards,

W.C.W

M/Sgt., M.I. S., A.U.S

Adr.

*　*　*　*

No one in my family would lay eyes on the home again until I pulled it up on Google Earth all these years later to find that it was now, among other things, home to a Mailbox Etc. franchise. As they turned away from the house and back onto Industriestrasse, they headed east to Neustadt, where they stopped at Wiedemeyer, yet another wine and Cognac merchant. The owner, a man of Russian origin, was from a German colony in the Caucasus. They bought some Cognac on the condition that they take 200.00 marks to a certain Carmen in Stuttgart—but for the love of God, not a word of it to anyone!

While they were in Neustadt, my father met an American woman who was very obviously an expat. He soon ferreted out that she'd been a supporter of Nazi propaganda and was no longer allowed back in the United States, but unfortunately he didn't expand on this brief encounter. They piled back into their truck and before long were about to pass another "maison de vin," when suddenly my father motioned to his captain to stop once again. Lafon must have figured out that when my father had that certain look on his face, with that pipe of his hanging in just such a way, there was little point but to see where he was headed and just let him go. My father got out of the jeep, determined, silent. He looked at no one. While his back was turned, he heard the sound of wheels rolling behind him. He turned around to see a German car pull up. It took but a moment, but sitting next to the beautiful girl behind the windshield was a young man approximately his age wearing a gray flannel suit. Flabbergasted, he closed his eyes and reopened them quickly to confirm what he saw. War can take people on very different trajectories, and when the swirling tornado calms, bring people together in haphazard ways. He approached them and said: "Ich habe den Eindruck, dass wir einander kennen. Ich bin Stabsfeldwebel Walter Wolff." (I have the impression that we know each other. I am Staff Sergeant Major Walter Wolff.)

The young man couldn't have looked more surprised. In fact, he looked as though he had the wind knocked out of him. Once he regained his composure, reinflating himself, so to speak, the color returned to his tanned face. He hadn't changed much since they were boys and wore the stress of the previous years well.

"How many years did you spend in the Boche army?" asked my father.

"Actually, I spent one year in a concentration camp in France, escaped, and spent the next six months in hiding. Mother was at Theresienstadt, near Prague. She just returned one week ago. She . . . has—that look."

Hans paused as he said this, his breath catching in his throat. As he did, my father told him that his aunt Meti had spent a short time in a camp when she refused to cede their house in Landau to the Nazis and was arrested. As their conversation fell into a moment of thoughtful silence, Hans's father walked out to the courtyard from the building to find his son conversing in German with an American soldier. Looking again at my father, Mr. Vogler took a subtle but more careful look at the young American.

"Papa, look who it is. Do you remember Walter Wolff from Belmunt? Say, how is your sister, Ellen? Has she married?"

My father shook his head no and was about to answer when the older Vogler interjected, "Walter, what a fine young man you've become. Look at you . . . and your uniform? Come in, come in—won't you, please?"

"That's very kind of you," my father responded, "but first, won't you pose for a picture with me? My parents and Ellen will scarcely believe this."

The older Vogler had been in prison for some time as well for resisting his wife's arrest. She was Jewish. Mixed marriages were forbidden under the Third Reich.

My father and Lafon entered a fantastically well-furnished house and joined their hosts. They ate, drank two bottles of wine, and, after inspecting the enormous cellars, bought two cases for their little side business. They exchanged news, joked around, and spoke of better times at Belmunt. After several hours, they said their goodbyes and left for Stuttgart, passing through Heidelberg for the second time in so many days. On the road, they picked up a young French girl who had to get to Augsburg, where she worked for the AMG (Allied Military Government) in Stuttgart. With no hotels for civilians, the young French girl had no choice but to sleep in the truck, so they emptied it of its fragile contents for the night, allaying any fears of midnight looters. My father gave the girl his bedroll and huge down pillow, neither of which he'd bought or expropriated, and turned the back of their truck into a protective cocoon of sorts. The following morning they reloaded the truck and left for Augsburg, dropped the girl at her destination, and continued on to Munich, then Salzburg, where they arrived at about 10:30 that night. Did I mention that when

My father and his old school chum from St. Moritz, Hans Vogler.
The elder Mr. Vogler is to his left.

they stopped in Munich they bought another two cases of wine and liqueur? What a racket!

You may be wondering what they did with all of this stock? Liqueur and "eau de vie" cost them $2.50 a liter. They sold it for $5.00. The wine costs $0.25, $0.30, $0.45. They sold it for $1.00. The aperitif wines (sherry, vermouth) sold for $1.45 at a 200 percent profit. According to my father, everything was strictly legal, and since their prices were reasonable by comparison to Italy and France, they were making a small fortune. Of course, at least for my father, it wasn't for the money they were doing this. Quite to the contrary, as we know, he had too much. It was for fun. Besides, the other soldiers were more than happy to obtain merchandise from them rather than elsewhere, because the prices on the gray and black markets were much higher.

However, he and Lafon encountered a bit of tragic chaos on their return:

Salzburg, July 21st, 1945

. . . Upon my arrival here, I found my room looted, but I have already replaced the stolen objects—which was easy with my "stock." But I was mad, because it was American soldiers who did this. Nothing has been recovered as yet, but tomorrow I'll light a fire under the feet of certain officers who are responsible for this. The bastards broke the door.

As a result, I moved. There was total confusion in the houses occupied by the army because the officers and NCOs [noncommissioned officers] do nothing but have fun twenty-four hours a day and could care less about the soldiers, so I decided not to care about them either. I rented a room in a private house, for the ridiculous price of $1.25 a month—RM 12.50. The room is good, the lady brings me breakfast (with the food that I supply her). Meanwhile, I maintain an official residence. What I'm doing isn't legal—but the officer responsible for my logic has three apartments himself, is never at the office, and has at the <u>minimum</u> five women. However, as an NCO I have the right to a particular kind of room. Merde! The people here are very glad to have an "Amerikaner" in their house. Oh, you should hear my magnificent American accent! I can no longer speak any differently. It shields me from my indiscretions and renders my propaganda more effective.

I have, however, come across a Jewish family from Poland who survived a concentration camp. They gave me a yellow star: it's for when I have business like what happened in Landau. It terrifies the Boches when they see that on a uniform. The Jewish brigade, which occupied a part of Austria before the "Limeys" pulled them out, made the countryside tremble with their little pogroms and their regime of terror. We should put them in Germany. This is a subject one can't publicize.

My mail is a complete mess. At least a kilo of your letters was sent back to Italy by some bastard who could care less about my mail or me. I think I'll visit his officer tomorrow—just because I won't tolerate these little manifestations of anti-Semitism! I too can be a bastard!

Last night, our little dog FINITO had a tragic accident. He fell two stories through a hole in the stairs. God, did he scream, the poor little guy. He was alive when we picked him up, and the captain brought him back to the hotel. I doubt he'll survive. He's so cute and beautiful. He's a little hunting dog, already 30 cm. long and completely brown, except for a white belly.

Kisses, Yours, Walter

*   *   *   *

Captain Lafon—quiet observer watching the drama of my father's past unfold as it became the present. The young superior officer was the only person to bear witness as my father recovered some of the shattered pieces of his former life. Lafon was also the only person to actually meet some of those who had played a part in that past when they coincidentally ran into my father's old friend, Hans Vogler, a day after my father had repossessed the house that had originally belonged to his maternal grandfather in Landau. It was there that my grandmother and her sisters had been born and raised before the house was expropriated and bought for a song from the Nazis. He alone was there to capture the expression on my father's face as he dealt justice to the occupiers while providing that the elderly Madame Hertel be permitted to remain in the house as he ordered the others out. The initiative my father took during this small but significant act of revenge at Industriestrasse13a likely offered him some much-needed closure. Certainly, this was an important part of the process that allowed him later to make the most of a promising future in New York City and to put six years of turmoil behind him as he compartmentalized the trauma and the complex emotions of his violent exile.

These defining moments informed my father's character, because to turn the tables on one's enemy is to restore one's place in the world—in his case, not only as a survivor but as a survivor with the ability to use his rank and new citizenship to regain a foothold as a Jew and as part of what came to be known as the Surviving Remnant.[6] In turn, my father could not help but be struck deeply by the desperation and the desperate condition of the thousands of other, far less fortunate survivors with whom he came into contact. He was so troubled by what he saw that he enlisted his family and friends to help as many of the Displaced People as he could.

The following letter was originally written on the stationery of the "DEUTSCHE PARTEI Amt des Volksgruppenführers" (Community Leaders' Office, German Party). Across that heading on the first sheet my father wrote: "See our latest success 'Behind Barbed Wire' contracts made for many years in advance" and on the second page "Under Completely New Management רשכ (kosher), רשכ (kosher), NOW STRICTLY KOSHER." Interspersed in the letter are several SS stamps. His humor was meant especially to ward off the censors.

August 28, 1945

...And now, to another very urgent order of business. Near here [in Linz] there are several Jewish DP camps. They live under really terrible conditions. The food is insufficient. They are lacking in everything. HIAS [Hebrew Immigrant Aid Society], HICEM,[7] JOINT [American Jewish Joint Distribution Committee], UNRRA [United Nations Relief and Rehabilitation Administration], etc., etc., etc., are doing NOTHING. They [the DPs] receive no medication. It is a crime. All of these organizations collect millions and do nothing. Because of this, I ask you to please send packages to my address marked like this [sketch] with [three vertical lines] M/Sgt. [address] P.M. NY, NY, so that I can recognize the packages. Do not put anything deluxe into the packages—simply canned foods or anything else that will resist the rigors of transport. I suggest: meat, coffee, sugar, chocolate, [condensed or powdered] milk, chocolate, ordinary soap, etc.—Ask all of your friends to do the same thing—it is imperative. Cher Papo, those on Wall Street can do the same thing. I will send confirmation to anyone who sends me a package. All of these packages will be distributed by the Jewish chaplain from the 26th Infantry Division, HQ Linz. A group of friends I was with ... gave me this urgent message. At the same time, and in the same vein I will write to Mrs. Rosenthal. She will know a lot of people. Anyway, my dear Ellen, show her this letter. If she seems interested, twenty something people at a time will do the same thing. May I suggest that this is done before the Xmas rush . . .?

Yours,

Walter

P.S. The mail is in complete disorder—nothing has been sent since peace was declared.

Then he decided to write to Eleanor Roosevelt. Perhaps he felt compelled because he had read these words of hers: "in order to be useful we must stand for the things we feel are right, and we must work for those things wherever we find ourselves. It does very little good to believe in something unless you tell your friends and associates of your beliefs." During World War II, Eleanor Roosevelt was known to have brought the cares and concerns of our GIs before Congress and the public, and she continued to do so well after the death of President Roosevelt. Perhaps for that reason, too, my father took it upon himself to draft a letter to the First Lady on behalf of the Displaced People whom he encountered as his intelligence work took him to some of the seven hundred DP camps throughout Austria and Germany during the first few months after the end of the war.

The conditions in which survivors were living were acceptable at best, but deplorably similar to the concentration camps from which they had just been released. Sickness, malnutrition, and the death rate during the first months was uncontrollable. Food and other basic necessities were in short supply. The soldiers were untrained in how to handle or organize the masses of traumatized homeless, stateless people who until just eight weeks before had been awaiting their annihilation in Nazi concentration camps. In fact, some of the camps that presently housed DPs had been built as slave labor camps by the Reich; some survivors who still lacked any alternative were left with no choice but to wear the infamous striped uniforms until other clothing could be found or requisitioned for them. The difference between their lives before and after the fall of the Reich was that they were no longer contained by barbed wire fences or guarded by the SS and threatened with imminent starvation and murder for being Jews.

The US government was just now beginning to take a stand and make a specific category for the Jewish victims of Nazi war crimes who would not consider repatriation as a viable option. For the first several months, no separate distinction was made for the Jews.[8] Further, during the summer of 1945, Israel was still a goal with no guarantee that Palestine would be opened to the stateless Surviving Remnant as a permanent home. Immigration laws were not amended by Great Britain or the United States until much later. Bills to relax immigration quotas were not introduced in Congress until 1947, and Great Britain, which held Palestine as a mandated territory following the defeat of Germany and the Ottoman Empire in World War I, did not want to stand against the Arabs, who did not want to see Palestine become the Jewish homeland. Anti-Semitism was still the norm, and the policy for granting asylum was a dynamic political process.[9] There was not yet even a specific term to describe what had happened. There was no "Holocaust" or "Shoah"; only later did these terms become part of the vernacular to describe the Nazi's war against the Jews.

My father saw his reflection in the eyes of the Surviving Remnant. In them, he found the unadulterated truth of Hitler's Final Solution and the profound reality of what he had escaped. He drew strength from their humanity and commitment from their plight. This is a rough draft of the letter he wrote to Eleanor Roosevelt:

Linz, Austria

30 July 1945

Dear Mrs. Roosevelt,

Enclosed you will find a rather interesting "publication," if I may call it that. [It was not attached to the draft because my father must have included it with actual letter.] Unfortunately, I could get only these fragments, but it amused me so much that I thought it worthwhile to send it to you.

At the same time, I would like to take the liberty to inform you that, while Polish, Yugoslav, and Italian refugees are generously taken care of, the remnants of the European Jewry are pushed around from camp to camp, with nobody taking any real interest in them. I was even told about some officers stating that we had come a little too early—had we come later we would have had fewer of these Jews to worry about. This, I trust, is not the general attitude of all concerned, but it does reflect a certain trend.

I was also told by some of these poor people, in a camp near Munich, that they had no contact with any American relief organization so far. The same appears to be true in the case of the Salzburg camp. I am telling you all of this in the hope that a reminder from a person of your prestige and standing should prod some of the organizations (whose moral duty it is to look after these unfortunate people) into action.

Respectfully Yours,
M/Sgt. Walter C. Wolff
32908561
H.Q. Documents Center
G-2 USFA /A.P.O. 777
US Army

*   *   *   *

I found no record of a response to his letter, but Eleanor Roosevelt's undying commitment shows in her speeches before Congress, in her *My Day* syndicated column, and mostly by the work she did with the UNRRA, United Nations Relief and Rehabilitation Administration, for which she took a great part in the drafting of the Declaration of Human Rights. She wrote, "There is in Europe at the present time a group of 100,000 displaced persons—the miserable, tortured, terrorized Jews who have seen members of their families murdered and their homes ruined, and who are stateless people, since they hate the Germans and no longer wish to live in the countries where they have been despoiled of all that makes life worth living. Naturally, they want to go to Palestine, the one place where they will have a status, where they will feel again that sense of belonging to a community which gives most of us security. President Truman has asked Great Britain for consideration of their condition and permission for their admittance to Palestine ... It seems to me urgent that these people be given permission to go to the home of their choice. . . . Our consciences can hardly be clear when we read about and see the pictures of these emaciated, miserable people who suffer while we sit comfortably and let them die at the rate of fifty per day—which is what is happening now, I am told. It seems to me imperative, also, that the Senate pass the UNRRA appropriation as rapidly as possible. . . . The need is great."[10]

Eleanor Roosevelt spoke publicly several times a week at fund-raising events for Refugee and DP organizations in the United States during and after the war mainly through United Jewish Appeal. Later, in the beginning of 1946, she began working on the DP issue through the UN, attending her first session that January and then visiting the Zeilsheim DP Camp directly afterward, in February 1946.

My grandmother was highly critical of the letter to the former First Lady and found it to be naive. My father wrote back that he wasn't asking for her opinion. He had chosen to send the letter home first in order to avoid the still-prying eyes of the censors, the idea being that his family would then forward it to Eleanor Roosevelt. What Omi failed to understand was that my father—along with every other Jewish soldier and the thirty or so Jewish chaplains in Germany and Austria directly after the war who took part in both the liberation of the camps and the military occupation—were the first American Jews to lay eyes upon the survivors as they made their exodus into the safety of the American Zone of Occupation. They were in the unique position of being the eyes and ears for a world just beginning to understand the extent of the atrocities committed.

In the heading of his letter to Eleanor Roosevelt, the place of writing is given as Linz, which was the site of my father's new posting. His close working relationship with Captain Lafon came to an abrupt end on Saturday, July 28, while he was preparing for a weekend trip with friends. The man who would become his permanent new commanding officer, Captain Scottie, came to him in Salzburg and declared that later that afternoon he was to leave with him—simply because Captain Scottie needed him. With great regret, my father's colonel "adjudicated" him to Linz, where there were several DP camps close by and where he would remain for many months. With that, he was forced to abandon not only someone to whom he had become quite close but a very comfortable room in Salzburg, where breakfast was served in bed, and his personally stocked bar with a considerable cache of wine and liqueur that he had yet to dispose of. He had only the uncertain assurance that all of his belongings would be forwarded to him shortly thereafter.

He bid Captain Lafon farewell and headed two hours northeast with Captain Scottie to the city on the Danube where Hitler spent some of his childhood. In fact, with his parents buried in a cemetery in the village of Leonding a short distance away, the Führer considered Linz his hometown, a feather in his Anschluss hat. Hitler's vision for this city reached far beyond its gray industrial past. It was to become the jewel in his Third Reich crown and a seat of industrial modernization and German Kultur, which was to rival any of the great cities in Europe. He invested enormous time and energy designing new buildings to fulfill his dreams of supremacy in urban planning and architecture to complement his quest for world domination. The new museums and cultural venues were designed to showcase plundered art and artifacts from every occupied country around the globe. Linz was to be the Hitlerite cultural utopia for the leader and chancellor of a modern global empire.

For the Great Dictator to rebuild a city to reflect his ultimate vision, he needed disposable slave laborers to quarry the stone and create building material. The SS brought in political prisoners first and Jews later to build three of the more notorious concentration and hard labor camps in the Linz area. Mauthausen and its subcamp Gusen were top on the list. They were both considered the largest and most ruthless as Level IIIs, "Return Undesirable." And then there was Ebensee, whose backdrop was the beautiful Lake Traunsee near Gmunden where my father would spend a winter he would never forget. They were all part of a network of camps created to support Hitler's massive reconstruction effort. Work them, torture them, annihilate them, replace them—all to build, build, build.

At the end of the war, Linz had been left in near total ruin by the Allied bombing campaigns, and the city was split geopolitically along the Danube by the Nibelungenbrücke Bridge. The Soviet Red Army was on one side of the river, in Urfahr, and the Americans controlled the other side, occupying Linz. Each of the Allied zones was poised to shape a new Austrian government as well as stamp out Nazism. In a race to sell each of the superpowers' governing styles, Communism was pitted against Democracy. During my father's first days in Linz, the airwaves overflowed with reports of Russian troops threatening the city. He reported in a letter of August 5, "The Russians have just occupied Urfahr. . . . It caused a panic and an exodus of people with a bad conscience, who in their haste withdrew into our zone. This really moved me, I assure you. These bastards here in Austria and naturally in Germany would like very much to see a war between the USSR and the Allies. For that very reason I'm glad to see the new British government. At the moment we're listening to the rumor that the Russians will take Linz and we will occupy Urfahr. This caused another panic."

In fact, my father had to spend a considerable amount of time calming his new girlfriend's fears, when this five-foot-seven-inch black-haired beauty packed her bags and was ready to flee after she heard the latest news reports. She came from Teschen, on the border between Czechoslovakia and Poland, and understood very clearly what her future held if she had to live under Communism. He explained to her that she should have faith in the British. Besides, they were having way too much fun together for her to leave, and these reports were just rumors and might never come to fruition. My father couldn't get enough information fast enough and waited anxiously for issues of *Time* magazine and *Stars and Stripes* to arrive so he could stay abreast of events and study the situation. In fact, the rumors didn't pan out. For now, Linz remained part of the American zone, with the demarcation line of the Iron Curtain falling right down the center of Hitler's one successful addition to the city—the iron and steel bridge spanning the Danube River. His "little friend" from Teschen stayed, and their romance continued.

*   *   *   *

My father sat on the threshold of an old school with one leg crossed over the other, guarding the POWs. The sounds of furniture scraping worn wood floors mixed with the heavy grunts of men whose rank, masculine odor overwhelmed the singular smell of my father's soap and walnut tobacco. How fantastic it was that this twenty-one-year-old German Jew now sat overseeing men might who under other circumstances would have murdered him. A Mogen David—the yellow star of David—was glued to his gun holster, with רשח (kosher) written over it. He found that a much more forceful reminder of his authority than the weapon the holster contained. It certainly did the job for the man who said of himself, "I am not the killing kind." The star forced them to face their captor, a Jew. He had survived them.

During the afternoon, one of the Germans approached. His face was red, and where his former rank had been displayed on either side of his gray lapel were a bunch of fraying holes. My father enjoyed a little psychological warfare. He lifted his arm and gave the POW a vigorous "Heil Moses!" and simultaneously clicked his heels.

Sweat darkened the POW's collar. His armpits were wet in the close August heat. He was one of eighty Wehrmacht and SS prisoners now charged with moving two offices, with all of their files and furniture, from another building close by to this one. Halls that should have been filled with the enthusiastic voices of children were filled instead with the complaints and grunts of hopeless men doing menial labor. The POW stared back at my father and said, "Sergeant, I have carried forty armoires today, und brought each vun up two vlights of shtairz. How can ve do all of zis ven ve are given only vun meal in ze day?"

My father grimaced ever so slightly before he very calmly answered the man in perfectly accented German. "Although regrettable, you do not run the risk of getting a bullet through your head if you are too tired—which would have been the case if the positions of the actors in this game were reversed. Verstehen Sie? HEIL, MOSES!"

With that, my father saluted the former SS officer, abruptly ending the discussion. The others stood by watching this exchange of politesse with their eyes focused on the star positioned at my father's hip. He then took his lighter out of his pocket, flicked it open, and pushed down hard until metal struck flint and spark turned to flame. He lit a cigarette and exhaled into the room, offering a more subtle form of torture, tobacco envy.

*   *   *   *

My father's first weeks in Linz were packed to overflowing. The dreary five-story red brick building that had probably been an old school had become the Documents Center where he now worked. It was surrounded by an eight-foot brick wall, just a short walk from the old monastery at the center of the city. His office had a nice view of its spires and looked out onto a small park. Damage from the war was evident in the crumbled buildings off to the side. It was a pleasant day, so he took some more photographs. As he did, he caught sight of Wehrmacht soldiers passing by the center on their way to be interrogated. An impressive sight, prisoners parading along the monolithic wall toward their uncertain futures. One at a time, they would be questioned and vetted to identify war criminals among them.

*Soldiers of the defeated Wehrmacht marching toward
the Documents Center, Linz, Austria.*

In a famous photo of Hitler taken during the last days of the war, he sits like a child, staring intently at a full-scale model of Linz. It was snapped sometime in March 1945, only a few weeks before his suicide. In the background of the photo, just to the right of his cap, are the spires of the monastery that show prominently in a photo my father took of the entrance to what became the Documents Center just seven months later.

They were a group of eight: three NCOs, four officers, and a charming blonde who worked at the "desk" facing his. His job was to inventory sacks of documents and stamp them with date of receipt and their provenance. Within a couple of weeks of his arrival in Linz, my father became the chief of his department, the name of which, for whatever reason, he fails mention in his letters. POWs and other soldiers did the physical work, and he oversaw their duties along with his lieutenant, whom he referred to as "a pedantic idiot." The man ran around like a chicken with his head cut off, coming in and out of the office with such frequency he was more disruptive than a good manager. Not one to keep his dissatisfaction a secret, my father eventually spoke to his captain, a man named Bodenheimer, who confided to him that he would have peace and quiet very shortly because my father was going to be given complete control over the department. He had great rapport with his captain. They had a lot in common. They were both German Jews who had escaped and lived in New York. The captain was originally from Frankfurt, about an hour away from where my father was born, in Koblenz.

Enemy documents to be sorted, Linz, 1945.

Meanwhile, geopolitical conflict continued to play out on the world stage. In Western Europe, the Russians posed one threat, and in the Pacific, the Japanese war machine would not give in to the Allies. While my father read and chatted with friends over Sunday brunch, Enola Gay dropped "Little Boy" over Hiroshima. The bomb's vaporizing power instantly killed and maimed over one half of the population of the city as it exploded before ever hitting the ground. Three days later, the Japanese would still not surrender, so President Truman ordered "Fat Man," a bomb three times the size of "Little Boy," to be dropped on Nagasaki. On August 8, with almost a quarter of a million dead or wounded and suffering from radiation poisoning, the Japanese were left with no choice but to surrender to the Allies. The Russians had declared war on Japan for failure to follow the tenets laid out in the Potsdam Agreement. The Soviets were after the eastern ports, and declaration of war allowed them time to secure strongholds in the warm waters of the Pacific.

With no particular interest in what he was doing, my father was more often than not bored with the exigencies of tasks he felt were better left to others. He had other things weighing on his mind that he wished to accomplish during his short window of time in Europe:

Linz

August 5th, 1945

My Dears,

. . . We can now go into Switzerland. You have a fairly complicated account there that does not accrue the maximum amount of interest in its present form. If you write, Chère Mamo, and you, Cher Papo, each of you to the bank, informing them that I have full power to do something in your name, I could transfer this account in a relatively short amount of time to the United States, where we can make the money work for us. How? It's simple:

1. The soldiers entering into Switzerland have the right to carry only 35 Swiss francs—to spend. As you know, this is nothing in Switzerland—especially if one has the intention of buying a watch or something of that sort. I had the idea of selling some checks from this account, taking in exchange bank checks from American banks or "postal money orders." To protect myself against rubber checks, I have the name and number of the soldier or officer—and in the army one can always track someone down. I personally know many officers and soldiers who will be very interested.

2. I could buy, in gross, Swiss-made watches—and they tell me that there is an abundance, and I can import them for you in the US.

I intend to go to Switzerland this winter. Not on "Cook's tour" as you would imagine—I prefer to travel solo (and I detest organized activities). They promised a furlough soon. I will go to Paris and then to Brussels or visa versa. I want to see the city, see if our things are still there and settle a little account with Mme. Jadoule (unless someone has already done that). I never forget!

The guys here are not terribly interesting. I spend most of my time with two Jews from Russia. The rest with few exceptions are German—Jews and Goyem. A few of the Goyem are prototypically "Bundiste"—and the Jews are Germans who, with two or three exceptions, get on my nerves. The officers are pretty much of the same caliber or worse. The CO is of Italian origin. He's a good boy—but that's it; the "exec" (his assistant) is nice. The other German Jews tend to pass their time discussing subjects of no importance in a language that contains elements of English. They sometimes forget that they're not in the German army and want to "play" officer. One of these gentlemen, by the name of Wolfsohn, of French origin, naturally, declared and I quote: "Ai ehm echehmed to bee a Tchewe, etc." Unfortunately, I was not present. Two of our other heroes were at Ghedi when I had that little "discussion" with the commander. They keep their distance from me—It is really interesting to see how a little "show of force" rests in people's memories.

I found an Armenian rug merchant in this town, and we're great friends. He's going to get me a room—which is difficult if you don't know anyone. I can already hear you saying the Armenians are "good kids"; I know that—I prefer them to the dear Austrians, who disgust me almost more than the other Boches. The Armenian M. Papzian, however, has shown me where to find the synagogue in Linz. I will go and take some pictures . . .

Well, Good Bye,

Kisses,

Your Walter

* * * *

Five days of rumor, speculation, and erroneous reports filled the air-waves preceding news that took but a moment to deliver. On one short-wave station in the BDN (Blue Danube Network, a postwar military broadcaster operated by the Armed Forces Radio Network), Cab Calloway's crooning was cut short by an agitated voice trying to remain calm in light of breaking news: "JAPAN—ACCEPTS—SURRENDER TERMS—OF—THE—ALLIES."

Seven words that shook the world, then a pause. The sudden silence in the absence of the reporter's voice was deafening. Nervous chatter. Teletype machines and typewriters set the beat as fresh news came across the wire. Reporters in the background tried to maintain on-air silence but couldn't contain their excitement and broke out in a chorus of whispers. The listener could hear them running to their typewriters. Trying to keep up with the rapid pace of events, they slammed keys to paper, tapping out new reports that were then slapped into a waiting broadcaster's hand, so he could pronounce them to a world anxiously awaiting confirmation.

"We have been told now to temporarily hold up that flash—to disregard it. So ladies and gentlemen, those of you who may have heard that flash as we brought it to you within seconds of the time it came upon our United States press tickers, please hold that flash. Temporarily, we resume the program in progress but keep tuned to this station." Dead air while they awaited confirmation and then a return to the scheduled program. The networks in those days relied upon wire service for their information, which filled every broadcast with the emotion of the moment. Finally, the news switches to London for the official announcement.

My father spun the dial on his short-wave Telefunken to the BBC station, his perennial favorite. He stopped. Celebrations from all over were being broadcast, with still no official confirmation, and then British Prime Minister Clement Attlee's voice broke through with, "Japan has today surrendered. The last of our enemy is laid low. Peace has once again come to the world. Let us thank God for this great deliverance and his mercies. Long live the King."

In an instant, my father's head swirled with notions of possibility. The prison of war had thrown open its gates and the inmates were finally set free.

"Qui vivra verra! My God, after six years of carnage it is finally over!"

Just hours earlier, at 4:15 a.m., eighty-nine-year-old Marshal Henri Philippe Pétain had been convicted and sentenced to death for his role in the Vichy regime; Soviet troops raced unchecked across Manchuria;

Times Square filled to overflowing with a roaring sea of humanity, surging to two million, as official word came from President Truman. The war was indeed over and a two-day holiday would follow.

At about 3:15 that afternoon, sure that the Japanese had surrendered unconditionally after hearing Emperor Hirohito's high-pitched voice accept the Potsdam Declaration in a prerecorded message from the Imperial Palace, my father grabbed his portable typewriter, a Triumph acquired from a GI for twenty-five dollars, and started to write home. The machine felt awkward to him: the letters were arranged differently, and he found himself hunting and pecking at unfamiliar keys. The black market was filled with GIs trying to make a few extra bucks, and my father was not immune to the perks.

"Well," he thought to himself.

"And I will give peace in the land, and ye shall lie down, and none shall make you afraid; and I will cause evil beasts to cease out of the land, neither shall the sword go through your land."

—Leviticus 26:6

*   *   *   *

He closed the door gently behind him, loosening his tie as it clicked shut. He was tired but not ready for sleep. He had just come back from a Saturday night double feature, both of which were filmed entirely on location in New York. Watching Deanna Durbin in *Christmas Eve* and Judy Garland in *The Clock* made him forget for at least a few hours that he was in the army. It created the illusion of what he yearned for so desperately—to be a free man again. His spirits had dropped significantly. He couldn't get over the date: it was September first, six years since this war had started. His mind wandered in every direction tonight, but he was sure of one thing, which admittedly was easy to say after the fact: he would have served in this war in any case, yet never would he have thought in his earlier life that it would be with the United States Army. If ever there was another war, and he sincerely hoped not, he would do it all over again. However, at the moment he had only one thought, and that was to get out, get home, and restart his life ASAP!

Even though they had only been on screen, seeing the city's most famous landmarks was like visiting with old friends. He could practically smell the city. Every time a new image appeared, the audience screamed out the location. There was even a shot of West 79th Street, which left him feeling even more homesick and bereft of what he was missing. It had been a great evening, and he was anything but ready to let it go.

The week passed quickly, and the first High Holy Days after the war followed on its heels. With nothing special to do on his afternoon off, he stayed home and relaxed before the weekend ahead. That night he and his friends were having a big party to celebrate Rosh Hashanah and had organized a sixteen-piece American orchestra for the dance. The next morning he left in the company of a buddy to spend his two free days in the country. He had arranged in advance with his commander to have a car. They headed to Attersee, a small Austrian village by the lake of the same name, and got a room at a hotel confiscated by his troops. His friend was an expert sailor, and they spent a great afternoon on the lake relaxing in the sun.

After dinner, they took their car to a dance in the nearby hamlet of Voecklabruck. With an hour left before midnight curfew, they stopped on their way back to take a little walk. On the road, they met a couple of very charming Hungarian dancers who were also out for a stroll. With no other language in common, they began to chat in German. Just as they returned to their hotel, they were stopped abruptly by a young GI.

"Papers. Who are you?"

My father didn't recognize him, so he responded curtly, balking at his tone, "None of your business. Good night." He and his buddy laughed it off and walked back to their room. A short time later, there was a loud and insistent knock at their door. They were already in bed. As the knocking continued, it became more forceful, so my father got out of bed to see what all of the commotion was about. He listened at the door for a brief second before unlocking it, and four soldiers burst in. Lining up to block the door, they shouted, "PAPERS!"

It took my father and his buddy a couple of seconds before they understood what was going on, and then they began to laugh like idiots. The suspicion that they were spies almost brought my father to his knees.

"What the hell are you two laughing at?"

Between gulps of laughter, my father explained who they were and that they were actually Ritchie Boys, former refugees themselves and now good American citizens serving with Intelligence. Regaining some of his composure, he said, "Your zeal is commendable, but now it's time for bed no? Cigarette?" Unable to help himself, he broke out in a quieter laughter and lit his own.

Defeated, the soldiers each took one. After all, they had hoped to at the very least to be taken seriously and at best to have taken two double agents into custody.

"Look, men, if you need any other references contact the general in the morning."

That was enough to nullify their zeal for arrest.

"Now, shall we all get some sleep?"

My father steered them to the door and shut it cordially behind them. The GIs left in a cloud of quiet smoke.

The next day, the soldiers graciously came to apologize, and he said, "No harm done, men. We were just having a bit of fun with you. So long."

Exquisite scenery is the backdrop to one of the most notorious concentration camps. Lake Traunsee is on the right.

They left town. With only a few kilometers behind them, they stopped at an inn and, in a little black market trade, exchanged goods for a hearty breakfast. Fortified, they drove on to Lake Wolfgangsee, set between the mountains like a giant deep blue sapphire, and continued along the southern side of the lake. The weather was delicious. Crisp mountain air and the strength of the mid-September sun made the scenery impeccably clear. They were deep in *Sound of Music* country.

Just before noon they passed through Ebensee, the town that only a few months before sheltered one of the worst concentration camps in Hitler's web of death camps. Before arriving in the village proper, they came upon a hundred or so graves of Jews and Poles who had been assassinated while interned there. My father's natural inclination was to shoot some photographs. As they approached the camp, he tried to photograph the cremation ovens but couldn't get close enough. They weren't allowed inside because, as my father states, rather tongue-in-cheek, it was "à présent occupé par des prisonniers de la SS" (at present occupied by the prisoners of the SS), in other words it was a DP camp. The unmarked graves along the road looked like so many hills of dirt. The graves had been dug under SS supervision—the photos show mounds of dirt in neat rows.

In the Torah, the Book of Numbers counts the contribution of the living. But what of the pasts of those buried in those hills of Hitler's graves, victims of his genocide decaying en masse by the thousands? Approximately 8,200 souls were lost at Ebensee from torture, starvation, privation, violence, and finally the flames of ovens hot enough to send their ashes to the heavens. At the end, the Nazis rushed to finish the job, killing as many as humanly possible, as fast as they could. The prisoners at Ebensee were used as slaves to dig tunnels deep into the mountains surrounding them. They wore wooden clogs if they were lucky enough to have any protection for their feet. How are their contributions counted? The numbers tattooed on their arm recorded one kind of census; but the measure of their contribution was their lives, for even in death they serve to remind the living.

It had been several days of incredible contrasts. Before going to bed, he wanted to write to his parents about the atrocities he saw at

Barracks at Ebensee Concentration Camp, September 1945.

"Here lie buried 1,000ds . . ."

"of victims of Nazi Kultur."

"probably the last days' harvest."

"They did not have time to bury the corpses." Ebensee, September 1945.

Ebensee. He decided to couch the unbearable in a bit of nonchalance and black humor; it was his way. Beneath the pile of other papers was the distinctive red border of the Nazi stationery he had collected from someone's ransacked office. He pulled out a sheet, rolled it into the typewriter, and began to write.

September 9, 1945
OUR NEW POLICY: LET'S FORGET ABOUT THE PAST
LET BYGONES BE BYGONES
NATIONAL SOCIALIST [SWASTIKA IN EAGLE]
GERMAN RULING PARTY
—now called: THE PARTY OF THE GOOD HEARTED?
INNOCENT?—SAUERKRAUT
EATING, JEW LOVING? GERMAN PEOPLE
(INDEPENDENT AUSTRIAN BRANCH)

My Dears,
     To begin with, chère Mamo, thank you for your letter dated the 28th of August of this year.

I have just finished my "midnight snack," which consisted
of bouillon, American Jewish ham, Austrian bread, and
German wine—extraordinary combination, but I must admit,
excellent. The meat, however, was furnished by my friend,
the French cook—in exchange for a couple of Slovakian
cigarettes, which I employ for just such "business." Oh yes—
the Columbia Broadcasting System is furnishing the South
American music.

The letter continued with descriptions of his weekend on the lake
and culinary adventures. In between, he gently placed his description
of Ebensee. It is so unexpected that the first time I read it, I actually
got nauseous.

Before noon we passed through Ebensee, a town that only a few
short months ago sheltered one of the worst concentration camps.
Before arriving in the village proper, we saw a hundred or so graves
of Jews and Poles who had been murdered there. Naturally, I took
some photographs. Later I tried to photograph the cremation ovens
in the camp—which is presently occupied by SS prisoners—but we
weren't allowed to get close enough, because the ovens are inside the
camp. Next we ate with a unit occupying Ebensee. We had chicken.

It is, if I may say, one of my favorites, and later when I found the
photographs from that day, the first thought that popped into my head
was, "Though I walk through the valley of the shadow of death . . .
I fear no evil. שְׁ‎ מַ‎ עַ‎ יִשְׂ‎ רָ‎ אֵ‎ ל‎ יְ‎ הֹ‎ וָ‎ ה‎ אֱ‎ לֹ‎ הֵ‎ ינוּ‎ יְ‎ הֹ‎ וָ‎ ה‎ אֶ‎ חָ‎ ד‎ (She'ma
Yis'ra'eil Adonai Eloheinu Adonai Echad)." By hand my father wrote
a caption across four of the photos: "Ebensee Concentration Camp—
Here lie buried thousands . . . of victims of Nazi Kultur . . . probably
the last day's harvest . . . they did not have time to [bury] the corpses."

*   *   *   *

Several days later he went on a special mission to Salzburg, to do much
the same kind of work as he did at Ghedi, sorting through the POWs
and interrogating suspected war criminals. He would remain there

for about two weeks. After he and his buddies finished their first day of work, they took a short drive to Hellbrun, the summer residence of the cardinal of Salzburg and then arrived back to Salzburg that evening, just in time to see a revue of the Rockettes from Radio City in New York, who were at Festspielhaus, which had been renamed the Roxy. Salzburg had changed since he was last here. It was much more lively, there was quite a bit of traffic and it was well lit.

While there, and for the third time since returning to Europe, a POW by the name of Wolff was brought to him for interrogation. The first time the soldier had been Jewish, the second time it was the notorious SS-Obergruppenführer und General der Waffen-SS Karl Friedrich Otto Wolff, and now here was SS Unterscharführer Walter Wolff: "Today I interrogated a Waffen SS Sergeant named Walter Wolff. That was pretty funny. No, not a member of our family. In any case I locked him up. Generally speaking, I don't like people using the same name as me, especially when they're members of the SS." An *Unterscharführer* in the SS was the equivalent of a noncommissioned senior corporal in the paramilitary rank of the Nazi party; his duties might run the gamut, but chiefly, the million-man army of the SS was in place to implement Hitler's order for the Final Solution.

Over the next few days, with the approaching change of season came a lot of rain. My father blew into the entryway of his hotel, swung his umbrella down, and shot it open and closed a few times, shaking the water off before neatly snapping it shut. He wiped his feet at the threshold then politely stepped aside to allow someone by.

"Hey Wolff, did you hear the announcement? Come winter, men with two years of service will be demobilized."

The other Ritchie Boy's accent betrayed his origin. My father turned, looking over his shoulder to the other young man and said, "Why, of course, on my TSF. It was all over the radio. Hope you're prepared. It's raining 'à la Bruxelles' today—cats and dogs! Why don't you wait a little while? Come in, have a coffee and cigarette with me until it lets up a bit?"

"Why not? Its been raining like this for days already, no?"

The two men found seats at the bar. As they peeled off their trench coats and settled in, my father continued, "That means I'll be

going home, probably sometime in May, because our unit can keep us
for three months more, in view of the special work we do."

"A lot of guys leaving for the States in a few days have all but
forgotten what it's like to be a civilian."

"In our department alone, there are two leaving. I'm having a
devil of a time getting the minimum requirements done. Personally,
I could care less. I think those guys are right to go, but at the
same time I have to show that our department is still functioning.
Naturally, I don't do anything myself, because that would set a
bad precedent. I've asked for replacements, so I suppose in two
weeks' time I'll get a couple of overzealous new Ritchies who'll do
everything I ask them."

They chatted for a while until my father excused himself. He
wanted to pass by his room before meeting a friend for a concert
later that evening. He walked back to his hotel the Gasthof zum
Eisernen Mann. He had an excellent bed, a table for his TSF, an
armoire, a pretty little buffet with cut-glass doors, a small dry sink,
and some couches and comfortable chairs. He had management put
up a chandelier with six lights. Very chic. By the time he redecorated,
there were ten electric light bulbs in the room—taking full advantage of the electricity, as he did when he added a new electric heater
to replace his old one.

On the wall were beautiful engravings. Not knowing what to
do with his excess of money, he bought enough to decorate and was
about ready to send thirteen home that he thought they would make
nice gifts if his parents didn't use them for their new apartment at their
hotel on the Upper West Side. He framed them, using Third Reich
stamps to attach the artwork to the mats. All in all, his new room was
pretty livable. It even had running water, central heating, and a bathroom next door as well as a toilet.

Omi's last letter said they had gone to Highmount in the Catskills,
where they may have spent Rosh Hashanah. He wondered how his
family would fare during the first Yom Kippur after the war. Always
one to mark holidays independently of their preordained place in the
ritual calendar, he still felt the peculiarity of these High Holy Days. He
never honored the fast, not then or at anytime after, but the unimag-
inable loss and the call to remember were palpable.

On Yom Kippur, in a tremendous show of unity and strength, services were held in unexpected locations around the world, from the ruins of felled synagogues to makeshift shuls in DP camps in Austria and Germany, and even as far away as Okinawa, where services were held by the sea at the oldest church in Japan. Every voice was an instrument in an orchestra, every word breathed in the promise of a new year. Across cultures, people had gathered by the thousands to mourn personal and collective losses, to find hope and seek a blessing in their family's absence. They gathered to pray with recovered and borrowed Torahs and prayer books sent from New York. Rabbis who had suffered devastating losses of their own led congregations of survivors and soldiers. Offering blessings of hope or just togetherness, they mourned and they renewed. The haunting melody of *Kol Nidre* was sung while unfulfilled promises made during the past year were forgiven.[11]

It had been five years since his family had arrived in Brooklyn. Five years, and my father was right back where he started from, but under very different circumstances. This time *he* was the pursuer when the police gave chase. Utterly remarkable. He glanced over at the pile of magazines and newspapers on his nightstand and was aggravated with Omi all over again. While others took up the violin, she was fretting about epidemics in Vienna where he had yet to set foot.

True, he was bored, but not bored enough to sit around all day and read or correspond with every branch of his family as his mother suggested. On the other hand, there were a couple of people to whom he felt sincerely obligated. His teacher, Monsieur Shoch from boarding school in St. Moritz, who was like a father to him when he was little, and Mr. Kresser. There was also his cousin Pierre. Pierre was different. In the last package that arrived from home, a letter from him fell from the pile. He was just bar mitzvah, and his father, Kurt, who was suffering from a heart condition, was due for an operation. My father made a mental note to send Pierre some coins and stamps for his collection as soon as he could. For now, though, he put his correspondence aside to meet his friend, who had just returned from a trip to Brussels. My father was anxious to hear about the condition of the city he had left behind.

That evening, as they found their seats before the concert, his friend turned to him and whispered, "Wenn der Mann den Kasten durch gesagt hat, wir heim" ("When that guy has sawed his thoughts through that box [meaning the violin], we'll go home"). My father was undone. The music was excellent, but every time he glanced at the lead violinist, who bore a look of extreme stupidity in the eyes of my father, he thought of what his friend said and had to do his utmost to muffle his laughter.

He saw performances with incredible regularity while in Salzburg. The evening before the Bach concert, he went to the ballet. The night after, he saw a play at the newly reopened Landestheater. During the rise of National Socialist Republic, the famous gold and Rococo façade did not project the proper image, therefore the German Reich gave the theater a million marks for a renovation that transformed it into a showcase for Nazi culture. On August 7, 1939, Karl Bohm presided at the reopening, with Hitler in the audience as he conducted Mozart's *Abduction from the Seraglio*. Mozart had been a court musician in Salzburg and his family prominent members of the community. In 1944, because the renovation reflected Nazi culture so perfectly, the theater was awarded an Allied bomb. It had only reopened just a few short weeks before the performance my father attended. Most in the audience were members of the Armed Forces, but a small percentage of tickets were distributed to Austrians.

Later, at dinner after the concert, they sat for a long time conversing in French. My father was impressed by how well his friend spoke. He took mental notes of everything they discussed, so he could offer a report to his parents in his next letter.

NATIONAL SOCIALIST PARTY [SWASTIKA IN EAGLE EMBLEM] GERMAN LABOR PARTY

My Dears,

. . . For the moment I don't think [my group] will get a furlough because so many personnel are leaving for the US. Qui vivra verra. Today, I also received your letter (rather, the copy) for Credit Suisse. Thanks a lot. I'll write them this evening, to inform them that I'm an American citizen and by virtue of this they can't block my account. For the moment, I won't be going to Switzerland, but still.

Other items that may interest you: report on Brussels, Sept. '45. Source: a soldier who had just arrived from there. $1 = 44.2 BFr.

Prices: higher than in peacetime but on their way down to an acceptable level. One can get EVERYTHING in restaurants. Price of a good meal, in a good restaurant: $1.65 +. Excellent meal, super special: $4–$5. The price of black market American cigarettes—which is a good indicator—only $.85, compared with the fantastic prices elsewhere. All consumer items are available in the stores and department stores as well as the restaurants. A lot of cars on the roads—large quantities of American-made ones, as usual. Even some from *1942* [the last year of production]. Luxury items are expensive. A portable typewriter costs in the $200 range. A fur coat, around $500 +.

There is rationing, but it doesn't seem to put anyone in any danger. The newspapers have 4–5–6 pages. Price 2 BFr. Auvers: the port is damaged, the city as well, otherwise essentially the same conditions. . . . The Belgians are very nice to the soldiers—that is not the case in France.

People seem to have a lot of money—and are spending it. Inflation? Maybe, but I've been told prices are on the way down. It's true that I didn't see all this myself, but the guy that I "interviewed" gave me the information. . . . I would really like to go see for myself—and I'd like to see if our suitcases etc. . . . are still there.

Well, I have other letters to write.

Good night

Madame, Mademoiselle, Monsieur.

Kisses, your

Walter

After the concert he went back to his apartment, finished his letter, and enclosed a government check for $175 in a separate envelope for deposit into his personal account. His parents would receive the letter sometime during mid to late November, if it didn't get lost in the army mail. Soldiers were allowed to send only their salary plus 10 percent back to the US each month and to return to the States with no more than $200. No matter how hard he tried, he could spend no more than ten to fifteen dollars a month. He watched as the rest of the money he'd accumulated lost its value. He then pledged to use his free time and resources to settle the family's accounts and property and somewhat begrudgingly to check on the whereabouts and condition of his parents' friends. It was against army policy for soldiers to communicate with civilian Germans, but he would try.

Along with his application for Brussels, he put in a request for a furlough to Paris to settle some accounts there and then he would focus on their Swiss bank accounts in hopes of transferring monies to the United States a few months hence. His real goal was to return to Brussels, and if Switzerland proved impossible, he figured it wasn't a bad idea to just leave the account open [so there would always be some money in Europe should the need arise]. Since he was returning to Linz on assignment after having been in Salzburg for two weeks, he used the rest of the evening to pack.

The next morning, with a voluminous amount of baggage and Private Pflug to assist him, he set off for the train station. Pflug was a good guy but simple—all brawn and no brain and rather square-headed, with prominent, distinctly Germanic features. He was just what my father needed. The rain had finally stopped. My father pulled his lapel a little tighter in the fresh, crisp air. Everything looked different in the sun. As they made their way through Salzburg, he noticed the light of autumn accentuating shapes and colors of buildings, highlighting this guilty city's morphology. After almost three weeks of living on the gray scale, color in any hue was welcome.

When they arrived at the Salzburg train station, Pflug unloaded the baggage while my father went to secure a reservation on the next train departing for Linz. He soon found that the special train he had hoped to take was no longer running.

"Look, I have urgent phone orders from my HQ to get myself to Linz without delay. And by the way, I'm with G-2." Verbal economy was my father's specialty.

"Lemme see what I can do, Sarge." My father watched as the train sergeant wrote something into a log book. There seemed to be no problem at all.

"Arright. The Mozart Express is leaving at 19:18 and will get you inta Linz at 21:30. It operates outta Vienna. When it pulls in, go right to 2nd class with your buddy and you'll find your compartment. Here." He handed him two tickets, and looked down as if to continue his previous task.

Without missing a beat my father said, "Who's conducting?"

No answer.

"Thank you ever so much for your kindness. Oh, and would it be too much trouble too use your phone?"

"Sure, but don't take too long."

He thanked the sergeant once again when he hung up, then walked off to find Pflug nearby, surrounded by the baggage. The private looked so empty-headed and dazed. They relocated to a café until it was time to board. As soon as the train was in motion, Pflug fell asleep with his head cradled in his jacket, buttressing the window. He looked like a child who had fallen asleep on a school bus, cheek stretched by the weight of his head and drooling slightly onto the fogging glass. With several hours to kill, my father wrote. He reached for his typewriter and opened the black box where it was stored. Leaning it against his lap, he reached for a piece of stationery from a file he always kept close, his fingers grazing the perfectly embossed Nazi state eagle in the upper left corner as he removed the sheet. He stamped "M/SGT Walter C. Wolff—Documents Center G-2 USFA" under the letterhead in black ink and began to write. The next time he looked up, the train was pulling into Linz. Pflug woke with a start as my father began to unload the baggage from the train to the waiting car.

"How did you pull that off?" asked Pflug through a yawn.

"It pays to phone ahead," said my father. "Now give me a hand loading this stuff and let's be on our way. We should have been here hours ago."

Once they were in the car, he turned to the driver and asked, "How are things here? Anything changed much in the past few weeks?"

"We had really bad weather, lots of rain. Today's really the first sunny one we had in weeks. Other than that, same ol' same ol'. Well there's the DPs. There's some kinda demonstration goin' on at one of their camps. They should be happy they're free, never mind this uprising shit. We've been told to keep the journalists out."

My father asked, "And why is that? What if the press did get hold of it? So?"

Keep the journalists out, indeed! He would see to it that Jewish agencies in New York would hear about the conditions these poor people had been forced to live under since liberation. He suppressed his anger. How, after all they'd been through, could anyone even fathom placing the Surviving Remnant, his coreligionists, with the very Nazis

who had guarded them and murdered their families? As soon as he had
a moment, he would write to Ellen. Demonstrating was a good sign:
it meant that the Displaced Persons were gaining strength in body and
spirit, breaking the silence they had been forced to keep for a dozen
years. Contradiction was a death sentence under the Reich, and they
were now, after all, in the First Amendment zone.

"Why do you care, Sergeant? It's just a small group of Jews
demonstrating."

My father ignored the query. They were almost at the residence anyway, and he had little if any patience for some cretin who couldn't put
two and two together. Just Jews! He had heard of a man named Simon
Wiesenthal who had approached the Americans almost immediately
after his release from Mauthausen with a list of every war criminal with
whom he had come into contact during his four and a half years shuttling
between death and forced labor camps. He must have quite a list. He would
make an appointment to see him this week. The war might be over, but
anti-Semitism was as virulent and persistent as ever. In Austria, the civilians
blamed the Jews for their own persecution. They believed that the Jews had
brought the Holocaust on themselves, the Jews were solely responsible for
their own demise, and it was because of the Jews and not the Germans that
Austria was in ruin. My father steadfastly hated the Austrians more than the
Germans, probably because he felt that the average Austrian civilian took
no responsibility for his part in the Holocaust. He'd find that man.

Meanwhile, his initiative to enlist help for the DPs, from his inner
circle back in the States, was beginning to gather momentum. After
Omi's disapproving response to his letter informing Mrs. Roosevelt of
the DPs' plight in the American zone, my father had resent the letter
to the one other person whom he was certain would take immediate
action, Mrs. Lee Rosenthal, his best friend Monroe's mother. He probably received her response when he returned to Linz:

September 28, 1945

Dear Walter:

Ellen has been very noble and is typing this letter for me
because I have had some difficulty with my writing hand. I want
to first apologize to you for not writing much sooner. Perhaps you
will understand when I tell you that I have been terribly worried

about that son of mine [my father's best friend, Monroe] from whom I had not heard for nine weeks until yesterday. Monroe went through the whole Okinawa campaign and two days after the island was secured—he was hospitalized for combat fatigue and an acute stomach disorder. Apparently, he was seriously ill, because he remained in the hospital for over five weeks, after which he was sent to the Philippines, where he is now. His letter was in a cheerful tone and he seemed to have recovered completely. As for myself, I believe I finally achieve a figure as a result of this war and my son's laziness.

Now, about the letter concerning the DPs in Europe. I was very much disturbed by it and immediately had photostatic copies made of it, one of which I sent to the Joint Distribution Committee after deleting your name and the names of your friends. The J.D.C. has apparently been deluged with complaints from soldiers in Germany and apparently found it necessary to send out many copies of the enclosed circular letter to men and women who were writing to them in a critical vein, because their sons were writing from Germany to complain about the condition of the Jewish DPs. Their obvious question was: "Why are we giving so much money to the J.D.C. if nothing is being done?" I am sure you will be amused to know that it was your letter which drew a reply from them. As I said before, I am sending you a copy of it. Also, your letter appears in the Jewish Morning Journal with your name deleted. Ellen will send you a copy. I think we have aroused some feeling in the public.

As for the practical end of all this, I have organized a group of women who will begin this week to send their first 500 packages and we hope to have at least 2,000 in the mails before October 15th. After that, of course, we will need requests from soldiers for packages. I don't know how you can manage that, but if you can get enough requests, I promise you that I can get enough packages.

Now, what worries me, Walter, is that we are perhaps helping a little bit in a small way the DPs in Linz. However, there are so many other camps which need to be serviced. I wonder whether we can get the chaplains and soldiers of those camps to organize, or do you think that, since General Eisenhower has appointed a man to advise him concerning Jewish affairs,[12] that this whole condition will be taken care of. Let me know about this.

I would appreciate it very much if your chaplain would drop a note to:

Mrs. Philip Silverberg
150 Mckenzie Street
Manhattan Beach, N.Y.

telling her how important these packages are and perhaps describe the gratitude of the DPs on receiving them. It will be very helpful, since Mrs. Silverberg has aided me tremendously in this cause, and, what is more important, she seems to have many untapped resources for more money and more food.

I think I have written enough now; Ellen will strike any minute, so I will close. I am delighted that you are having such a wonderful time at the expense of the US Government. Be a good boy.

Cordially,

Mrs. Lee Rosenthal

P.S. You will be amused to know that I waved such a big stick at Mr. Sobel,* the head of the J.D.C., that he offered to send me to Europe, I think, perhaps to get rid of me. So, don't be surprised if I call you sometime soon.

Will you ask Cpl. David Aronson if he knows a Mr. Mankuite who is general manager of the Rokeach Factories? Mr. Mankuite insists that he know this man, that he loves him dearly and I don't care whether it is the same David Aronson or another one. The name certainly produced a great many canned foods for us.

As if he were running a postal relay race, after receiving the letter from Mrs. Rosenthal he wrote another one home to empower his sister to do more:

---

*Louis H. Sobel, assistant executive secretary of the JDC.

HQ DOCUMENT CENTER, G–2, USFA
APO 777, C/O PM, NEW YORK, N.Y.
LINZ, AUSTRIA

October 10, 1945

My Dears,

. . . I received a letter from Mrs. Rosenthal . . . to be expedited to Vienna. It will go by special courier, but I have no guarantee that it will be delivered to the proper hands. It will be expedited by civil courier in Vienna. I put Austrian stamps on it.

Good work, Chère Ellen. Congratulations. Now, slowly but surely the US is moving. The propaganda effort must continue in favor of our "coreligionists." I have just written to this Mrs. Silberman, whom Mrs. Rosenthal mentioned. I gave her the Gabriel Heatter[13] treatment, very flattering. I don't know the woman, but it is always effective. Here are some examples:

"Our cause is important and very urgent! A severe winter is rapidly approaching, and our DPs are not adequately cared for. I don't believe our conscience could ever rest if the women and children, and men who managed somehow to escape and survive the horrors of the Nazi extermination camps—would now perish, perish after we delivered them, after we had the chance, the privilege, the honor, and the responsibility to feed and clothe them."

"These people depend on America and expect almost miracles from America—because there is hardly anything else they can hope for!"

"Citizens of importance and high standing like you must lead and direct help for the remnants of European Jewry; it is your moral duty!!"

I hope that this will have the desired effect. All means are good to achieve a goal. I suggest using the photos that I sent yesterday, I mean the ones of the concentration camp, for the same goal.

Well, good night.

Kisses,

Walter

*   *   *   *

The raw smell of sweat and perfume. Couples jitterbugging across the dance floor, skirts flying, sweat dripping, loud Big Band music. The wine just kept flowing. The commander sat across the table from him, flirting with one of several romantic candidates my father had invited along for the evening. Spellbound by his sudden popularity and the attention he was getting, the commander ordered another two bottles of champagne. My father pulled a black leather pouch from his jacket pocket and shoved his pipe into the tobacco, filling it with one hand. Conversations faded. The rhythm of the sixteen-piece orchestra blended with the noise of waiters carrying silver trays of drinks and food as he lost himself in a moment of thought.

He'd been back in Linz for a week, and along with his return came news that he might be transferred to Vienna. Join the army, see the world. Mrs. Rosenthal and Ellen's outreach program in New York was bearing fruit. Packages for the DPs had begun to trickle in, and it occurred to him that if in fact he was transferred to Vienna, their distribution would be affected if he weren't present to oversee it. He reminded himself to send his sister copies of the sole article to appear in the paper about the demonstration the other day, with instructions to forward it to every Jewish agency in New York. Goddamn Austrians and their bloody propaganda. They were still planting articles in the papers telling their readers of the wonderful conditions provided for the refugees! He would never forget the "what might have been," and it weighed heavily on him. What debt must memory and good fortune pay to insure clarity of conscience and soul?

When he looked up again his pipe had gone out, it was after eleven, he was sucking on stale air, and an Austrian orchestra had taken over and were playing their last song. He wasn't sure why, but the evening had flown by. He, his commander, the lieutenant, and two of his friends were the last to leave. By the time they got back to their residence, dusk had turned to early dawn and he was stone-cold sober. Not four hours later he was back at his desk. His office was almost empty. He thought, Long live the Documents Center, the Documents Center is dead—well, almost! They were supposed to shut it down during the next couple of months, and there was a ton of paperwork and loose ends to wrap up, so it was odd there were so few guys in that morning. Normally, there were more than a dozen typewriters working at a furious pace between the two adjoining offices, with a radio going at all times.

This morning the office was quiet. A lot of the men were already on their way back to the States. If he was to be transferred to another section of Intelligence, he hoped it would be CIC, the Counter Intelligence Corps. They lived better than anyone else, and they had the same privileges as officers without the actual rank distinction. Even though he'd rather continue on with his old unit until demobilization and return, CIC would be a fine substitute. Anyway, when the office was quiet, he could get twice as much done in half the time. He decided to stay until lunch and then sleep for the rest of the day. He picked up the phone and put a call through to Mr. Wiesenthal. Maybe he could see him this afternoon. When he made the appointment, he discovered that the address was just four doors down from the War Crimes Unit, and down the street from his office at the Documents Center. Later my father learned that the man's living quarters and office had first been located in an old schoolhouse in Leonding, just outside of Linz, overlooking a small dwelling that once had been home to the Hitlers and adjacent to a cemetery where the Führer's parents are buried. As soon as Mr. Wiesenthal found out, he asked to be moved. My father hung up the phone and went back to work.

When he left the Documents Center, he stopped at the PX to buy birthday presents for his mother and Ellen, even though it was a bit too early. The mail system was in such chaos that it was the only way to ensure receipt of their gifts by the first and the eighteenth of December. With that errand off his list he went back to his room and read for awhile before taking a nap. He was in the middle of reading an anti-Semitic tract, *The Jews in France*, which sought to prove that the government and the press were entirely in the hands of the Jews. If all that were true, thought my father, we're a lot stronger than he ever thought: "It's very amusing, and I'll send it to you along with a collection of anti-Semitic and anti-American books. Some are so stupid you can actually read something else while reading them. Now we can laugh—but it wasn't long ago that it wasn't funny at all."

The books are crumbling and in various states of decay, but seventy years later they still run a chill up my spine. After a nap he left for his appointment.

Since liberation, Simon Wiesenthal had recovered enough to become the president of the Executive Committee for Jews in the region. By now, the DPs were really organizing themselves. It was sometimes easy to forget that before the war, they came from all walks of life and weren't stateless and destitute, on the verge of starvation and death. Within days of his release from Mauthausen in May, the man volunteered his services to G-2 to help capture Nazis. Dying of hunger when he first approached the Americans, he was so frail and sick at ninety-nine pounds that they turned him away. He spent the next week trying to gain weight. He had to. Before approaching the Americans for the second time, he rubbed his cheeks with red paper. His list with the names of every high-ranking Nazi who had crossed his path was a compelling recommendation.

A man about my father's height opened the door to an office accented by a big map marking the location of every concentration camp. On his desk, piled high, were files and index cards. He was balding, had dark hair, and wore a slight mustache. His ears stuck out inquisitively as if he were waiting, attentive for someone. He was extremely thin and weighed no more than a hundred plus pounds. His dark suit was too big on him. Yet his eyes were set with such an intensity they dispelled any sense of physical frailty. The man was not yet the person whom the world would come to know as the most famous Nazi hunter of all time. He was just an extremely determined survivor who understood that in order for him to live with the losses he suffered, he had to serve as a voice for those who were no longer able to speak or act on their own behalf, and he would see to it that the world would know and never be allowed to forget the genocide Hitler's armies had inflicted on his people. He had sworn that, if he lived, he would see to it that every single war criminal was brought to justice. A former engineer, he had lost everything, including, he was certain at the time, his beautiful wife. When they were reunited several weeks later, they counted eighty-nine family members between them who were murdered by the Nazis. Eighty-nine. The thin man was resolute.

The two men stood for a moment at the threshold, two very different kinds of survivor. One who had eluded the web, and the other who was caught in it until the moment of liberation on May 5 of that year. My father's outstretched hand reached for the man's, who gripped it firmly for just a moment too long. The survivor's accent leaned east toward his Galician roots, while my father's leaned west toward Germany and his. They spoke in German. My father explained his effort to organize care packages for the DPs, and then continued on with the subject of retribution and restitution for the living.

"My family still has finances in Switzerland. We're currently deciding what changes will need to be made in terms of actionable sales or what have you. I just received a report from Crédit Suisse informing me of what is left between our accounts. The *Gerichtskasse*[14] doesn't seem too badly damaged, but the road ahead for our coreligionists will be a long one toward restitution, and the Swiss are not exactly warming to the idea."

They spoke for some time. Before parting, Mr. Wiesenthal said to my father, "Finances aside, everywhere we go we see misery, especially in Vienna, but what is missing now is not so much food as clothing. Henceforth, food is more or less secure, since the UNRRA[15] has assumed complete control. Your packages should not stop. No, sir, keep those coming. If I say, dear man, that food is less of an issue, it simply means that UNRRA has assured us that they will see to it that no one shall die from hunger any longer. However, one has to do more than that for us. And the packages are well received. Clothes, clothes are essential."

"Has the UNRRA not distributed enough?"

"Yes, but winter is coming, there is not enough to go around, and they are projecting extreme cold. We cannot continue to live under such conditions. We are, after all, the victims. Did you hear about the uprising at Bindermichl?"[16]

"I caught only a glimpse of it on my way in from Salzburg, but I did hear about it. It was meant to be kept out of the papers. I would like to help."

"I see that. Please keep doing what you are doing and keep the agencies in the States informed. Now I must get back to my work. The Military Tribunal begins in Nuremberg on the eighteenth, a week from today, and there is much to do before then."

Wiesenthal paused for a moment, drawing his open hand across his face as if to wipe away the incomprehensible. With tears welling in his eyes, he continued: "I survived, but I will not rest until every last Nazi is brought to justice. There may be millions of us dead, but each one of us has a story. Buried with each of the dead are theirs. Behind every single man, woman, and child are the Nazis who tortured, raped, and killed them. They are the murderers among us. We can never let the world forget. Never."

My father looked once more into eyes deeply set from witnessing years of depravity and cruelty. Offering his hand he said, "The hunters are now the hunted. Thank you for your time, Herr Engineer."

"Indeed, and you for yours, Herr Sergeant Wolff."

*   *   *   *

After his meeting with Simon Wiesenthal, he wrote the following letter to his friend Monroe's mother, summarizing the conditions under which the DPs were living and the state of postwar anti-Semitism in Austria:

Dear Mrs. Rosenthal,
It was indeed with great joy that I received your letter today. You seem to have gone all out for this very important cause—not that I expected anything less from you.

Yes, Cpl. David Aronson knows the owner of ROKEACH foods very well—the gentleman being a relative of Dave's. Furthermore, he worked right there. I suppose the world is small.

You mention my "chaplain" being a very bad Jew. I have not seen him yet—but I shall do that tomorrow, to arrange for the distribution of the packages when they arrive. Anyway, the man is part of the 26th (Yankee Division), which is leaving for the States shortly, to be replaced by the 83rd Division. At any rate, we can handle the distribution ourselves, since we can easily get one of our trucks for the weekend. I will also tell the acting Jewish chaplain of the 26th Division to write to Mrs. Silverberg and I shall write to her about the matter tonight.

We will also mimeograph a letter of thanks to be sent to the ladies who sent the packages.

As you seemed to imply, these packages are just a drop in the bucket. I fully agree with you on that point, but something is better than nothing. Unfortunately, though, it will be rather difficult for us to do anything beyond the immediate vicinity of Linz, the army being what it is.

I even anticipate some trouble because of the hundreds of packages that will arrive, I mean from the Army Post Office and the Inspector General, but that doesn't bother me in the least, since there is hardly anything they can object to, if they're informed of the purpose of the matter.

As far as organizing the Jewish soldiers of other areas in a similar manner, I think that that could be done best from the States. I suggest you consult the New York Times about what division occupies what area; I am rather certain that they could give you that information. Then, I would write letters to the Jewish Chaplain of these Division, or Corps, or Armies, urging them to organize a similar action among the Jewish men under their jurisdiction. These letters should be addressed to the Chief Jewish Chaplain, Jewish section of the XX Division. Very often there will merely be an enlisted man acting as chaplain, as is the case here. In Salzburg and the surrounding area, I happen to know, is the 42nd Division (Rainbow). Maybe you can think of something better, but I don't have any ideas off hand.

Since they removed Patton from his post,[17] and because of the subsequent scandal about DP camps, things have improved somewhat, but still, there is PLENTY to be done. At least, they are making an effort to better things. A few days ago we had a big demonstration of Jews from a neighboring camp. Our coreligionists, about 300 strong marched through Linz with posters, protesting against the removal of the camp where they wanted to put the survivors of the con-centration camps and crematoriums into barracks without windows, cooking, or sanitary facilities.[18] To top it off, the place was surrounded by barbed wire and guarded by sentries. The military had threatened to remove them by force, because they wanted to return the pres-ent location to the Austrians who wanted to establish a children's camp that used to be there years ago. So the men marched up to the military governor's office. They were received very courteously, and General Reinhardt, Commander of Upper Austria, is said to have known nothing of the matter. He immediately fired the commanding officer of the camp and rescinded the orders for removal. I understand the matter went up to General Clark's headquarters. Now, I want you to understand, their present camp is by <u>no means</u> paradise. It is extremely overcrowded and far from satisfactory, but the other place was even worse. Now large apartment houses, several miles outside of Linz, near Neu-Muenchen, are going to be made available to the people. These will have central heating and proper sanitary and cooking facilities, and there will be only about four to a room, which is a great improvement.

Enclosed you will find an article on these demonstrations in the local paper. Unfortunately, I don't have time tonight to translate it, but I'm quite certain Ellen can do this in a very short time.

Now that we've talked business, let's come to our more immediate problems. I was almost certain that there was something wrong with Monroe, but I didn't dare mention the possibility to you. Gosh, was I glad to hear when the Okinawa campaign was all over. I do hope that he is entirely OK and back soon. Please let me have his address; although I don't expect an answer to my letter from that lazy so-and-so, I want to write him anyway. Are you really coming over here? If you are, by all means, see me—if you can. I am certain you could do a lot of good, and fight with some of the more obstructionist brass-hats. I personally hope to return by late spring, when I shall have three years of service. No, I'm not complaining. I was very lucky in this war, in the first and the second part of it.

The music I had tuned on my radio turned out to be a Russian station. They interrupted their broadcast with: "Anti-Semitism is Fascism." Such appeals are very necessary, since we persistently hear of anti-Semitic riots in Slovakia and of regular pogroms in Poland. These bastards have not changed—and never will. Anti-Semitism is still strong here and everywhere in Germany—it is a subject not even up for discussion anymore—but taken for granted. Yes, naturally, they all say now that you should not exactly have burned them alive, but—

Well, there is so much I could say on the subject—but I guess that all these things be known in the States—only they don't get

enough publicity. Speaking of publicity, I sent Ellen several nega-
tives of pictures I took of the Ebensee concentration camps showing Jewish graves marked with "Mogen Davids" side by side with
Christian graves. These shots are quite good, and could very easily
be used for propaganda purposes—such as appeals for help for the
survivors or to get across the idea of "Let's not forget" etc.

Well, that will be all for tonight. Now I am going to write to
Mrs. Silverberg a letter thanking her for her great effort.

So long—and write me soon—and <u>thanks</u>.

Sincerely,

Yours,

Walter

HQ DOCUMENTS CENTER, G–2, USFA
APO 777, % PM, NEW YORK, N.Y.
LINZ, AUSTRIA

October 12, 1945

Dear Ellen,

. . . In between time, I had a conference on the subject of the
packages with the president of the executive committee for Jews
in the region on the subject of retribution for the living. If I must
leave, naturally, it will be a bit complicated, but everywhere we go
we see misery, especially in Vienna.

Now you need to act on the clothing. That's what's missing now, more than the food, which henceforth is more or less
secure, since the UNRRA assumed complete control. No, the
packages should not stop; if I say that food is less of an issue that
simply means that UNRRA will see that no one will die from
hunger, but one has to do more than that for the survivors, and
the packages are always gratefully received. The food is more or
less good, but nothing special. Clothes are still needed. Yes, the
UNRRA distributed some, but more are needed. As you must
have certainly read in the newspaper that I sent to you yesterday,
there was a demonstration here in Linz. Contrary to what the
Austrian newspaper reports, the camp where we wanted to put
the DPs was not good at all. The mistake has been corrected since

that time—very good lodging has been found, but it is significant that I learned it was meant to be kept out of the presses. In view of this fact, I will send you another copy of the paper. The Jewish agencies should certainly be notified. To give you an example of the extent of the annihilation of our race, here is a very significant number: in the camp neighboring Mühldorfer Hart [originally a subcamp of Dachau, located in a suburb of Munich]: there are among the 800 occupants only 15 children. Facts such as this should be employed in our propaganda to receive aid. If you would, dear Ellen, inform Mrs. Rosenthal of everything that I've written to you on this subject.

*　*　*　*

It was the middle of October. With the volume of work decreasing in Linz, my father was promoted and placed in a new department in Gmunden, about halfway between Salzburg and Linz, but wouldn't elaborate in his letters home as to what exactly he was doing, other than to say, "I got really lucky— they posted me in a new department here, and for [my commanding] officer they gave me this really nice guy that I had at Ghedi in Italy, who was also my Order of Battle instructor at Ritchie. . . . The work I'm doing can't be described in precise terms, but at least I'm not glued to a desk and I'll see the country—at least I think I will." During the first couple of weeks he sometimes made the trip between the two cities twice in a day.

He set out on an unusually warm morning, with his new commander to return to Linz for a high-level meeting. He hadn't been back to Linz since he was promoted. As he got into the back seat of the jeep, he said, "C'mon, come on then." He patted his leg and invited Lieutenant Sirkin's dog to jump in and sit beside him. The dog was happy to comply, resting his chin warmly on my father's lap. Linz was about a two-hour drive from Gmunden, and the dog stayed fast asleep for most of it. Occasionally, he'd pop up and reach his head out the window like a small child. With the wind caressing his face, the dog let his ears blow around like little propellers. When he'd had enough, he'd flop back onto my father's lap, nuzzling his little nose between his paw and my father's gun holster. That morning, man's best friend was getting an unusual amount of attention as my father thought back to his own dog, Finito, who succumbed to an untimely death a few months back. The little orphaned puppy made it all the way from Verona to Salzburg.

The meeting was at a bar somewhere near his old office at the Documents Center. My father listened intently to their every word. He was the only noncommissioned officer in a room filled with lieutenants, captains, majors, and colonels from both the Western Allies and Russia. He was sitting among the elite command of the army, feeling a bit like a little fish in a big sea. Relations between the Allied and Soviet occupied zones had become strained. Behind the scenes, the political rhetoric was heating up. Austria leaned toward building a neutral democratic state, leaving the Communists in the minority, which incited a demonstration of anti-Western feeling in the Eastern zone. Among friends, the Allies spoke more and more of the next war or wars to come. As time passed, my father could feel a distinct chill growing in the room as relations between the personnel of the two countries seemed to stiffen. While overtly they remained extremely cordial and amicable toward each other, they sounded like the meetings at the Munich Conference in 1938 must have been—filled with interminable pleasantries and formality without concrete results.

My father excused himself after the meeting to check the mail. The postmaster handed him an avalanche of packages for the DPs, and one for him. Every single package would have to be accounted for and an appropriate thank-you sent to its proper donor. There were so many that he needed to corral at least three of his coreligionists to help him, but before he could do that he wanted to see what was sent to him. He knew better than to open anything from home publicly, so he found a more private spot before ripping open the box. He dug his hand in and pulled out—underwear.

"For the love of God, when will she learn?!"

Thank God he was alone. Underwear, a scarf, a cap, two sweaters, a comb and mirror set, magnificent Yardley gloves, a military shirt, candy, pralines, newspaper clippings, *Collier's*, and the *Saturday Evening Post*. He would pass along what he didn't use to the DPs. But did she have to send him underwear? And to top it off had no interest in popular watered-down periodicals for the masses, especially *Collier's*!

(This was odd, because *Collier's* was one of the first magazines courageous enough to publish an article, by Jan Karski, about Polish
concentration camps months before the end of the war. Karski had
been a Polish resistance fighter who was captured and then viciously
tortured by the Nazis. He later escaped to the United States and was
one of the first to break the story of the systematic murder of Jews
to the West. Odd too, because *Collier's* had in its stable an illustrious
list of contributing writers ranging from Churchill to Hemingway
and Martha Gellhorn.) He noticed that he had overlooked a letter
in the pile of mail. Nice stationery. A girl's handwriting, it looked
familiar. He opened it, unfolded it, and began to read it on the spot.
It was from his friend Doris in New York:

Dear Walt,

Just got your letter today and thought I'd answer pronto! I
want to make this kind of fast because Floss is going out and I want
her to mail it. I'm in bed with one of my yearly colds and feel perfectly awful. It seems colds are going around fast and furiously . . .
and it wouldn't be right to miss one.

Was in our old hometown a couple of weeks ago to do a little
shopping. Had a wonderful time. The one thing I really enjoyed
(you're going to laugh) was walking on Fifth Ave. <u>at night</u>. The
more I go to New York, the more I love it. I don't know what it is,
but the whole atmosphere makes you feel like living and working.
Do you know what I mean?

You're quite the important young man over in Linz. I don't
know what they're going to do without you!?! Seriously, Walt,
I think it's wonderful (the work you're doing). At least this job
sounds interesting, which is more than I can say for a lot of other
Army jobs I've heard about.

Walt, I think it was awfully sweet of you to think of me, and I
know the perfume will be something wonderful.

You mentioned something about a car. What are you going to
do with it after you come home? It would cause quite a sensation if
you were to bring home a European car!! Can't you picture yourself driving around New York in a low slung something or other.
<u>Ahem</u> I can just picture the young ladies of New York and what

they'd say to each other. "Darling you know Walt Wolff's in town, and you ought to see him, he's looking wonderful, but you ought to see his car. What I wouldn't give for just one date with him— not that he hasn't always been quite attractive, but <u>now</u>." See what happens to people when they have nothing to occupy their minds? By the way, that picture you sent me was very much appreciated and you shall be rewarded—if you can call it that.

Gotta close. Write.

Love,

Doris

Suddenly the prospect of going home no longer felt so remote. He smiled and lit a cigarette. It wasn't so bad being him. No, not at all, but he better hide the letter. His girlfriend might get hold of it, and God knows there was enough talk of war going on right now! Mady was an older woman. She was engaging, fun, and he just remembered they had a date that night, and he was still in Linz. She was twenty-three, an actress, and she spoke more languages than he and his sister put together. Before his group left for Gmunden, he phoned her and invited her for drinks and supper at nine. They arrived back by eight thirty. He ran up to his apartment to change and on the way in checked his bar. Full. He had just gotten a new ration of liquor, so it was flush. He quickly changed into his new shirt, then brushed back his hair with his two bristle brushes and a bit of pomade. A last look in the mirror and he was ready. When Mady walked in, she sat down on one of his couches, carefully removed her gloves, and placed her hat beside her.

Breathily, she said, "What a lovely villa, Walter."

He described his villa in a letter home two weeks later:

U.S.D.I.C.G-2,USFA
APO 777, C/O PM, NEW YORK, N.Y.
Linz, Austria
Gmunden, the 30th, October 1945

. . . I now have a new room in a little ultra-modern villa, and this room is the epitome of chic. It has a bed, two leather couches (the type employed by the legendary millionaires to smoke their

$10 cigars), a little modern table—black, a beautiful armoire that matches the rest, and a little buffet-bar. There are rugs, lamps, curtains etc. It's really deluxe. I also have a little room the size of your kitchen to wash myself in, etc. The bathroom is across the hall. I am the only one to have a private room—I suppose because I am the highest ranking in the unit. All of the old ones left, that's why.

Otherwise, I have some pretty important work now, and it's really interesting. That's the real reason why I've been writing less often—I have a lot to do, because almost everything that comes into the department has to go by me—and naturally the lieutenant. We still get along really well—with him, one can act freely without worrying that it will filter through to the "upper-level commander."

I also have a new girlfriend, very nice. She is an actress, 23 years old, pretty intelligent (speaks more languages than Ellen and me combined)—She is excellent company. There is a captain interested in her as well, but she seems to prefer me—for which I am obviously honored!!!!

That Saturday, my father and six of his friends left after breakfast and drove up to the Berg Hotel am Feuerkogel, located on the mountain overlooking Lake Traunsee and the town of Ebensee. Before it was requisitioned by US forces, the hotel had been used by the Waffen SS to house wounded soldiers returning from the Eastern Front. The men dropped their bags, settled in for a quick coffee, and then made their way up the mountain. The view was magnificent. They picnicked on a large rock overlooking the slopes, with the Alps extending as far as the eyes could see and in every direction.

Finally, his years of anticipation disappeared in a moment. He laid his skis down in the snow and clipped into his bindings. Resting his eyes momentarily on the horizon, he adjusted his equipment one last time. His muscles tensed against six years of forced abstinence. Last night's moon still held her steady gaze, white against the azure sky. In one smooth motion of muscle memory, he leaned toward the blinding powder and dug his wooden poles deep into the snow. Then, with the dexterity of a racer, he propelled himself forward and pushed off the crest. Freedom nipped at his boots, a rush of powder sprayed into the windy periphery as he pushed himself to find his groove. He found his old slalom. With every passing meter he shed his private war through the decompression chamber of gravity and lost time, exhilarated by the fantastic rush of speed on his victory run down the occupied mountain. Small, complicit villages rested below; concentration camps and gutted ruins were made invisible from his bird's-eye perspective. The coming privation of winter was but a blurred detail on a scarred panorama, which looked for all the world like a Tyrolean snow globe in a toy store window.

*   *   *   *

If there is one thing from his wartime service that struck my father deeply and remained with him throughout his life, it was the plight of the DPs in the early aftermath of the war. He never spoke about it, other than to describe a Chanukah party he gave, but he never forgot the faces of the survivors or the scarcity of children left in the aftermath of the war. In fact, during his Shoah Foundation interview in 1998, he was asked if he had a relationship with any of the survivors. He responded with surprisingly animated warmth to his voice and said, "Oh, yes . . . We took the utmost care of them." His voice trailed off for a moment, memories echoing their way forward despite his control: "I have to go to a Chanukah celebration—which really doesn't interest me, but the mayor of Gmunden will be there and I'd like to arrange for a license to open a butcher shop for three of our coreligionists—this is an excellent occasion to do that—we will distribute the things from the Wolff Relief Agency, and I would like to see who gets what."

Coincidentally, the first night of Chanukah that November in 1945 fell on the eighth day of the Nuremberg Trials. That afternoon, a one-hour documentary was shown in court, depicting footage the Allies had collected during the first hours and days after liberation. For the first time, the condition of the survivors at the concentration camps was forced upon the perpetrators. The film left defendants and prosecutors alike stunned into silence as the extent of the atrocities and crimes against humanity were brought directly into the courtroom. There was no denying in those pictures. As darkness fell in

Nuremberg, candles celebrating the miracle of this festival of lights were being lit at nearby synagogues and at makeshift shuls all over the occupied zones. Several nights later, my father attended the Chanukah party that he had organized for the DPs at the Ort Castle in Gmunden. With the help of some friends, he brought along forty sacks of packages to distribute personally, only a fraction of the 1,500 that he would eventually receive through the army mail system, turning it on its ear.

My father would not live to see a remarkable moment that occurred during the writing of this book and on the heels of Chanukah. One evening, while I was looking through a wooden wine box that contained his notebooks from high school and university, a contemporary-looking thank-you note fell to the floor. It read:

Dear Mr. Wolff,

Sorry I took so long with these . . . It has been very busy! I have enclosed copies of pictures I have. Thanks so much again for your kindness in sharing your remembrances. . . .

Stay Well,

Judy Zeichner

P.S. If the Felix you refer to in your photos is Felix Opatowski—

I am in contact with him in Toronto.

In the box were seven pages of Xeroxed photographs. I leafed through them, and not far from the top lay a photograph of my father in uniform sporting his yellow ascot, which I knew so well, and his army beret with a US insignia pinned to it. And then, as if by magic, there were copies of the photos that had been taken at that Chanukah party.

Someone had saved a picture of my dad until the day they died and was as touched as he was by the memory of that party given on that cool November night in 1945. It did not take me long after I sat down at my computer and Googled Judy Zeichner and Felix Opatowski to find them, and I called them immediately. Although in his nineties, Felix was ebullient and so warm and welcoming. He got so excited that he put his wife, Regina on the phone as well. Together, sometimes

Chanukah party given by my father and army personnel for survivors of Nazi concentration camps at Schloss Ort Gmunden, Austria, November 1945.

Survivors celebrating Chanukah, November 1945. Among them are Felix Opatowski and Jacob Artman.

talking over each other, they recounted their time in Gmunden after surviving several forced labor camps as well as Auschwitz. Two phone calls later he told me how he and Jacob Artman, Judy Zeichner's father, had become fast friends at Auschwitz and remained as close as brothers for most of their lives. Jacob was five years his senior and took care of Felix as if he were the little brother he never had. Both young men were alone and would never see any of their families ever again.

Jacob had arrived at the camp three weeks before him and already knew how to act and what to do and how to stay out of trouble. He explained to Felix, who was originally from Lodz, in Poland, that he should never go anywhere by himself and always do absolutely everything as a group to attract as little attention as possible. Sometime during his first weeks at the camp, Jacob explained that the smell permeating the air and the ash falling to the ground was that of the Jews being gassed and cremated in the ovens at the camp. Felix remembered the day a transport arrived from France with busloads of children who were immediately marched to the crematorium—to their deaths. They came from Drancy, the transit camp outside of Paris.

Felix and Jacob stayed together throughout their internment and found each other again at Ebensee in Gmunden—which had been transformed from a concentration camp to a DP camp after liberation. There, they eventually made money stealing food from the American mess and selling it in Linz on the black market. Felix and Jacob met their wives while at the camp before emigrating to Canada and the United States.

When Judy answered the phone, she knew immediately who I was and began to cry as she exclaimed, "This is the best Chanukah present ever!" She explained how, after her father, Jacob Artman, died, she came across the photo of my father while going through his things and tracked him down in New York. They never met, but they spoke at length over the phone and he shared memories of Gmunden and the DPs with her. She was struck by a couple of things he said when, in the rarest of moments, he shared memories of Gmunden and Ebensee with her. He told her about the swimming pool at Ebensee, which he saw a few months after liberation. By the time he got there in September, it must have been emptied, but he had seen photographs or heard that when it was first drained of water, it had been piled high with the striped clothing of the dead, who had been stripped after they were killed so the Nazis could collect their uniforms. The other statement that left an impression on her was his description of the survivors with whom he came into contact. He gently told her that they all looked as though they had not eaten in a very long time.

Felix and Judy on behalf of her father both told me what a wonderful thing my father had done for them, not only by organizing that Chanukah party but through his care and kindness in procuring the many packages for the DPs. I had just identified two people out of hundreds of strangers in my father's archive of over two hundred photographs. Nothing short of a miracle.

*   *   *   *

When my father and his group returned to the mountain again a couple of weeks later, they brought their girlfriends with them. As they got closer, they could see that a fresh coat of snow blanketed the Gmunden glacier and would make it too difficult for them to drive further. When they noticed a red and white cable car coasting toward them, they left the car at Ebensee. Floating above the majesty and serenity of the mountain reminded him of Corviglia in St. Moritz, except here the vast wilderness silenced the ghostly screams of those who never made it to liberation. They found a chalet on the trail a short distance from the cable car. In an act of questionable authority, my father requisitioned the house, and pronounced it their new weekend retreat and a perfect place for a celebration. He had brought something very special, which he had secreted away under every bathroom sink in every residence since summer: bottles of wine from my great-grandparent's home in Landau, taken when he reclaimed the house from its occupiers. He wanted to raise a glass to my grandmother on her birthday. The wine was perfect. It tasted of champagne without the carbonation! Every sip was an elixir distilling the freedom that had hung in the balance for so long. After a full day on the slopes, he sat by the fire and shared some wine. My father proposed his long-anticipated toast among his good friends, "To my chère Mamo, on her birthday. To her health, and may I be home to celebrate with her next year!"

Together they raised their glasses. "Hear, hear!"

And one of his friends replied: "And to our friend, Wolff of the Gestapo, who had the czar of Austrian industry and the Bohemian and Moravian Protectorate cleaning his office yesterday!"

"Really, it was nothing," said my father in mock modesty. "You should have seen him. He was an enormously fat man, typical of a Generaldirektor who not long ago was giving orders, telling others what to do without ever doing anything himself! He was so funny, all I really wanted to do was put a bullet in his head. He wasn't used to taking orders from anyone, let alone from a nice boy like me! To the Jew and the Nazi janitor!" He raised his glass. "I'm sure I'll be one of the main accused in the next edition of the war crimes trial. If only I were the killing kind. . . . The bastard!"

*   *   *   *

By mid-December my father was on the road again. After a weekend of skiing, he walked into the adjutant general's office with the intention of protesting the fact that he had never been given his famous furlough,

The Nazi slogan "One Reich, One People, One Leader" and destruction in Vienna 1945.

"We thank our Führer," Vienna, December 1945.

when it suddenly materialized. The AG let him talk for a couple of minutes before nonchalantly pulling the orders out of a drawer and handing them to him.

"Wolff, you've been granted a ten-day compassionate furlough. Where are you headed?"

"Brussels, sir. It was the last place I lived with my family before the Nazis invaded. We left four days before they bombed."

"Good luck to you, Sergeant."

"Thank you ever so much, General." My father gratefully saluted.

Three days later, he left in a station wagon with the courier from Vienna and a fellow named Rudiger who was on his way to Holland to marry his prewar girl—who, while awaiting his return, had become a leader in the underground resistance. They stopped over in Linz and ate at the Documents Center Hotel before continuing on to Vienna. Normally, the journey should have taken less than two hours, but the roads were slippery, so they were forced to drive slowly. On their way, my father noticed a very thin garrison of Soviet troops—he could almost count all of them. A group of them wanted to buy cigarettes and watches, so they obliged and sold them several cartons. When they finally arrived at US military headquarters in Vienna, it was evening. My father was immediately notified that he was in trouble because of the packages that had arrived in his name for the DPs. Over a bottle of wine at the "Zebra Club,"[19] he prepared his case thoroughly, writing out all the possible charges along with his accuser. It made for quite a list. Given the results he achieved the next morning, he must have cut the figure of a rather convincing defense lawyer when, the first thing the next morning, he walked through the door to his appointment and presented himself before a colonel in the adjutant general's department. In a letter, he described an encounter that went something like this:

"Sir, if you would check with Corporal Katzman, acting Jewish chaplain for the 26th Division, he can vouch for the honest distribution of these packages. I can assure you there has been no wrongdoing. I quite simply received an overwhelmingly positive response to a request I put through to relatives in New York."

"Master Sergeant, you've gone against all regulations! Fifteen hundred packages?! Do you realize what this has done to the mail system in Linz?!"

"Yes, sir. I wish to reiterate that the whole matter arose from a misunderstanding and that all parties responsible for the mailing of the packages had absolutely no intention of infringing upon any regulations. Quite to the contrary, all involved were motivated by the best of intentions and a sincere desire to help some unfortunate victims of Nazism."

"Who did you expect would distribute that many packages?"

"Colonel, I can assure you I never imagined my request for a few packages would be answered with the quantities that finally arrived. I never had any intention of taking the responsibility for the distribution of so many, but I have and will continue to do my best honestly and justly until each one has been handed out."

"We have had serious problems with the black market, and I sincerely hope this matter won't cause any further difficulties."

"Sir, yes sir. I can promise you that in the future I'll be careful to avoid any possibility of such embarrassing misunderstandings. I believe all the persons who know about the matter can attest to that fact. I have taken the liberty of putting together a list of references who would gladly vouch for my good intentions. In addition to Chaplain Katzman of the 26th Division, there is Mr. Segman, who represents the American Joint Distribution Committee; the chaplain of the 83rd Division and the president of the Executive Committee for the Jews in the area, who has been given an office just a few doors down. His name is Simon Wiesenthal. I have spoken to him extensively about the conditions at the DP camps."

My father pulled a document out of his dossier and handed it to the colonel. "I would like to give you a copy of a formal letter of apology that I'm sending to Lieutenant Colonel Condiff.

"Very well, Master Sergeant. I'll take all of this under consideration. Diisssmissed."

The case was quickly settled by "compromise." In other words, my father got what he wanted. He always did, nothing and no one was going to stand in the way of him delivering those packages no matter what he had to do. Several weeks later, after his reprimand from Lieutenant Colonel Condiff, my father sent him a formal note of apology.

GMUNDEN 6 January 1945

Lt. Col. Carl H. Condiff

Staff Postal Officer

HQ U.S.F.A.

A.P.O. 777, U.S. Army

Dear Sir,

In the course of our interview of 11 December 1945, you requested me to forward you receipts for packages received. As I told you then, I am not in possession of all the receipts, now, since I sent most of them, covering some 25–30 mail bags, to the United States; those included account only for part of the total received.

Although Cpl. Katzman, formerly acting Jewish Chaplain for the 26th Division, in Linz, has been redeployed in the meantime, it should be possible for you to contact the Chaplain of the 83rd

Division, who knows Cpl. Katzman and is most probably informed about the packages too.

Mr. Segaman, representative of the AMERICAN JOINT DISTRIBUTION COMMITTEE with the 83rd Division headquarters, who took over the remaining packages when Cpl. Katzman left, can further vouch for the honest distribution of these.

Again, I wish to reiterate that the whole matter arose from a misunderstanding, and that all parties responsible for the mailing of the packages had no intentions of infringing on any regulations, but, were, on the contrary, motivated by the best intentions and a sincere desire to help some unfortunate victims of Nazism. As for myself, I can assure you, Sir, that I never imagined that my request for a "few packages" would be answered by the mass which finally arrived. I had no intentions to take the responsibility for the distribution of so many packages, but did my best to do so honestly and justly after they had arrived. I believe that all persons who know about the matter can attest to the fact.

Russian troops parade in Vienna, December 1945.

In the sincere hope that the matter will not cause you any further difficulties, and with the promise that I will, in the future, be careful to avoid any possibility for such embarrassing misunderstandings,

I Remain Dear Sir,

Respectfully Yours,

Walter Wolff

In fact, for every package my father did received, he created a form of confirmation that he sent to each person from whom a package was received:

Gmunden

Austria

1945

Dear:

Your package for Displaced Persons has arrived. In the name of the recipient, I thank you. Your package will be turned over to the Jewish Chaplain of the 83rd Division, with headquarters in Linz, Austria. In the future please address all your packages directly to him. (APO 83, % P.M. N.Y., N.Y.)

I also want to urge you to pack future packages in wrapping paper, since the last shipment arrived in deplorable condition.

Right now, winter clothing is of the utmost importance for our coreligionaries. Hoping that you will send whatever excess clothing you have, I remain,

Sincerely yours

Walter C. Wolff

Overnight, weather conditions worsened, making a flight to Paris—the next stop on his way to Brussels—impossible. With planes grounded until further notice, he decided to take advantage of being stranded in Vienna. Anyway, if the weather took too long to improve, he could always take a train. After his meeting with the colonel, he stopped to do a little creative banking for the next leg of his journey. The old military schillings and the Reichsmark were in the process of being replaced by new Austrian schillings, and Belgian francs were unavailable until he arrived in France, so he bought as many French francs as he was allowed in an effort not to lose money during the switchover. Then he met a friend who had once lived in Vienna and had offered to show him around town. They walked and talked for hours. The city center wasn't as badly damaged as everyone had reported. Some neighborhoods suffered much more than others, but the heart of the city was fine. Trams were functioning, windows were being replaced, streetlights were restored, and cultural and café life was lively, to say the least. By comparison, the town center in Linz was in worse shape, having suffered more damage. He found the people here much more pleasant than other Austrians. They were well mannered, nice enough—and the Americans were their favorites. His friend spoke a perfect Viennese and, more often than not, found himself explaining the provenance of his accent. The Viennese, in turn, were really impressed that one of their own could be an American soldier—unlike the Austrians from Linz and the Boches from Gmunden, who considered a countryman in an American uniform to be an act of treason.

That evening, the two officers went to the opera and saw an excellent performance of *Don Pasquale* given to a completely international audience. Seated in front of my father and his friend was a high-ranking British colonel the size of a small blimp. Next to him sat a French pilot who, upon hearing my father speak, swore that he was a "Parigot."[20] Next to him sat a charming Jewish girl from the Bronx in a civil service uniform accompanied by a corporal who was also from the Bronx. Behind them was a row of Russian officers. During the intermission, the corporal from the Bronx began to converse in Yiddish with a Russian commander, who insisted on holding his machine gun while he propounded on the merits of the German language. In heavily accented German he said, "Aberr Daitsch Sprach nix schwer—ichk nemen Daitsch Frailein, soo Lerrer, na, ich fleissig studieren, und ich sprechen Daitsch mit Kurzer Zeit in Wein." Translation: "But . . . speaking German isn't difficult—I speak to German women. They good teacher, I diligent student. Before long I [learned] to speak German in Wein [Vienna]."

The conversation became a free-for-all between Russians, Americans, French, and English, with each one translating for the other. It was fantastic! After the opera they went to a cabaret, where a Cossack captain approached my father and presented him with a leather military button engraved with the star, hammer, and sickle, a little token he had nonchalantly just plucked off the floor to use as a bargaining chip. Picking up the hint, my father mistakenly offered the Cossack a cigarette to show his appreciation, until he realized that what the Cossack really wanted was to buy a carton at the black market price of $100 to $150. My father quickly explained to him in his best Russian and with a few pointed gestures that he could offer him only a smoke: "Nyet—nyet—nyet!"

The next day, with no improvement in the weather, he continued his tour of Vienna, until evening when he met his friend. They went to the famous Theater in der Josefstadt, where performances of Beethoven and operas by Wagner were presented. They got tickets to see a superb performance of *Der Schwierige de Hugo V. Hofmannsthal*.[21] They were the only military in the audience. Afterward, they moved on to the Zebra Club and then to the Esquire, another famous nightclub, where he was introduced to a girl through an acquaintance. She was nice enough, but when she began to explain to my father why exactly she preferred the Americans to the Russians, he excused himself. She said to him, "You zee, vit an Americanisher, I can if I vant to, but mit de Russichs, I have do or elze!"

In general, he found the women were not exactly a bargain. They were desperate but more restrained than elsewhere in Austria. Vienna, it seemed, was as Socialist as ever.

In the morning, my father awoke to clear skies. He took off from Vienna on a C-47 at 0900 hours, arrived in Salzburg in time for a second breakfast, and landed in Frankfurt at 13:30, just in time for lunch and news that atmospheric conditions over Paris prevented them from traveling any further. They were grounded for the night again. He left the airport with his traveling companion, Rudiger, in search of lodging. As they drove toward the city from the airport, my father's eyes began to focus. Frankfurt was a sea of destruction all the way to the boulevards on the outskirts of town, where some residential quarters still existed. Those structures were flanked by the IG Farben building, which sat in the middle of the rubble. The largest building in Europe was now the headquarters of the American army and Eisenhower's main office. Notoriously, IG Farben had been the biggest campaign contributor to the Nazi party, was ultimately instrumental in bringing Hitler to power, and

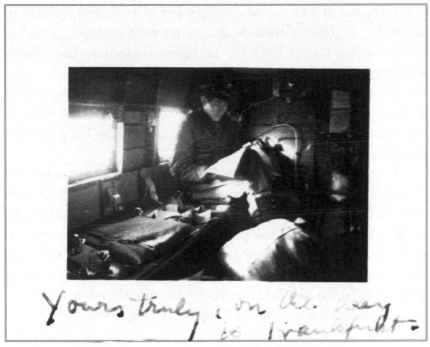

"Yours truly" on the way to Frankfurt, December 1945,
in a C47 troop transport plane.

remained a huge collaborationist with the Nazi regime. Many have
said that the Nazi war effort could not have been possible or successful without them. They used slave labor to produce war materiel
and among other things held the patent for and produced Zyklon
B, the pesticide used in the gas chambers during the Holocaust.
Twenty-four executives were tried at Nuremberg for crimes
against humanity. The building was not returned to the German
government until 1995. It is now part of Frankfurt University.

Finally, near the railway station, they found a belt of hotels still
standing in mostly livable condition. They took a room for the night
at one that had been requisitioned by the army. Later, as a precaution,
they walked over to the station to make arrangements for the first train
out in the morning. On their way out my father asked rhetorically,
"Rudiger, not that I really care, but, where do you think the Frank-
furters live if we have commandeered almost every building in this
depressing and unpleasant city?" The chill air caused him to pull in on
himself and draw his cloak closer around him.

"The hell if I know? Maybe they live like rats underground in what's left of some of these buildings? It's warmer down there. Say, there's the Red Cross Club, Wolff. Let's go in. It's too cold and hideous out here."

"We may as well spend the of rest of the evening here. At least it's one of the few places we can go without being forced to be in the same room with any of those Boches bastards. They talk too much!"

They found a table, and my father slipped out of his jacket and carefully lay it over the back of his chair. Just as he was about to enjoy his first bite of a nice piece of cake and a hot cup of coffee, a loud whistle resonated. MPs with machine guns ran through the room in an effort to occupy every entrance. Coming out of nowhere, a lieutenant grabbed the microphone away from the singer and yelled, "Everyone get up, put your hands on the table, and don't move. I repeat, Do not move!"

"What the hell are they looking for?" Rudiger whispered.

"Contraband weapons."

Rudiger blanched and started to say something, knowing my father was armed, but my father cut him off. He had a loaded pistol in his jacket. He never went anywhere unarmed, especially after what had recently happened to a bunch of soldiers in Munich. Neither man moved. It was over quickly, and my father finished his cake and coffee with no further interruption. He wasn't worried. All he had to do was to declare that he was with MIS.

In the morning Air Traffic Command sent word that there were two seats on General John C. H. Lee's[22] plane departing at 9:50.

"We had better hurry," said my father, cigarette flapping between his lips.

"What the hell, he's like second in command to Eisenhower! That's Jesus Christ Himself's plane! How?"

"C'mon Rudiger! Run now, ask later. Let's go before we miss it!"

They boarded the general's private plane with about twenty other guys and were flown over the Siegfried and Maginot lines, over Metz, then west to Paris. They landed at Orly and took a bus to the ATC depot at Place Vendôme. Although he had never been to Paris before, it felt like déjà vu. Everything about the city seemed familiar, natural, normal as they came through the Porte D'Italie. It was good to be back in France again—the posters, the French advertisements, people his age, the Citroen and Renault cars. He was so happy to see everything looking as normal as it did that, although there was no mention of a stopover in his orders and a train was leaving for Brussels that evening, he was determined to stay the night. For the first time in years, he was at home in his skin. Here he felt, somehow, unburdened by his past. They stopped for a bite to eat at the GI mess at the Gare du Nord.

When his waitress came over he smiled at her flirtatiously and asked, "Pouvez-vous me donner le nom d'un hôtel, s'il vous plaît?"

His French shocked her so that the flirtation went over her head and she gave his uniform a second look before she answered. "You are Français?"

"Uhh, non. It's a long story, but . . . un nom d'hôtel, s'il vous plait?" he said half in English.

"Hôtel Bonnes Nouvelles. 17 rue Beauregard." The waitress scribbled it down on a napkin and handed it to him. "Near de Louvre, Rive Droite." She left him with a quizzical smile.

Rudiger and my father took the métro from Gare du Nord to rue Strasbourg-Saint Denis and asked for directions. Around the corner, they found the hotel neatly tucked away on a side street. The Bonnes Nouvelles was little, old, non-requisitioned, and very French—but clean enough. It was perfect. He checked in.

His room was small and simply furnished. He dropped his bags and quickly changed into a clean uniform. To complete his look, he donned an olive-colored tie, cap, gloves, and a white scarf. Then he slipped his US insignia into his pocket and grabbed his camera as an afterthought. When he came downstairs again, Rudiger was waiting by the door. The weather had completely cleared, and Paris felt like spring. They took the métro to the Etoile. Again he had a feeling of déjà vu. Everything, including the names of the stations, seemed familiar. They arrived at the Arc de Triomphe, saluted the Tomb of the Unknown Soldier, and continued along the Champs-Élysées.

They ate and drank their way through the city that December day, strolling along the Champs-Élysées as though it were May instead of a few days before Christmas. With the exception of cafés and cinemas, everything was closed, but through the windows my father noticed how well stocked the shelves were. Before long, they stopped at the

Champs-Élysées, Paris, December 1945.

Lido Café, home to an American mess with excellent service and fantastic food prepared by the French.

"After we finish here, there's a shop I want to visit. I released a man several months ago who made me promise that when I came to Paris I would go to his wife's glove store so she could give me a pair as a gift for my mother. He had been a POW in German hands for five years before he came to me for interrogation. I let him go. He was a lone Jew in a crowd of surrendered soldiers."

"Where is it?" asked Rudiger.

"In the Lido Arcade. It should be right over here. We can duck in; it should only take a few minutes."

The glass canopy captured the winter light, enriching the colors in the mosaic floor. The arcade was reminiscent of another time and was untouched by the war. They found Mme. Payen's little storefront. Closed. How unfortunate that she would not reopen until the next afternoon at one. They left and walked again along the Champs-Élysées, following de Gaulle's footsteps through a liberated Paris. They turned down Rue Saint-Honoré, passing La Madeleine. I wonder if my father was aware that below the Greek architectural wonder of a church dedicated to Mary Magdalene stood the footprint of a synagogue from the twelfth century? During the first expulsion of the Jews from Paris, the synagogue was confiscated by the bishop. Continuing down Boulevard des Capucines, they finally stopped for a *digestif* at Café de la Paix, just as any tourist should. A strange silence permeated the city on that day, which my father couldn't quite justify until he realized that the noticeable lack of soldiers throughout Paris was creating a rather beautiful quietude. It gave the city a sense of normalcy that he had not experienced in years.

"Here's a table with a rather lovely view, soldier," said my father.

"Of the Opéra or of our neighbor?" asked Rudiger, whispering out of the side of his mouth. Their evening began with a cigarette and ended with a Pernod long after my father and the neighbor, Gina, accompanied him back to the métro to catch his train.

> He wanted to arrive in Brussels that evening to proceed to Rotterdam the next day. Gina (my acquisition from the Café de la Paix) suggested that we go to Clichy, where the prices are more acceptable—which we did, by métro. We wasted no time. . . . Eventually, we went to a little restaurant—typical of the small restaurants we know so well. The meal and the price were excellent. . . . Following the meal we went to Bal Musette—which was really fun. All sorts of dancers—rather chic couples. There were two Americans there, myself and one other. While there I also put on my US insignia, because no one, including Gina, wanted to believe I was an American. We stayed until closing—Gina was crazy for dancing.

Afterward, they left the narrow street of *bals musettes* on Rue de Lappe and walked along Boulevard Beaumarchais for a while, enjoying the warmth of their night together. As dawn broke over the City of Lights, they parted. He had done everything he could do in one day. Back at his little room in the Bonne Nouvelle, he slept for a few hours and woke at 7:30. As he pulled himself together, he tuned the dial to Radio Monte Carlo just in time to hear Rina Ketty crooning one of his favorite songs, "J'Attendrai" (I'll Wait). On his way back to the Gare du Nord, he captured the calm of the liberated city in black and white. In one unforgettable day, Paris had left her mark on him. He was certain he would return some day.[23]

CHAPTER 10

"I Found Your Gold Bally Shoes"

Irwin Shaw once wrote: "When we look back into the past, we recognize a moment in time which was decisive, at which the pattern of our lives changed, a moment at which we moved irrevocably off in a new direction. The change may be a result of planning or accident; we may leave happiness or ruins behind us and advance to a different happiness or more thorough ruin; but there is no going back. The moment may be just that, a second in which a wheel is turned, a look exchanged, a sentence spoken—or it may be a long afternoon, a week, a season, during which the issue is in doubt, in which the wheel is turned a hundred times, the small accumulated accidents permitted to happen."

While slaying his dragon, my father confronted the terror he faced during the war years. Throughout his odyssey he encountered a thousand heroes with a thousand unforgettable faces, while witnessing the violence and death visited on countless people who were lost during the Shoah. He knew what a miracle it was to be alive.

And so it was that on December 17, 1945, he finally boarded the 12:30 express from Gare du Nord to Brussels and returned to the only place he had ever called home. Two cigarettes and a bit of kidding around bought my father a spot in first class. He spent most of the trip chatting with his neighbor, a banker from Ghent. In 1940, just days after his own family's escape, Ghent was trapped in the pincers of the German advance toward France. Hand-to-hand combat broke out on its streets,[24] and the city was caught in the midst of one of the world's largest battles. As the Allies ferociously defended control of the English Channel, the fighting was so fierce that neither army could restrain its firing, which resulted in massive civilian casualties.

When the train pulled into Gare du Nord, my father bid the banker farewell and rushed through the great hall of the old railway station toward the exit. A few hours earlier, while he was on his way to Brussels, Aunt Ellen was celebrating her twenty-fourth birthday on West 79th Street, while on the East Side of Manhattan a bugler was warming up to play Taps during the first tree lighting ceremony on Park Avenue. As soon as the trumpeter blew his last note, Boy Scouts were to light memorial bulbs in what has become an annual ritual dedicated to the supreme sacrifice of our fallen servicemen.

Returning to a city scarred by war and occupation, he was eager to discover what remained of their old lives, if anything was left to be

Coming full circle, my father arrives at Rue de la Loi, Brussels,
in December 1945.

found. Once outside the station, he stopped and held Brussels in his embrace for a moment before hailing a cab.

"La Residence, 155 Rue de la Loi."

He fell back against the seat as the taxi pulled away. He lit his pipe. The suspense was too much to bear. Before another moment passed, he leaned forward to look out of the window. He rolled down the glass just enough to sniff the cold, familiar air. He couldn't help it, he smelled everything, always. To his surprise, Brussels had barely changed. Cars were rolling, trams were functioning. At first glance in the dim light of the late December evening, the buildings around the station appeared to have suffered no harm. The window across the street at Le Bon Marché was full of merchandise. They passed the department store L'Innovation. Boulevard Anspach was busy. The city was alive. From the corner of his eye he spotted La Coupe Glacée, his favorite ice cream shop. As they passed Chez Mayol, he saw an enormous bunch of grapes cascading from a basket like a waterfall. Delicacies would have to wait a little while longer. He snapped photos along the way. The last time he saw his building was as he craned his neck from the backseat of their crowded car while his father sped away. All he could see from that painful angle was the enormous geometric blur of one of Brussels' most imposing buildings fading into obscurity as they drove through the normally busy artery of the city. Just a few short days later Hitler dropped his bombs.

Remarkably, nothing appeared to have changed. La Résidence Palace was just as he remembered it. He was all about the business of the moment and curtailed his emotion, but one thing is certain: when a child loses his home, he loses his sense of place and along with that a formative part of his young identity. My father had lost his anchor that awful day of May 1940. When the German army occupied the city, they forcibly evicted the remaining tenants to requisition the building, and the home from which my family escaped on Rue de la Loi became Wehrmacht and Luftwaffe headquarters and residences. Ironically, the château where they lived for the first six weeks after they escaped from Brussels also became headquarters for the Wehrmacht. They were caught in Hitler's crosshairs from the start, but they somehow were not captured. They escaped from Germany to Strasbourg, then to Belgium before fleeing to France in a hailstorm of bombs and gunfire. As with many other German Jews, they put their trust in the two countries that fell the fastest and collaborated most willingly with the Reich and its plans for the Final Solution. I am positive that this was not lost on my father once he became aware of just how close they had come to a different fate.

Information about the building's use during the occupation has either been buried or lost. The Belgian government recently destroyed documents relating to that period, and no amount of research uncovered anything different than the following description pieced together from Wikipedia and the latest brochure describing the history of 155 and an architect's plans for transforming it into the architectural centerpiece of the European Union.

Following the end of the First World War, Walloon businessman Lucien Kaisin planned the building to be a luxurious apartment block for the bourgeoisie and aristocracy of Brussels in response to the housing shortage caused by the war. He also expected to address the shortage of domestic workers at the time, by providing housing and making the domestics available to all residents. The complex of buildings, which were designed by Swiss architect Michel Polak, was created to be a small town within a city. It was divided into ten sections with a total of 180 apartments of varying sizes and contained amenities such as hot and cold running water, central heating, and electricity. The Art Deco building included a theater hall, a swimming pool, an indoor tennis court, a barber shop, and other commercial services such as two restaurants, a conference room, a bank with safety deposit boxes, a post office, and small luxury shops. It was a prestigious housing collective for the most privileged layers of society. Its commercial success was short-lived, though, because of its requisitioning in 1940 as headquarters of the occupying German army. In September of 1944, the day after the liberation of Brussels, the building was taken over as headquarters for SHAEF (Supreme Headquarters Allied Expeditionary Force) and RAF (Royal Air Force) Second Tactical Air Force.

When I think of 155 in all of its grandeur, I think of it as my grandparents' home; a place where, if things had been different, I would have visited on Sunday afternoons for tea instead of visiting my Omi in her Park Royal Hotel suite on West 73rd Street, where she spent the remainder of her days sitting quietly in her chair comforted by her elegant blue bathrobe. She was like a grieving widow who never parts with the memory of her lost love. The three keys on the old key ring that I found at the bottom of her alligator bag opened the door to her home in her former life. In the forty or so years that she lived in New York, my grandmother never lived in a proper home again; she lived in a residential hotel because, as my mother confirmed, she lost her faith when she had to leave every home she ever knew. All that is left of those days, besides her set of keys, are a few remaining odds and ends and my father's chronicle written on his return: an objective account of belongings found and what transpired at the building during their absence. He slowly and methodically takes us on a tour of his lost city, and brings to my grandparents and aunt a part of their life no longer within their grasp. They never returned.

My father paid the cabbie, then looked up and around for a moment, taking stock while he adjusted his cap. He fixed his tie, picked up his bag. With measured steps, he began what felt like a slow walk to the building's main entrance. To the guard positioned at the entry he said, "Pardon me, sir, but I used to live here."

The Canadian soldier stood firm and would not let him through. As the building was now British headquarters, my father had no choice but to find a hotel for the night and come back in the morning. He waited at the curb for another taxi. He decided where to go.

"Le Savoy."

They drove toward the hotel, and as they approached, he could see evidence of the bombing. The street suddenly ended. The hotel was the last building standing. After that was a rather large pit where a good-size river could run through, dividing the Botanical Gardens in two. He whistled through the side of his mouth and said in French to the driver, "That's the first damage that I've seen."

"Ehh-heh, I'll take you around a bit on the way to your hotel, monsieur. The Boches SS tried to burn down the Palace of Justice before their hasty retreat last year. There is no longer a cupola. The fire lasted more than twelve hours, the cupola melted. Now, if you did not know it was there before, well, you will see, you will hardly be able to tell."

They continued on. My father saw Brussels with her gloves off. The Shell building had windows blown out and had been requisitioned by the Americans as the CHANOR Base Section. My father lit

155 Rue de la Loi, Brussels.

a cigarette and asked the driver while he exhaled, "Tell me, how is the press here? I've just come from Paris."

"Oh, compared to Paris, Bruxelle's is excellent! We still have *Le Soir*, which is pretty good as usual, *La Dernière Heure*, *La Libre Belgique*, which is very good, several Leftist and Catholic papers, plus the noontime *Paris-Soir* imitations. From these, my friend, you can tell what the prevailing conditions are here. How was Paris?"

They talked and drove through the city, dodging people, bikes, and trams until they reached the Savoy. The cabbie waited while my father inquired about a room. No luck. He climbed back in to the car.

"Requisitioned by the Canadians. Hotel Métropole, s'il vous plaît. Place de Brouckere."

"Except for that fire and the big crater near the gardens, we would have fared pretty well. So you're an Americain? But your accent, c'est impossible."

"Yes, I lived here before the war. We left before the bombs dropped. In fact, we were in Dunkirk having dinner when the first ones fell."

"Ahh, okay. I wasn't so lucky. I was here for the duration. It was very hard. Leopold was a coward to leave us to the Boches. A king who abandons his people! Please let me drive you around and show you a bit more of the city. I'll give you a tour then, the longer way to Brouckere."

He checked in at the Métropole. The next morning he went straight back to Rue de la Loi and the guard let him in. Near the door he saw a familiar face. An old man wearing a black Hamburg hat and a black coat, with a decoration on his lapel. The war had not been kind to him. The man had aged. My father approached him and said to him in French, "Are you M. Huber?"

He answered, "Yes I am, and what about it?"

As my father identified himself, M. Huber's eyes changed. They hardened with recognition. He responded very curtly, "I thought you all dead, because you never gave me any sign that you were alive."

Watching this exchange was another man. My father had his name on the tip of his tongue, when from behind him emerged a fat woman of a certain age, with a mop and bucket—that she almost dropped. She recognized him immediately. She began repeating, "And I can still see him in front of me, such a nice little boy, and look at him now, an officer in the American army! Ah, you know, I often said to Jeanne, whatever happened to Madame Wolff, her children, and Monsieur Wolff ?! I can still see him in front of me, look at him!"

When the excitement of the moment passed, my father calmly asked Monsieur Huber the whereabouts of his belongings, full well knowing that finding anything was as unlikely as his own return. He immediately asked that anything remaining be handed over to him as he had sole power of attorney. A still-hardened Huber brushed him off and explained that a certain Monsieur Weiss would have to give him permission on behalf of his parents. Right about then, my father, feeling increasingly frustrated, wanted a word or two with his own father. If only he hadn't given Weiss permission to intervene during their absence, there would be no issue. He would either have to convince Huber or find Weiss, but someone had to trust him. Now. How could this possibly be so complicated? He was obviously who he declared himself to be, and considering the incredible extenuating circumstances, surely there should no problem. Finally, after my father calmly explained to Monsieur Huber that he would do anything he asked, that time was truly of the essence, and that his parents now lived in New York, Monsieur Huber relented as suddenly as he had dismissed him. He began to open up and tell my father the lengths to which he and others had gone to safeguard the Wolff's possessions.

Huber recounted that, when Monsieur Weiss was interrogated about the absent tenants, he purposely did not declare "the issue" to the Belgian government, because, as my grandparents were German nationals, he didn't feel it necessary in view of the country's political neutrality. He further explained that Monsieur Weiss had apparently lied to the Gestapo during interrogation at Avenue Louise, telling them that he had not inspected the contents of a certain chest in which my grandparents had hidden a box containing a piece of gold! Monsieur Huber knew the whole story and continued to explain to my father that actually Monsieur Weiss had shown spectacular courage during questioning and had landed in prison for a period of time afterward. Had he declared anything at all, everything would have been lost.

"When you come back, see the pharmacist Monsieur Demeure. He will show you to your things."

My father excused himself and went to the Société Générale, where he hit another stumbling block. The manager told him that their accounts were blocked because my grandfather was declared as a German citizen and not a displaced person. Belgium had been neutral, and at the time the country's Jewish population was not required to declare their religion. After my father explained his situation to the banker, he sent several telegrams along with a detailed letter to my grandfather, explaining exactly what needed to be done to secure their accounts: write a letter to a Monsieur Wonters at the Office of Seizure, Minister of Finance, 38 Blvd. Bischoffsheim, containing an extract from the German Monitor citing loss of nationality and have it witnessed by the Belgian consulate in New York. Send back a proxy declaring my father as my grandfather's business agent for the entire affair, and another declaration giving him permission to take any and every step necessary to accomplish what he needed to do, along with his written blessing that any action or decision my father took was final. Next, my father needed to get in touch with the US consulate to learn the terms required to effect the transfer of funds to my grandfather's account in New York.

As soon as all of that was put in motion, he returned to La Résidence to find Monsieur Huber, who brought him to the pharmacist Demeure, who didn't recognize him either. Armed for battle, my father pulled out a letter with my grandfather's signature and his passport number identifying himself to the pharmacist. Demeure then quizzed my father on the events of May 14, 1940. After he was satisfied that my father was indeed representing the owner, Demeure led him to the cellar, where to his astonishment he found just about everything. Moments later the baggage was liberated. My father thanked Monsieur Huber for his kindness and offered each man a bottle of Johnny Walker he had brought along to ease the situation, with the promise of future libation.

"We can never repay your kindness, Monsieur Huber, Monsieur Demeure, but on behalf of my family I hope you'll accept this token for all you've done."

"C'était la guerre!" they exclaimed as each man took a bottle. Demeure paused for a moment before he said, "Monsieur Wolff, I must apologize for taking a pair of ski boots for one of my eight children . . . and . . . a suitcase to have some shoes made. It was a long and difficult war. Wait, here's your mother's fur coat. My wife took very good care of it."

My father immediately and inconspicuously grabbed the shoulder of the coat and felt something stiff ruffle to his touch. He found it. He carefully folded the coat over his arm so that the shoulder rested against him.

Demeure said, "I must say, you do look very different than when you left. We really didn't recognize you. My regards to your family. Let me help you bring your things out."

The three men gathered the things and brought them out of the building to the front, where my father flagged down a taxi, and together they loaded the precious cargo.

"La Grande Synagogue. 32 Rue de la Régence."

The Romanesque building built in 1878 by a Christian architect is one of very few synagogues to survive the war unscathed after Kristallnacht. It has now been dedicated as the central focal point of European Jewry and renamed the Great Synagogue of Europe. Inscribed above its main doors in Flemish and French is, "Have we not all the same Father? The one God, did he not create us?" My grandfather was quite religious, and, although my father felt otherwise, he was bar mitzvah there in 1938 or 1939. No fewer than 25,000 Belgian Jews died during the Holocaust, and in December of 1945 only a small 5 percent had made their way back, with almost no children among them.

When the taxi arrived, my father had everything brought to the building just behind the synagogue that belonged to the Jewish community, where some family friends named Enoch were living. Monsieur Enoch had been put in charge of family research for the JOINT and was second in command to a certain Madame Margolis, who was an American and the first woman to be put in the leadership position for the American Jewish Joint Distribution Committee (JDC) overseas. They had been a lot more effective in Belgium than anywhere else my father had seen so far in Austria or Germany.

There, in complete privacy before he did anything else, he tore open the lining in the shoulder of the fur coat. Nothing. Too bad, it had felt like the real McCoy. It was the starched lining in the pad that had caused the rustling. He would have to insure the coat for a lot less than it was worth, or customs would smell a rat. He put the coat on a chair nearby. Moved by the moment, he took a deep breath and began too take inventory. He could smell their old Brussels life in the cold contents of the trunks, suitcases, and boxes, permeating the air in a cloud of familiar smells. He peeled away layer after layer to discover what was left. Everything was neatly folded or carefully wrapped. There was his mother's sewing kit, a gift he remembered my grandfather giving to her for her birthday. Ellen's beautiful art books were her treasure. He held up a pair of pants, his old undergarments, then a shirt. He put his old clothes aside. Then he found a treasure of his own. In the warmth of his surroundings, in the building next to his old synagogue, he saw the light blue paper with his initials embossed in navy blue ink on the upper left-hand corner. His bar mitzvah stationery. He wondered what had become of the medical student who tutored him in Hebrew. Where was everybody? They were supposed to come back. They were supposed to come home together. His father had told him so, but now such a long time had passed while the world was consumed that his old clothes recalled with their size only the end of a boyhood that war had so frivolously squandered.

Bruxelles, 25 Dec. 1945

My Dears,
If you have a good memory, you'll recognize this writing paper—I once received it as a birthday present—7 or 8 years ago. It pleased me so much to find it that I've kept it to bring back with me.

Thanks so much for your two letters from the 17th, which were at M. Huber's office on the 21st of December! That's incredible.

As to the letter to the Société Générale, I reserve the right not to expedite it. Reasons: a) the damage has been done, and your nationality was not registered in time at the bank. For this reason, even if the bank had made an error to begin with by registering you under the wrong nationality, it happened as a consequence. b) The wrong can be repaired very easily, by sending a copy of The Moniteur, thereby un-blocking the $617. c) If we have the choice to resolve this amicably or in the courts, I assure you that amicably will take less time, and certainly it will be free, whereas otherwise it would certainly not be. In view of the amount in question, I think that what I am proposing is more reasonable—especially because if the account is unblocked you can't transmit it automatically to the US, because special permission is needed from the Minister of Finances. In creating bad blood, this permission could be delayed, etc. You know very well how tiresome his could be . . . legally, in view of the export laws for capital. As to the latter, the consul will give me the details.

BRUSSELS . . . Has barely changed . . . the stores are well stocked—and one can find virtually EVERYTHING. Deluxe items can be found in abundance. You can buy everything, from an American automobile (by special order) to a house, a dress, to shoes. . . . At all of the pastry shops there are at least a dozen different kinds of cakes. . . . At Mokafé (Passage de la Reine, near Arenberg) the coffee is excellent, as always. The restaurants have EVERYTHING—steak frites, trout, sole, chicken, turkey, shrimp. In the streets the women yell, "One and fifty for thirteen!" selling sandwiches to the soldiers late into the night.

I was at the Métropole for two days, but they wouldn't give me the room for 10 days because everything was reserved for Christmas weeks in advance. All of the other big hotels are still requisitioned, Grand, Albert 1er, Palace, Cosmopolite, Siru, etc., etc. So, I took a room at the Ancien Hotel Scheers, next to Le Bon Marché, facing the train station; it was very practical . . .

Here is what I've done with our baggage: . . . I had the impression that all was almost as we had left it. Most of the things have lost their value to us: things are either too small or too old. I think some of the clothes were missing—but the war was hard on these people; they have 8 children.

There were none of your dresses, Chère Mamo, and none of your suits, Cher Papo. Of Ellen's, there were some of the things from childhood and one evening dress in excellent condition, with some Bally shoes in gold. Those I sent. There were all of the little things, not worth the freight—used underwear, etc. And pots, dishes, your horse lamp, Chère Ellen. Your alarm clock [sketch], Ellen, I took with me. Then there were books: of those, I only sent the ones with some value, like art books, and dictionaries. There was a 1932 edition of Larousse. That I didn't send.

The pharmacist Demeure told me that he took a trunk and used it to make shoes for his kids. Here is what there was of our baggage: the big trunk: it was necessary to break the locks because the key was broken. With a screw driver, it took less time than writing about it to you. After making some inquiries on the cost of shipping it, I decided to give the monster to M. Enoch, who will need it because he's moving . . . Enoch has twins, a little boy, Pierre, and a little girl, Anne. Little Connie is all grown up, but she's very frail, she looks sick. Enoch was in France during the war. He was a captain in the Maquis and tells stories that remind me of the Scarlet Pimpernel. Aside from his dangerous missions, he was a gunner and TSF [radio] operator, who played the peasant during the day and worked at night for the government of Vichy at the supply office helping with the distribution of rations cards. To his friends he was known as The Belgian, and he had an identification card to prove he was Belgian—but he was really born in Darmstadt [near Frankfurt].

He had already been in a concentration camp. and was a prestataire.[25] He escaped from St. Cyprien camp simply by leaving through the main gate, on foot, at the time when the officials were leaving. From time to time, he went to see his wife in Belgium—having himself photographed with her once on the Blvd. Adolphe Max. Then he took her and the little one back to France. Near the end of the fighting, but when the Boches were still in his village, he put up a large antenna across the main street, attaching a piece of wire to the roof of the town hall and the other one to the church. His wife was the one who told me that story. He modestly said that he sent many a Boche to the other world. When I went to see him, he didn't recognize me—only when I told him who I was. His wife didn't recognize me either, and the little one even less.

Next, there were two bags: one big, one small. The big one I sent to you, the little one I took with me, I just needed one, since I'd accumulated quite a lot of stuff on the road. Then there was the big blue trunk of Aunt Mete's, which hadn't been touched. I put some of our things in it—anyway, you have only to open it. . . .

I used Wallon Frères as the shipping company to Auvers, and from there WSA for Mete's trunk and the wardrobe. To protect them, Wallon crated them. I wrote an accompanying letter, asking that it be insured. The sum doesn't represent its value, but if I insure it for too great a value, then you'll have trouble with customs. As far as <u>customs</u> is concerned, I'll write you stating exactly what the provisions of the law are that permit me to send these things without paying any entry taxes. I have the information from the US consulate in Brussels. Naturally, to facilitate the process I gave them the impression that this was American property in Europe, to be "reimported" to America. Anyway, before the things arrive, you'll have the details. I don't have the dossier in hand.

The rest of the things I gave to M. Enoch to distribute—and believe me, there are people who need it. The radio I sold for 2500 Fr. B. = $60. One bulb got crushed (sorry!), the transformers didn't work. Otherwise, the isolators were dry and the rubber cables need to be replaced . . . In Austria, I could have sold it for double . . . I sold it for a good price. The stores are full of TSF, of all kinds, more than the US.

I couldn't find old Jadoule. I probably could have, but it would have taken too much time since La Résidence is the British general headquarters—that bitch is certainly not worth wasting my precious time on. I did go see Mme. Wolfers. She spent the war in Switzerland and just got back seven months ago. M. Wolfers died shortly before that. She lives in a family "pension," near the Bois de la Cambre, 100 meters from Avenue Louise [the notorious Gestapo Headquarters where countless people were interrogated, tortured, and imprisoned during the occupation]. She is doing well and has not changed. She's happy to be back. I brought her a beautiful pot of flowers—she was so pleased. I telephoned her first and introduced myself as Wolff. She asked how my daughter and son were, and I let her find out in person that I was actually the SON. The black market is really very interesting . . . The rate changes every day, and after 1300 it is CLOSED. It's like a factory. All the workers stop at 1300. To get the rate for the day, one only has to call certain men. . . .

In the meantime,

Kisses your,

Walter

He sat at the bar at the Ardennes drinking a beer and watching as a chorus of Cole Porter's song "Don't Fence Me In" moved across the room in a wave of what had become Brussels' new anthem. The moment he spotted her in the crowd, he couldn't maintain his usual reserve. He watched her hair move gracefully across her shoulders as she sang along with her friends. They rocked, arms linked, keeping time with Bing Crosby and the Andrew Sisters. He never thought blond hair could be so beautiful. It was the darkest shade he'd ever seen. She was very pretty, well dressed, not at all his type but totally intoxicating. Her simple elegance gave her that very particular look of someone who was clearly well educated and from a good family. Her dark blue eyes drew him to her. The moment she caught him admiring her from behind his drink, the exigencies of the past several days and the ordeal of the past five and half years just fell to the wayside. When they smiled at each other, it was as if no one else existed. They shared themselves uncompromisingly. On New Year's Eve he left Brussels for Paris a changed and more complete man than when he arrived the week before. It was a gallant affair. They parted vowing to see each again, with no obstacle too great to impede their love.

* * * *

Bargaining with another two cigarettes, he was back in first class on his way back to Paris. He left his baggage at the checkroom at Gare du Nord and took the métro to L'Opéra and went directly to the

European Air Transport Service to reserve a seat on the next plane to Vienna. When that proved impossible, even after he explained that he had been on a compassionate furlough, he made his way to ATC (Air Transport Command). The French secretary who was in charge of reservations told him nicely but firmly, "Non!"

So my father began to explain his dilemma to the young woman in French.

"You can save yourself the trouble of asking because it is reserved for American military or paying passengers only!"

"Come on, wait a minute, now. I don't believe you understand, mademoiselle. Just a moment."

If my father had a dollar for every time he was forced to explain his accent, he could have paid the young woman in cash for the airfare back to Vienna. He took out his special MIS pass, and she immediately apologized. He explained to her that he had lived in Europe for quite some time, and trying to charm her, "I lived in Paris for two years in between—thus my 'Parigot' accent."

She called her superior officer. My father laid his papers on the counter and explained to him that it was essential he return to his station as fast as possible, and that he had no time to waste on military trains.

"Unfortunately, there is no plane until January first." The officer looked at my father and stamped PRIORITY 3, reserved for big shots on a mission, boldly in red on his ticket.

"January first? I guess you're forcing me to stay in Paris to ring in the new year. Quite unfortunate, really," said my father in a most lugubrious tone, a smile peeking out from the corners of his mouth.

The next day he went to the office of *Stars and Stripes*, where he found his old friend Albert from Brussels. It had been a number of years since they'd seen each other, but he recognized my father immediately. Albert was just back from his trip to southern Germany. They walked around Paris all day taking pictures and settled into a café for a couple of shots of some very fine Cognac and to compare notes on how they had spent the last few years. Albert told him he was hoping to return to the States shortly, because he just about had the sixty-five points necessary to complete his tour of duty.

"On the road I saw a lot of Ritchie men—in every town I passed through, Brussels, here in Paris, as well as Vienna and Frankfurt.

The progenitor of Ritchie can be found a little everywhere! To the Ritchie Boys!"

Albert lifted his glass and they toasted.

"To the Ritchie Boys!"

That evening my father went to see the play *Bichon* at the Edward the VII Theater on a little street between L'Opéra and La Madeleine. For New Year's Eve, with no specific plans, he wound up at Montmartre. After passing half a dozen clubs, he settled on L'Heure Bleue on Rue Pigalle because it was lively, fun, and there were very few soldiers. He sat at the bar and ordered a Cognac. He took a sip and almost spat it out. The officer next to him looked at my father and asked, "What's the matter my good man?"

"This is undrinkable. I'm sending it right back to our little barmaid."

My father politely explained to her, "I had asked for Cognac and not for rubbish. You could take the varnish off the table with this swill!"

The barmaid's eyes grew wide. She looked at my father's uniform up and down and then, in what seemed like a single gesture, swept his glass away and returned with a freshly poured shot.

"Now that is a Cognac. Look at the color. Merci."

My father and the RAF pilot began to chat, and he told the pilot about his experience running his RAF compatriots to safehouses when he lived in Lyon. Before it got any later, he excused himself to call the airdrome, to confirm his departure time. He thought he had an early flight, so he had already left his baggage at the ATC Terminal and given up his hotel room and he had absolutely no intention of going to bed because it was much easier to stay up than to wake up. His departure had been delayed to 10 a.m., though, and suddenly he was without a room in Paris on New Year's Eve. Within ten minutes, he had a room at the neighboring hotel. By 2:30 he was ready for bed. Before going to sleep, he asked the woman downstairs to wake him at eight o'clock. She swore up and down that she would. At 9:30 the next morning, the telephone rang. "Sir, was that you who wanted to be woken up this morning?"

"Why, yes, and my plane is leaving at 10:15!" He couldn't even take the time to really yell at her. "France never changes!"

He jumped out of bed and into his clothes. No taxis. He took the métro to Gare St. Lazare and found one there.

"Aérodrome d'Orly. Vite! Wait! Oh, my God, my baggage! First make a quick stop at Gare du Nord. Keep the meter running. I'll run in and grab my bags! *Vite!*"

In the car, he changed uniforms. He took off his long jacket, switched his tie for a white silk scarf, and switched his shoes for boots while the driver careened through Paris at the extraordinary speed of twenty-five to thirty kilometers per hour. The driver was crazy with confidence they'd arrive in time, but he got lost halfway there. They arrived at the airdrome at 10:30 and my father paid the driver, grabbed his bags, and ran into the terminal just in time to hear, "Last call for Master Sergeant Walter Wolff. Last call. Please report to the scales to be weighed in. Walter Wolff, please report to the scales."

He ran to the weigh station and heard them announce that the plane would not take off until 12:30. Join the Army and see the world. Hurry up and wait.

The plane had every comfort. In an hour and a half they were grounded in Frankfurt due to a change in the weather. This time, because of the priority stamp on his ticket, he was given a comfortable room to share with the pilot and the radioman. The next day they left at 10:30, had lunch in Prague, and arrived in Vienna for tea. When my father finally reached his destination, he readied himself for an onslaught of hostile questions relating to his whereabouts after his furlough had run out. He had been gone twenty-five days on a ten-day furlough, but all they said to him was, "Oh, you're back. Very good."

Since they hadn't even missed him yet and he could easily have stayed for another week, he applied for another furlough to ski in Chamonix and then decided to push the envelope and stay for another three days to catch up on the pleasures of culture in Vienna.

By the end of January, my father received notice that his tour of duty was coming to a close. He left for New York from the port of Le Havre on the USS Le Jeune in March 1946. After he returned from his furlough, his letters home slowed to a trickle. The returning soldiers marched on board to the beat of a military band playing farewell songs, and as the sun set over the damaged French landscape, the ship pulled out to sea. Finally, after nearly six years of war, his life could resume in safety and in peace for the first time since he was very young. My father always found the orchids among the ruins no matter where he was.

New York harbor, April 1946. My father is second from left, facing Weehawken, New Jersey, as the Le Jeune pulls up the Hudson escorted by a tugboat with a band playing and the message "Welcome Home Troops" on the shore.

9 April 1946
Au soir

Hello, my Darling,

Yes, I'm home now and I'm a civilian again. Again an individual instead of a number in a card file. I was demobilized on the eighth, and this is my 2nd evening home. It really feels wonderful. As a pleasant surprise, I found a letter of yours in my little apartment—the letter you wrote on the 14th of March. Thanks—it was a nice thing to find it right on my table.

My Darling—I feel so guilty—guilty about having made you love me—and thus unhappy. I long for you too, believe me; I long for your tenderness, for your pretty smile, for the softness of your lips—for you. But let's both be reasonable—and not "chase rainbows."

You tell me in your letter to please help you—"if I ever loved you." Francine, Chérie, there shouldn't be any doubt in your mind:

I did love you—and still do—and will in the future. You are one of the most beautiful events in my life so far. I have liked many girls, and thought I loved some; but I never told a girl that I loved her, except playfully—before I told you—"je t'aime, je t'adore." And I still mean it.

But you know, my Darling, life is not that simple; there are so many factors that separate people—even people who sincerely love each other. Only few people are fortunate enough to be able to enjoy the privilege of true love. Most people have to be content with a reasonable facsimile.

Darling, as your picture on my desk smiles at me—the only picture on that desk—I feel so sorry for having met you, for having loved and having held your body close to mine—sorry for you, because doing so you came to love me. I don't believe I'm worthy of such beautiful sentiments. I would be much happier to know that you hate me—hate me for having done that to you. If you did—I wouldn't be an obstacle to your happiness—But then again—I'm happy if you just love me a little—because I DO—and will never want to forget you. Let's keep our relationship as a beautiful thing to remember—it was brief—but pure. I say pure because I see nothing impure about those unforgettable nights when you gave yourself to me.

April 14, 1946

Well I carried this letter around for days now, and it is time that I mail it—and finish it. My family and I have gone to a beautiful resort some two hours from N.Y. For ten days. I am not used to such luxury any more—I have to get used to it. Plenty of girls here—but there is not so much beneath their pretty smiles and nice clothes. I still feel a little awkward in civilian clothes—but keep changing shirts, ties, suits, shoes—just for the hell of it.

I still can't believe it!

All my love
Yours,
Walter

CHAPTER 11

The Key to the Wine Cellar

"Are you getting off at Noyelles-sur-Mer?" I asked the blond boy traveling alone, after he stopped talking on his cell phone. I looked out the window. Rain was coming down in sheets moving sideways. Wind was whistling through the closed doors of the train.

"Eh, oui," he answered.

"Perhaps you'll know, then, where the Château de Noyelles is?"

By this time I had taken my rain gear out of my suitcase and pulled my British oilcloth hat over my head, before folding my overweight garment bag and yanking it toward the exit. What was I thinking I'd need for a week's expedition? The boy looked at the map on his iPhone for a moment and answered that in fact he only knew the château where he was going and that it had been in his family for generations. For a fleeting moment, I thought my story might not be so uncommon, if châteaux in the region were so numerous. No matter, we left it at that. The train finally pulled out from between the vast fields of Picardy wheat, dotted with white cows and horses whose manes blew in the wind as they galloped through the summer rain. We came to an unceremonious stop, and the train conductor in her short blue skirt and high heels announced our arrival at Noyelles-sur-Mer and proudly blew her whistle.

"Voilà, madame, vous descendez içi." As the conductor helped me pull my suitcase off the train, I watched the boy climb into his grandfather's car. I quickly went over and knocked at the window.

"Oui?" he asked nicely. The boy told him what I needed.

"Je vous apporterai. . . . Mais," he paused, "ce n'est pas loin, madame." (I'll take you. . . . But . . . it's not far, madame.)

Okay, I thought, and blew air through my cheeks. The website did say it was close to the station, and I was completely forlorn. It had been a bit of an exercise getting to Noyelles in the first place, after missing my 8:13 train from Brussels Midi to Paris Nord in the morning. Things were looking up. The man explained that, since he wasn't expecting another passenger, and with a full trunk and a small car, he would try to accommodate me, since it was raining like a monsoon. Had this been a silent movie, his facial expressions and constantly moving hands would have been explanation enough.

"Vous êtes tellement gentille. Merçi, monsieur." I thanked him profusely for his kindness, took the boy's suitcase, and put it on my knees. Voilà! The doors were shut, and we were on our way. Like a Marx Brothers movie, piled in the car as we were, the man drove over the train tracks, went a few hundred feet, and announced once and for all that we had indeed arrived at the château. With a certain degree of panache, I thanked them once again. That degree of politesse has been lost in other countries, particularly in America, to a much more casual set of manners. I threw my worn leather knapsack over my shoulders and pulled my suitcase up the wet gray stone steps of the château. I walked through the old metal and glass doors and was greeted by a young woman, Ludivine, the concierge and caretaker: the one in charge.

"Bonjour, je suis Madame Feld," I announced, letting the "e" hang off the end of "Feld-e" just for a moment. I would never sacrifice my well-cultivated Parisian accent, no matter how tired and jet-lagged I was.

"Ah, oui."

The words rolled out of her mouth and a smile broadened across her face as she realized who I was. Finally, I took a breath and looked around. I had crossed a personal Rubicon and made it to my family's past. This quiet, exquisitely restored château had held its own through not one but two world wars and within its stone walls kept the secrets of generations of people. I was going to caress some answers out of it for the following three days. Without missing a beat, Ludivine left my bags at the tiny front desk and asked if I would like a tour. I smiled and said, "Absolutely." We walked through the rooms on the main floor and we got to the dining room, with the huge wooden fireplace and wood stove. Original plans and elevations for the château hung on the walls. I stared out of the window, looking for the famous garden and the strawberry patch. Later, when the rain stops, I promised myself.

"La cave, do you want to see the cellar?" She knew.

I smiled and said, "Plus que vous pouvez imaginer!" (More than you can imagine!)

The wine cellar. I have never wanted to see any place so badly. We descended the winding wooden steps and she opened the door.

"Watch your head."

The stone ceiling would be a firm reminder of the building's age, and mine, if I smacked my head. No concussions today. No time. I took it in slowly, one step at a time. This was it. I walked toward the rear of the cellar; Ludivine unlocked the door and switched on the light. Once upon a time, a young boy sat and faced fear with comedy. You could hide the boy from the dangers of falling bombs, but you couldn't take his playfulness away from him. In this cool, moist place, they had sat together, five Jews and a bunch of scared Wehrmacht soldiers, waiting for the air attacks to stop. How my father ever kept a straight face while those guys drank the olive oil that he'd switched with wine, I will never know. Or, as I like to remind myself, the clues were always there. Even comedy has a price tag. His life depended on the outcome of the prank, and with that kind of straight-man tactic he became an intelligence officer and followed in Mr. Kresser's footsteps.

After the cellar, we went upstairs to the area where my family had lived. It had been totally rebuilt after it was damaged in a bombardment. The footprint remained, and I couldn't help but notice how small it was. The windows faced the front of the château, from which you could look out into the distance as the sky changed with every passing cloud. The driving rains ended and the sun was now dominating the Norman landscape. Simplicity lay in the details, allowing my imagination to transport me. As if on cue, to fill in another blank, a group of red planes flew past the château in formation. That was a sound I was looking for: the planes were from that period. Their rumbling through the cloud-filled sky reverberated clearly in the gusting wind. The loud buzzing sound got even louder as they approached. This was an answer. They could look into the distant sky and hear as

well as see incoming aircraft. They had a built-in warning system to go
to the cellar and enough time to get there.

"Ludivine, did you see the planes?" I asked rhetorically. "Now
I know, it's not at all different than I imagined. C'est incroyable!"
(It's incredible!)

We stood in the room a moment longer, wondering how five
people had lived for six weeks in such a small place. I followed her out,
and she locked the door. The rain had stopped, and we headed outside toward the garden. The garden. We walked over the white gravel
toward the open wooden gate to the trees already heavy with summer fruit. Everything was growing in neat rows; any remnant of the
past lay buried in the earth below. I looked for the strawberry patch
where the bomb fell, leaving my father unharmed in the crater. We
walked through another open gate at the other end of the garden, and
I noticed that the thick walls were made of flint bricks. Before we left,
I pulled a pear off a tree and bit into it. Through the garden were a
second garage and some living quarters for the Polish groundskeepers.
In the distance I could see a crater and asked if that was left over from
the war.

"Non, mais c'est un peu bizarre." (No, but it is a bit weird.)

"Oui," I said.

Ludivine excused herself and walked back to the château, leaving
me to my thoughts. I wandered everywhere. I went off the manicured
grounds, sometimes sinking into the thick mud. I looked deep into
the ground wishing to find something, anything. I walked carefully
over a path made of broken tiles and bricks, remnants of old houses
laid like a carpet so a person wouldn't sink. They created a bridge,
from which I could observe my surroundings in the forest behind the
château. I looked at the trees, hoping to see my father's initials carved
deep into the bark. I took a walk around the perimeter. I walked along
the Rio River, staring deep into its waters for a shadow of its war-
torn past to surface with a clue. When I got to the end and turned
down the narrow path, the white cows stared at me, looking for their
own clues. We had a lot of questions for each other. Anyway, they were
too young to remember anything, and so was I. The river was much
too narrow at one and a half meters wide to be the one that my father
spoke of, when he explained during his interview that, while he was

standing at the side of the road, enemy tanks were approaching from one end moments before the firing started, and he turned around and saw a small French troop behind him across the river. Yes, it had to be Le Dien; it was just up the road behind a farm. That was where the firefight took place, requiring them to hide under their car. I absorbed what I saw and began to walk back along the banks of the narrow Rio, passing a couple of farms until I reached the main street and followed the flint wall to the front gates of the château. I felt strangely at home in a place where I had never been.

Instead of going back in, I walked toward the train station. Wet grass, smells of lavender and chamomile wafted in from the fields. Le Relais de la Baie stood on the corner across the street. I wandered into the café. To my surprise, my French was greeted with a Scottish hello. I ordered a tea for the jet-lagged me and some crêpes with cream and jam. A bar in the middle of northern France run by a Scottish painter who came on holiday and never left. It was a quirky place, with beautiful landscapes done by the owner, Pippa Darbyshire. Art books were stacked on tables and overflowed from the bookshelves. After I ate, I got up and took a walk around. Swing tunes carried my thoughts back in time. As if on cue, I turned to find a piece of the old wall exposed but framed. I looked closely and read:

> Pte. B. Mc Cubbin, 7th Argyll's f. Sutherland, Highlanders;
> PTE. R. Bowerman. No.17276 2nd Oxford A. Bocke, Light
> Infantry BE 7.

Behind me I heard gravelly, heavily accented voices ordering a bottle of wine and turned to see who had walked into the bar. Pippa introduced me as "l'Américaine" to her Belgian and Dutch friends, Christine and Jaan. Christine was a potter from across the road, wearing clay-covered overalls and a green T-shirt that was never changed during my three days in Noyelles. She rolled and lit one of her many filterless cigarettes, inhaling deeply.

"I like de smoking," she would always say as she blew smoke through a deep, hacking cough.

I dubbed her "Crazy Christine." She had a heart of gold. This was a woman with a past. She soothed her darkness with alcohol and

cigarettes and could not have been kinder. Both she and Jaan took a
keen interest in what I was doing and wanted to help find people and
information for me. Crazy Christine thought of someone who might
have more historical background about Noyelles and offered to get in
touch with her friend Jean from Vron. If he was available, she would
take me to see him the next morning.

I found it impossible to believe that such a bucolic place could
play a role in the theater of not one but two world wars. The odd
thing was, this little village was a shell of its former self. From the turn
of the last century through World War II, it was home to many small
hotels and shops of all sorts. There had even been a movie theater in
what appeared to be an old carriage house. In the days to come, history would reveal itself and people related to my family's past would
appear by degrees. I watched from the café window as cars sped by on
the narrow road where General Heinz Guderian, the champion of the
Panzer assault, once passed through to congratulate his troops. Hitler's
train had no choice but to stop, for the Führer to gaze upon his prize.
The move toward the Channel had occurred so quickly that it left
even Hitler confused about how the troops should proceed. Rumor
has it that on his way to Abbeville the tracks had been sabotaged and
Hitler was delayed at Noyelles for a short time. The château was only
a one-minute walk from the train station, so it's possible that he even
spent a short time there.

Later that evening, another storm blew in off the Channel,
shaking the château, with every long gust whistling through the trees,
knocking branches to the ground. I could hear layers of sound. Doves
coocooing, seagulls wailing plaintively as they flew above. I looked out
my window and watched the gusts in the trees for a long time. A train
whistled into the station, its sound echoing in the wind; a car here and
there and a lone truck pulled through and waited for the train to pass.
From my round porthole window, I looked into the distance.

At dinner, I sat by the window, staring out at the garden. I looked
so deeply that my imagination conjured images of what must have
been. I ran my hand across the soft, tooled edge of the old fireplace
in the dining room while I ate. I wished my father was there to talk
to me. Everywhere I looked, I felt their presence, and didn't want to
miss a detail. I felt strangely at home, yet in the weeks to come, as I

looked back to those three days, blurry details began to clear and the bold colors of occupation dressed my mind's eye. The swastika. The flag billowing in the wind, signifying the château as command center. The new order. I spoke to the couple across from me. They had won a trip to the château with all the amenities in a lottery on the Internet designed to attract retirees. I had become somewhat of a novelty with my story. We finished our warm apple galettes and left the dining room.

"Please save the other half bottle of the La Coste for tomorrow's dinner. Bonne nuit et merci," I said over my shoulder to Sylvie, the cook by night and maid by day, as I left the dining room. I stood outside for a few minutes to get some air before I decided that I was better served by a good night's sleep. I had a lot to think about.

The next day I took the steam train to Saint-Valery and Le Crotoy on the Baie de la Somme and walked all over both towns, thinking about the incredible battles that were fought on this land. In Saint-Valery a plaque marked where Joan of Arc passed through after she had been captured by the English in 1430. I took it as a sign that I should have faith in myself and the courage to pursue this project. I wandered all day and ate lunch in Saint-Valery and dinner in Le Crotoy before settling in at the château for a nightcap. For a long time before going to sleep that night, I just listened to the silence.

As promised, Christine had arranged for me to meet with Jean. She arrived promptly a ten the next morning, motioned for me to get into her van and threw a map in my lap. We drove to Vron, where we were welcomed with open arms and hot tea. Although fascinating in themselves, his collection of early twentieth-century postcards of Noyelles proved to be a dead end as far as my research was concerned, so we stayed with him only briefly, as I was on a tight schedule. Olivier, the owner of the château, had arranged a luncheon at noon with the grandson of the former caretakers. He had a feeling that if there was anyone in Noyelles who could remember anything about the occupation, it would this man. I arrived back to the château just in time to see the men pull through the front gates. Before sitting down to lunch, I took a tour of the grounds with Olivier and the now-elderly caretakers' grandson. As we walked, I asked the man if he remembered anything about the battles that took place in May and June of 1940. He had quite a vivid memory, in fact.

I showed him the precise spot where my father said he remembered the German soldier with a crush on my aunt had been standing when falling bombs killed him and my father landed in the crater of one that didn't detonate. The man gestured so strongly that he almost knocked me over.

"Là," he said, pointing to the wall where the pear trees were, beside the Polish caretakers' house. Precisely where I had chosen to pick a piece of fruit the other day.

"Il était enterré là." (He was buried there.)

I shook my head and thought: The coveted strawberry patch had turned to jam and the nemesis was buried there too. Ah, la guerre!

The next day I rode my bicycle deep into the countryside and left the road to travel between two fields at sunset. The heavy black bike was difficult to maneuver over the dirt that separated the land into neat pastures on which the white cows of Picardy were grazing. Yet again, we stared at one another for a long time, looking for some kind of answer. As I moved further down the path, westwardly toward the sunset, the cumulus clouds battled, changing the light. Before long I saw the same pattern of broken tiles, a mosaic in the landscape. I couldn't risk going over them with the heavy bike, and crossed them on foot. I was too far from the château for a flat tire.

It was the night before my departure. I was feeling a deep sense of loss as this door to the past was closing and I had to return to my present life. I found the mosaic over the dirt paths curious and wanted them to be pieces of the destruction of war. They told their own story of the lives lived within walls that were now laid to rest on a path between pastures with inquisitive cows grazing. I stood leaning against my bike, which rested against a tree, for a long time, until daylight gave way to dusk. I ached, wanting to stay longer, not sure of what answers, if any, I would find.

When dusk turned to night, I pulled my bike away from the old tree and rode back toward the paved road until I reached the broken tiles and walked around them until it was safe to ride. I headed toward Noyelles, past Pippa's café, now closed and locked for the night. I rode through the gates of the château and lined the bike up with the others one last time. Instead of going upstairs, I went into the garden, slowly walking through, past the Polish caretakers' house. It was quiet, private.

I walked a little further until I was directly behind the château. Hidden by a large bush, I lay down, staring up at the sky. I suppose if I could, I would have found a car and hidden underneath, just to feel. I would have engineered my own fear by adding the sounds of planes flying overhead strafing with their gunfire, and the noise of a nearby battle as ground troops fought. I felt cold dampness pushing through my clothes. I lay there for a long time, absorbing. A car pulled in through the gates. I got up with a start, walked back to the front and unlocked the door to the château, holding it open for the two guests back from their long day of sightseeing.

I had an ache in the pit of my stomach. I felt as though I was grieving. I got into bed, and fell into a deep sleep and awoke the next morning having dreamed of the broken tiles. There was something about them. In my dream I walked slowly alongside a friend over a hill of destruction. We were talking quietly, I was trying to make a point. It was then that I looked down and saw a sepia-toned photo on a heap and pulled it out from under the glass. There was another photo underneath. Another layer. And another.

On my last morning, I walked along the road to the river Dien, watching the sun cast its rays of white light upon the haystacks rolled in the fields, like Monet's paintings. I was looking for the Chinese cemetery but couldn't find it. The cemetery is the resting place for 838 Chinese laborers who died from the Spanish flu after being recruited by the British government during World War I. I followed the sign and walked along the narrow sidewalk, now a couple of kilometers from the château. I should have taken the bike. As I walked on, I looked down at my watch, and in front of me were two broken ceramic tiles. Just a little farther, I thought. My throat was parched, I hadn't taken any water. Plums from a tree hung heavily over a fence, so I picked one and coated my throat with the juice from the ripened fruit. My father would have done the same. I couldn't reach any others but saw one that had fallen onto the sidewalk. It tasted even better than the first. The road was clean, I didn't care. An old man leaning against a ladder was fixing the tiles on his roof and I asked him for directions. Time was short, he had trouble hearing me, and I had to repeat myself over and over.

I had an eleven o'clock rendezvous with the mayor of Noyelles and needed to find my way back. I had wandered a lot farther than I had anticipated and began to follow the parallel road, assuming it was a shortcut. Finally, I found the path along the Rio and took my shoes off as I walked through the wet grass to the château. Just in time, I thought. I would not be late for the mayor. As I walked in, the phone rang and Ludivine answered it.

"Elle est juste à côté de moi, Monsieur Maire." She handed me the phone.

"Allô, oui, Monsieur Maire. No, I'm sorry." He had another engagement and couldn't meet with me. C'est la vie in the fast lane at Noyelles.

Almost as soon as I hung up the phone, I saw Jean approaching, the Frenchman with a German last name whom Crazy Christine had brought me to meet two days earlier. I smiled and waved him in. As he climbed the gray stone steps, I took a better look at him. At almost sixty, he had a youthful way about him. Shy and reserved. A gentle giant. He arrived with a gift, a CD loaded with turn-of-the-century postcards of Noyelles from his enormous collection. The casing enclosed a note:

> We wish you a nice trip back to the USA. With the hope that these few days spent in the country at Noyelles-sur-Mer have allowed you to get close to the spirit and memory of your father, who during those uncertain times spent several weeks at this château that has welcomed you.
>
> With friendship and the hope that your book will see the light of day.
> Yvette and Jean Willig

I thanked Jean and thought for a moment, then asked him if he wouldn't mind driving me to Saint-Valery, since he was on his way to work. I had hours before boarding the 3:30 express to Paris and wanted to do a little sightseeing. As we drove through the gates of the château, I took a last look at my father's room and at the garden where the strawberry patch once stood. I didn't want Jean to see, but my eyes welled with tears, which I discreetly wiped away.

Later, over a lunch of possibly the worst Italian food I've ever consumed, Jean sat across the table from me and quietly told me his story. "As I remember," he began between bites, "my mother was working in

May 1940 at the RAF mess installation at the Abbeville-Drucat aero-
drome and evacuated at the same time as the British stationed at the
base, and went as far as Avranches. That was where the last of them
left for Great Britain. They invited her to come along to England. She
refused, telling them, 'La lutte n'est pas terminée!' (The fight isn't over!)"

She parted ways with the RAF soldiers, headed for Paris, and
settled in with some cousins until September 1940. Then, having been
issued new identity papers to cross the border of the occupied zone,
she returned to her mother's in Abbeville, where her mother was in
charge of the kiosk at the train station. How she came to work as
a cook for the Germans, I don't know. However, sometime around
Christmas of that year, at the station in Abbeville, she never forgot the
small man with an oversized uniform walking erect, speaking loudly,
slicing the air with his hands as he made a point. Flanked by other military, he stood apart, distinctly apart. It was Hitler, seen close enough
to discern his features and gestures and the resolve in his eyes. Close
enough to elicit the enormous courage it took to resist—to fight back.

Jean Willig, half German, half French. His mother played an
important role in the Resistance. As a cook for the Nazis in Abbeville, she smuggled dynamite to the saboteurs. During shopping trips,
she layered the explosives beneath the groceries at the bottom of her
sack, letting the vegetables and other supplies stick out at the top. The
dynamite that Jean's mother carried was used to destroy stretches of
railroad tracks to derail trains. She belonged to the Fer Réseau, a resistance group that diverted freight shipments to the wrong location and
also sabotaged switches to cause derailments. Because the ground was
level in northern France, train derailments varied in their effectiveness
but were fairly simple to execute. Jean's father used to alert the train
engineer to the time of sabotage so they could collect the valuables on
the train, wine and cigarettes among them, and offload them before
the derailment. She met Jean's father at the newsstand in Abbeville,
and they fell in love. He was a German officer. They had a baby. Jean is
normally careful not to talk about his family history.

Once, when Jean's son was a boy, he asked his grandfather about
the gray uniform in his closet. It had a Nazi pin on the lapel. Jean
wasn't clear as to the significance of the pin, but his son never spoke
to his grandfather again. Jean has asked his ninety-two-year-old father

what he did during the war, and he won't answer. Suffice to say that there is a coffer that Jean will receive on his father's death that will explain everything in detail. As one would whisper a mantra during meditation, the old German soldier repeats, "You will see. . . . There is nothing to be ashamed of."

Jean will have his box, as I have mine. Two German fathers, each with a box of documents, giving their children a link to the past. "You may as well have it," mine said as he gave me his. My box, cold, green, dusty, metal with raised letters denoting "US Army." What of the other box? What secrets will it contain? Mine has loving letters home, some on the red-bordered stationery of the Third Reich. Stolen stationery, like a banner, his proof positive of the enemy's defeat.

*　*　*　*

Later that evening, in Brussels, I was so exasperated that I started a conversation with the ladies next to me. One was an elderly woman, not much younger than my father would have been. They listened and laughed along with me as I told them why I was so aggravated, agreeing that the old Métropole wasn't kept to its old standard, and no, I certainly shouldn't have been my own bellman, when I showed them the bruises on my arm from the weight of my heavy bags hanging awkwardly while I maneuvered my luggage to my room by myself. Maybe if I didn't act like a teenager all the time, people would be more willing to treat me like the woman of a certain age that I am. They asked me where I was from. I explained and told them that my father had stayed at the Métropole during Christmas week of 1945, when the city and the hotel were reborn with the future's promise. Then, the hotel was lively and festive, not old and stale, the way it was now.

When the waiter came back, I ordered salad and a smoked salmon platter. The ladies asked what brought me to Brussels. I explained that I was there to do research, that I was looking for answers to my father's past. As we continued to chat, I noticed the old woman's face change as if lit by flashbacks of the terror that must have enveloped her during the war. Her jaw went slack and stayed that way until I finished recounting my purpose here. As we sat in the café, she began to describe the day she lost her home and her playmate to the Blitzkrieg of bombs and tanks assaulting the city. Her eyes were wide shut. She gripped her patent leather taupe handbag more tightly with every detail, her hands trembling. I ordered more champagne for all of us. She was only ten on May 10, 1940, the first day of "La Grande Exode"—the great exodus when waves of Jews fled Brussels as the Germans poured through the embattled city. Everything had been lost; it was rubble. She spoke of never being able to return to her home, but not of how or where they survived the war. Then, suddenly, her eyes betrayed her will. I could see the tears well up as she told me about her little friend who had been killed. At some point, she sucked in and appeared angry as she said, "Thank God for the Americans. If it wasn't for them . . . They saved us. I get so angry when anyone says anything negative about the Americans!"

Her daughter said, "My mother is very passionate and loyal when it comes to the Americans."

During our conversation, the woman's daughter sat motionless and listened as if a passive observer. I gave them my card, hoping to keep in touch, invited them to see my website and hear my father tell his story in his own words. The old woman loosened her grip on her handbag, and her fingers flushed with color as her blood began to recirculate. As they got up, I rose to shake their hands and bent to give the older lady a kiss on each cheek. For days afterward, I was haunted by her expression. Perhaps the pain of reliving those days was too jarring for her, and I worried that I might have made her sick. The invasion and subsequent occupation of neutral Belgium came as a huge surprise to the country, as it found itself very suddenly under occupation and at war. It was obvious that the fear this woman felt as a little girl had endured in an anger that would last for the rest of her life. I left for the airport early the next morning after breakfast.

*   *   *   *

Weeks passed after I came home. I began to write. I assimilated my trip, and, as I wrote, emails arrived and details emerged that required research. I was stuck on certain points and enthralled by others. My imagination was held captive by history, and what needed to emerge for me was a more complete story of those early days of war. I hungered to hear the voices of the radio reporters, Churchill, Roosevelt, and the BBC. I wanted to know exactly what my father heard as he carefully spun the dial through the crackling static looking for whatever sources could provide accurate news devoid of the propaganda that poisoned listeners.

I read with a voracious appetite, trying to grasp what this war was about. An old friend of the family emerged as a main character in Herman Wouk's *The Winds of War*. Leslie Slote was now my personal guide, leading me through history. When the characters in the novel discussed current events, I fact-checked and researched the details. So accurate was Wouk's account that, during one conversation between two characters at the end of the novel, one asked the other if he had read a certain issue of *Time* magazine. The issue to which Wouk referred was dated September 22, 1941. I located a copy and immediately ordered it. When it arrived a few days later, I read it cover to cover. In the first few pages were a photograph and a small article about the arrival of the SS *Navemar*, the ship that brought the Wolff family to the United States. Toward the back I found an article that linked the FDR Drive in New York to the Battle of Britain.

I realized with an overwhelming sense of pride that there was a very specific relationship between the arrival of the *Navemar*, the overcrowded freighter carrying European refugees, and the other ships that crossed the Atlantic. After delivering materiel to Great Britain, the ships' empty hulls were filled with wreckage from the Luftwaffe bombardment that demolished Bristol, England. The city was a major port for American supply ships. Unable to make the crossing empty, the ships were loaded with the rubble for ballast. Thus balanced, they sailed back to New York. The foundation for the roads in the New World was literally being laid with rubble from Hitler's bombs.

Originally placed on a footbridge over the East River Drive in June of 1942 by Mayor LaGuardia, the plaque was relocated and rededicated by Cary Grant in 1974, when construction on the apartment complex Waterside Plaza was completed. It reads:

BENEATH THIS EAST RIVER DRIVE OF THE CITY OF
NEW YORK LIE STONES, BRICKS AND RUBBLE FROM
THE BOMBED CITY OF BRISTOL IN ENGLAND
.... BROUGHT HERE IN BALLAST FROM OVER-
SEAS, THESE FRAGMENTS THAT ONCE WERE HOMES
SHALL TESTIFY WHILE MEN LOVE FREEDOM TO THE
RESOLUTION AND FORTITUDE OF THE PEOPLE OF
BRITAIN. THEY SAW THEIR HOMES STRUCK DOWN
WITHOUT WARNING.... IT WAS NOT THEIR HOMES
BUT THEIR VALOR THAT KEPT THEM FREE....
And broad-based under all
Is planted England's oaken-hearted mood,
As rich in fortitude
As e'er went worldward from the island-wall.

ERECTED BY THE
ENGLISH-SPEAKING UNION OF THE UNITED STATES
1942

From the rubble of war a foundation was laid and a road built.
I don't believe that my father ever knew this detail. It seems that few
people do, but it resonates. Both the *Navemar* and one of the ships that
carried the rubble now lie at the bottom of the Atlantic, having been
sunk by the enemy upon their return to Europe.

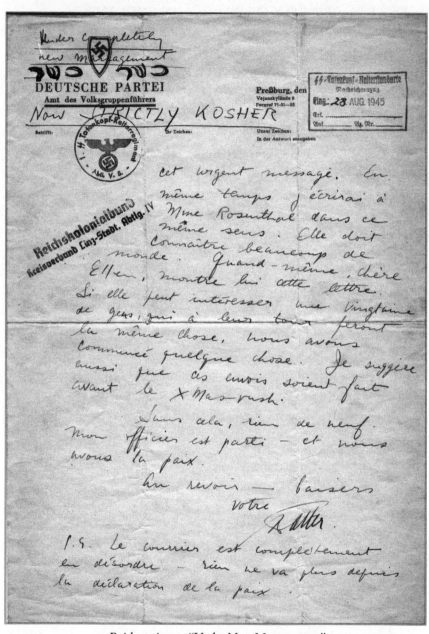

Reich stationery "Under New Management."

CHAPTER 12

Details Are Confusing, and Freedom Is Just Another Word

"Nothing is less real than realism. Details are confusing. It is only by selection, by elimination, by emphasis that we get at the real meaning of things."

— *Georgia O'Keeffe*

If propaganda was the fulcrum of Hitler's regime, then comedy was its antithesis. By all accounts, laughter is healing. How does one package freedom, or liberate a particular shade of red from the devil? One word: comedy. Charlie Chaplin did it as the Great Dictator; Mel Brooks wrote "Springtime for Hitler"; and my father? He "requisitioned" stationery from the Nazis and wrote caustic remarks in English to fend off the censors. Mel Brooks said, "[B]y using the medium of comedy, we can try to rob Hitler of his posthumous power and myths."[22] My father took something once meant to fanatically enslave the minds and hearts of a people and made use of it for the exact purpose and by the exact sort of people or person it was meant to destroy. His was a unique position of freedom.

I often think about him sitting over his writing paper, oval face and high forehead peeking over the typewriter keys as he tapped away, Acqua di Parma and pipe smoke surrounding him in a distinctive amalgam of scents that have transcended time. Words, one to the next, flowed from his fingers as from the hands of a seasoned writer, and a portrait of his life as a Jew in the army emerged on the paper whose sole purpose was to convey the assigning of orders to plunder, torture, and ethnically cleanse to the end of propagating Aryan purity.

No longer a threat, the stationery served as a mnemonic device for the defeat of the Nazis—and freedom.

By writing these lines in English instead of French at the top of some of the letters, he left the reader little choice but to laugh at the incongruity: Strictly KOSHER kitchen !!!!! UNDER NEW MANAGEMENT!; Try our HOT PASTRAMI sandwich Special; See our latest success 'Behind Barbed Wire'; Contracts made many years in advance; Under Completely New Management, NOW STRICTLY KOSHER; HEIL MOSES!; AMT. DES N.S.REICHSJUDEN Führer'S ISRAEL WALTER C. WOLFF now called: THE PARTY OF THE GOOD-HEARTED? INNOCENT? SAURERKRAUT EATING, JEW-LOVING? GERMAN PEOPLE (INDEPENDENT AUSTRIAN BRANCH) [Office of the Leader of The Nationalist Socialist YOUNG JEWISH FÜHRER]. The juxtaposition of his words next to the Nazis' is a form of appropriation and disambiguation. All of a sudden, the object that was once so toxic, so venomous, used for a state-sponsored murder campaign to kill millions, is transformed, creating a break from the past. The symbol of Nazism is desensitized, neutralized. By altering the semantics, my father reorients his readers so they may easily see the writing for what it is: a letter home to family and friends. He has asserted his freedom by obliterating the original intent of the stationery with his comedic tagline, often enough from the anti-Nazi context of a Jewish deli. More than that, humor becomes a tool for other meanings.

Ten of the letters burst with that particular hypnotic shade of red associated with the Nazis. But, with the heading of "Under New Management," as he wrote, they cross the line from horror to laughter, revealing a strange metamorphosis of purpose. He turned them out like a short-order cook preparing a blue-plate special. On those particular sheets of stationery, whether typed or in longhand, he began each one with his genre of black humor emblazoned across the top, before continuing on. One letter describes the atrocities committed at Ebensee, the concentration camp in Austria that he visited, sandwiched between a rather Proustian description of lunch and his midnight snack. He found no humor in what he witnessed, but in order to deliver the news of what he saw he found that he had to speak around the subject. Seven decades on, his anecdotal descriptions are an invitation through the looking glass.

They are indeed a metaphor for freedom. With every new reading, he forces us to look, to face his enemy once again before closing the door and rooting himself in his future, rarely if ever to speak of the subject again. Present fell into the dust of decades past, forever linking us by an invisible chain. There is no delusion or denial in his writing. Liberated from the clutch of the devil, the stationery boldly bears the eagle gripping a wreath and balancing the swastika in its claws, as if the bird of prey were stopped in flight. Only much later, as Death's door slowly opened to welcome my father, did unspoken memory find expression in hallucinations and then in words tangible enough for me to grasp. I am haunted by a few of his final words. They are the ultimate reminder that he never forgot. "When I hear that sound, I think, I am a Jew. I am a Jew. I am a Jew."

I never understood exactly what he was referring to, but his remark was a watershed moment for me during those last few days of his life. It made my hair stand on end and ran a chill down my spine. Something awful had occurred in his distant past. Though I never got to ask him what happened, or why that particular sound elicited such a strong reaction, I have the letters, which have painted an extraordinary picture of his youth and young manhood.

There is other, more sterile stationery that leans less on the drama of a colorful border but is no less startling. It is as white as the Nazi paragon's hair was blond. A perfectly embossed Nazi state eagle sits in the upper left corner. The bird holds a wreath with a centered swastika in his claws. Just underneath is printed:

DER GAULEITER UND
REICHSSTATHALTER
IN SALZBURG

Looking at the letterhead, I couldn't help but notice the striking resemblance to Helvetica and felt compelled to research the Nazi's use of typeface. Hitler was the one who decided to abandon the traditional German Fraktur for a more legible typeface: easier to read, easier for the Nazi state to spread the word, simple. The newer typeface clearly reflects a Bauhaus modernist trend in its design. Which is rather paradoxical, considering Hitler closed down the school because it didn't reflect his ideal of an Aryan Germany, since many of the students were Jews and modernism was too forward-thinking for the Thousand-Year Reich. The typeface, however, is not Helvetica. That was created in the late fifties. The developers of Helvetica had no ties to the Nazis and were not anti-Semitic, but it is absolutely fascinating how a typeface such as that or Futura can be so universally absorbed by the masses.

Futura, for example, was originally developed by Paul Renner, who was opposed to Nazism but whose typeface was adopted by the Nazis and is still one the most post popular ones today, used by companies ranging from Volkswagen to Louis Vuitton and Domino's Pizza. Futura somehow led me to look for the original owner of this particular sheet of stationery. Once I found out who it belonged to, every time I clicked on his name in the Google search engine the same frustratingly banal if damning information popped up, until, lo and behold, a portion of his Nuremberg interrogation report surfaced on a fabulous website called fold3.com, which provides access to military records.

The stationery my father used for a letter dated October 9, 1945, belonged to Gustav Adolf Scheel. Hitler appointed him, in his last will and testament, to be the new acting minister of culture in his post-suicide cabinet. Scheel, the son of a minister, had studied theology and medicine, and according to his Nuremberg interrogation file, joined the SA (Sturmabteilung—the Geman Nazi paramilitary group formed in 1921 that was called the Brown Shirts) in 1930, rising steadily through the ranks from Studentenführer during his university years to the advisor for cultural matters, as it related to the Nazi Party, for all of the instructors in every category of education and for every scholastic organization. He earned every position he held and ultimately was appointed the acting head of the administrative district and imperial lieutenant of Salzburg until May of 1945. He had an extremely high rank in the SS as the head of the police in several districts, including Salzburg. And finally Adolf Hitler appointed him minister of culture in his last will and testament as the twelfth appointee on his list. "In order to give the German people a government composed of honorable men,—a government that will fulfill its pledge to continue the war by every means—I appoint the following members of the new cabinet as leaders of the nation. . . ."

This sheet of paper definitely belonged to him. Scheel was also single-handedly responsible for the deportation of the Karlsruhe Jews, who had roots there since the seventeenth century. He sent most of them to their deaths. After the war, during the peaceful handover of Salzburg to the Americans, he fled and was later arrested and tried for crimes against humanity. He was very cooperative during his interrogation and implicated others. Upon his eventual release and "denazification," he settled in Hamburg, where he worked at the harbor for a time before returning to medicine as an assistant doctor at a hospital. The British arrested him once again in the 1950s for taking part in the illegal underground extremist group called the Naumann Circle. Scheel held close to twenty different positions in the Nazi Party, and denazification apparently was not an option he chose to live by.

After the Holocaust, in the mid-fifties, when he formed his first home furnishings company, a precursor to Bon Marché, my father designed a letterhead that I've always found alluring. He chose a trendy new typeface developed by two Swiss designers who aptly named it Helvetica, Latin for "Swiss." Helvetica was modern and neutral. Perfect to represent a company whose designs would forever be steeped in modernism and Bauhaus tradition.

But, instead of using black, he chose that particular shade of red. I realized this at some point with the shock of recognition and the sudden realization that my father's memory was porous, not at all immune to the color and graphics of Nazi propaganda. Once the reader sees both sheets of paper, the Nazi stationery and his, side by side, the accident of its influence is unmistakable. My father created his new letterhead using three distinct but equally important components. His choice of Helvetica is a clear signifier of the modernist tradition in design with a nod to the safest and loveliest years of his childhood spent at a boarding school in Switzerland. His use of our family insignia is a nod to his German heritage; and lastly his choice of that red is a signifier of freedom from the oppression of tyranny.

In Chinese culture, red signifies good fortune and joy. Call it a Jewish spring. A short time later, as his business developed, he reduced Bon Marché's logo to its purest form. He set the wolf in the shield and crown between the words "Bon" and "Marché," exactly like the Third Reich stationery with the red border. In other words, he clipped the enemy's wings. Unconsciously, at least, he was forever caught between the two worlds of his past and his present. In an effort to free himself from his wartime memories, he suppressed them, but the aesthetic influences of that era were too strong even for him. With the gift of one green box, I have woven threads of history into a portrait of my father as the man he became.

*   *   *   *

At the end of his video testimony, when asked if he had anything else to say, he took a breath and without looking directly into the camera, his voice broke over his silence. "It is a great pity that so few of us lived to tell their story and lived even to smile about it." Then, with a smile, he said, "I mean, I can't help it, but giving some Kraut a bottle of oil to drink when he is expecting wine still amuses me. I can't help it, but those are just moments that happened there." During a time when the promise of a tomorrow was so uncertain, it took courage to temper the atrocities of death, loss, and ruin with moments of happiness and laughter.

APPENDIX

To the Editors of *The New Yorker:*
A Letter from Austria

My father's advocacy for the Displaced Persons did not completely end after his return to the United States. In April 1946, after his demobilization, one of the first things he did was to draft a letter to *The New Yorker*. The rough draft survived in the green metal box and is reprinted here in its entirety.

New York City, 24 April 1946

To the Editors of The New Yorker/ "Letter from Austria"

Reading reports on the political situation within the American Zone in Germany, it occurred to me the situation in our zone in Austria is very much the same; I have just returned from Austria. Most of the blame for this preposterous situation must go to the individual Military Government officials. To anyone who has been in Austria for any length of time, it is an open secret that the Military Government officers have in most cases no qualifications other than their military rank, for the job they are holding.

Most of the men who formed the core of the M[ilitary] G[overnment] when it was still in the hothouse stage, who had received proper training, and who had been selected for their special abilities, have now gone home. If a unit had any excess officers, who, because of their inefficiency, general ignorance, or their character, could not be used to command troops, they were promptly assigned jobs commensurate with their rank—positions for which they were utterly unqualified. A pitifully low percentage of these officials are acquainted with political past of Austria, and their knowledge of present political trends and recent developments is almost completely missing.

Many have no interest whatsoever in their job, and devote much of their time to the improvement of their lavish villas, or maybe the apartments of their mistresses. Their primary interests in life are wine, women, and song, loot and cheap flattery on the part of their civilian "friends," who make it a point to call them major, colonel, or captain at every turn. It is not an uncommon sight to see some of these "ladies" riding around in powerful automobiles, run on American army gas. As appears to be the case in Bavaria, some of the girls occupy very important positions in the military and civil government, and their direct and indirect qualification for these jobs seem to be their sex-appeals, or possibly their ability to speak English. The knowledge on the part of the MG personnel is indeed rare, and their reliance on politically shady interpreters of varying efficiency is complete.

As a typical example of these prevailing conditions, I can mention the case of the civilian supply officer for the city of Linz, in Upper Austria; he has been a 2nd Lt. for several years, never having been promoted because of his inefficiency, and general ignorance. Previously he had served as a supply officer for a small unit, his duties being largely taken care of by his noncom. When that unit was reduced in size, he requested a transfer to the Military Government, so as to be able to remain with his mistress, a known Nazi sympathizer. After he received the job he appointed some shady characters, with very doubtful political pasts, to assist him in his duties; one of them was arrested when he attempted to appropriate property under American control, presumably for the Military Government. Upon questioning it was established that he was "arrestable" on several counts.

As is the case in Germany, the Nazis in Austria, are slowly but surely infiltrating into positions of importance, regaining some of their lost influence. The three major parties now recognized in Austria are the Social Democratic (Socialist), Christian Social

(Rightist) and Communist parties. The Christian Social Party, supported by the US officialdom—unofficially, and the Catholic Church openly, is the one which won the recent elections. Why? Well, the Church always has a strong position in Austria; furthermore, the party included in its election program a plank which openly advocated that Austrians should let "bygones be bygones" as far as the "little Nazis" were concerned; they also used the familiar catch-phrases of "anti-Communist bulwark" etc. It is true that the former members of the NSDAP were deprived of the right to vote, but then again it is a well known fact to students of the Nazi Party that a very large number of Nazis never became members of the party proper. As a matter of fact many applicants for membership in the NSDAP were turned down when National-Socialism was riding high, and the party was supposed to be an organization of the elite! Thus, many convinced and fanatical Nazis were never enrolled in the NSDAP, and are today, not only voting, but in many instances appointed to or running for office, the only condition for running for office being, that the applicant never belonged to the Party.

Of course, there is what is commonly referred to as "screening" by the Counter Intelligence Corps; this procedure, however, often merely involves questioning of the individual. In a minority of cases a serious investigation is conducted. Even these insufficient attempts at establishing a person's loyalty is frequently conducted by Austrian employees of CIC. Instances where such civilian personnel of CIC turned out to be notorious Nazis, are, unfortunately, not rare.

Although there have been no large scale actions by enemy resistance forces, such organizations are being assembled in towns and villages, under various guises. In Upper Austria and Salzburg for instance, insignias representing an Edelweiss, made of barbed wire from the American concentration camp for Nazis, are being distributed, and are openly worn. They are manufactured by the inmates of the above mentioned concentration camp; upon close inspection a swastika is plainly visible, as formed by the leaves of the flower. Many instances of discrimination against genuine Anti-Nazis on the part of the US appointed officials and the local populations are given. In other words, it really doesn't pay to be an Anti-Nazi these days, since the US administration make few attempts to support its real friends. It appears that it has become the unofficial policy of our forces to support the Christian Social Party, which I have described before. The Social-Democrats, about as red as our New-Deal Democrats, are actually shunned, but they are really the middle road party which we should encourage.

If another attempt at establishing Democracy on the Danube fails—and it surely will unless we radically change our methods— we have nobody but ourselves to blame; we certainly did little more than arrest most of the well known Nazis, but not all, and to intern hundreds of unimportant and inoffensive small-fry.

After almost a year of occupation we have not established policy covering all the exigencies of the situation, providing adequate punitive measures, scaled uniformly according to the seriousness of the crime. If we are to improve our administration, it is imperative the MG, MIS, and CIC receive carefully selected and well trained personnel—and soon.

Yours Truly, Walter C. Wolff

Acknowledgments

It has taken a village to write this book, and I have been incredibly fortunate, from the beginning, to have received encouragement and support from people across the globe who wanted this story to become part of the vast archive of Holocaust writing.

To my mother, Lila Wolff, whose love and devotion to me and to my father is endless, I thank you from the bottom of my heart. You are an example to us all, and I love you. I am so proud to call you a friend and a role model.

I owe an incredible debt of gratitude to Isabella Pia Ayoub, who urged me from the moment she heard about it, to go through that dusty green box carefully because in it lay my greatest inheritance. You encouraged me to move mountains to accomplish my goal. By continually raising the bar, you have given me the confidence to believe in myself and surpass my own expectations. You, my friend, refine my broad strokes. Thank you for reopening my creative soul and giving me the time and the space to use every tool in my toolbox, and for listening to and reading every sentence of this book, often while we were separated by an ocean of time zones. Our friendship is a sisterhood replete with the beautiful sounds of laughter, tears, children, and enough stories to fill volumes. I cannot think of anyone whom I would rather have by my side and whose boundless love and esteem for my parents helped bring this project to life.

To Jennifer Lyons, who brought me to Arcade and did not give up until we found a home for the manuscript.

To my editor, Cal Barksdale, who gave this book its ultimate shape and whose guidance allowed the story to flow so that my father's voice could be heard. Thank you for taking a chance on this project.

To Rhoda Fiedler and Shelley Fiedler for taking the bull by the horns and championing this project from the start.

To my closest family, friends, and allies who have listened patiently whenever I asked to read to them. Thank you.

To my father's first cousin, Doris Wolff Bendheim, and family friend Gerda Preuss, who lived through that perilous time and have known my family intimately since they were children in the 1920s. Thank you for giving veracity to my words by sharing and reliving your memories to confirm details about your surroundings before and during the war.

To Roberta Haselkorn for listening and actively promoting me from the beginning. Thank you.

To my first literary agent, Rosalie Siegel, who somehow knew at "hello" and has been a pillar of support ever since.

To the many scholars who have taken the time to answer my queries and given their time and energy to a novice, but specifically to professors and authors Volker Berghahn, the Seth Low Professor of History at Columbia University, who took an early interest in this manuscript and opened a world of knowledge to me; Anne Nelson, professor in New Media and Development Communication at Columbia University's School of International and Public Affairs (SIPA); Atina Grossman, Modern European and German History, and Women's and Gender Studies at Cooper Union; Dr. Frank Mecklenburg, director of Research, chief archivist at the Leo Baeck Institute; Dr. Guy Stern, Ph.D., distinguished professor emeritus at Wayne State University; and the many scholars at USHMM, thank you.

To the staff at Apple, in particular Seth Bengelsdorf and Matt Forte, who almost fell over when they saw the collection of letters in the archive, and to all of the Creatives at Apple who guided me so beautifully through the technical aspects of building this project.

I also want to thank the teachers and students who invited me to take part in their Holocaust Education programs at middle and high schools all over New York City. Their enthusiasm, questions, and letters after my speeches are a continuous source of inspiration.

And to my cousin, Alan Kaufman, who has endeared himself to me forever for lending his ears and his heart while we searched for a home for this book.

Notes

1. On January 1, 1942, President Roosevelt, Prime Minister Churchill, Maxim Litvinov of the USSR, and T. V. Soong of China signed a short document that evolved into what became known as the United Nations Declaration, committing the signatory governments to the maximum war effort and binding them against making a separate peace. Representatives of twenty-two other nations added their signatures the following day. *https://www.un.org/en/aboutun/charter/history/declaration.shtml*.

2. During World Wars I and II, "square heads" was a disparaging slang term used to describe Germans, especially German soldiers.

3. Two years before my father's pledge, shortly after the outbreak of World War II, Congress changed the original stiff-arm salute to the raised hand or hand over heart gesture. Prewar photographs show American schoolchildren and adults—including some saluting Roosevelt—looking like Fascists with their arm outstretched, the gestures were so similar.

4. National Archives and Records Administration, *www.archives.gov*.

5. Alois Schicklgruber was the name of Hitler's father. Adolf was his bastard child born out of wedlock. His mother remarried a miller with the last name Heidler. After she died, the young Hitler was sent to live with his stepfather's uncle for unknown reasons. He later took his adopted father's name Heidler, which was misspelled on a legal document, resulting in the name Hitler.

6. *Sh'erit ha-Pletah*, Hebrew for "Surviving Remnant," is a biblical term that originally referred to the Jews who survived and remained in Jerusalem after the destruction of the temple.

The Jewish Displaced People came to refer to themselves this way after their liberation from the concentration camps in 1945.

7. HICEM resulted from the merger of three Jewish migration associations: New York–based HIAS (Hebrew Immigrant Aid Society); JCA (Jewish Colonization Association), which was based in Paris but registered as a British charitable society; and Emigdirect (United Jewish Emigration Committee), a migration organization based in Berlin. HICEM is an acronym of these organizations' names. The agreement between the three organizations stipulated that all local branches outside the United States would merge into HICEM, while HIAS would still deal with Jewish immigration to the US. However, Emigdirect was forced to withdraw from the merger in 1934, and British wartime regulations later restricted the JCA from using its funds outside Britain. Thus, for a while, HICEM was funded exclusively by HIAS and could be considered as its European extension. (Wikipedia)

8. In her book *Jews, Germans, and Allies*, Atina Grossmann states: "Already during the war, before the scope of the Final Solution was fully understood, Jewish officials had warned UNRRA that a 'great number of people,' of whom the 'overwhelming majority would be the Jews,' who had been 'deported or expelled to foreign countries and also many of those displaced within their own country would be unable or unwilling to be repatriated.' ... For the most part, however, the Allies did not specifically focus on the Jews, assuming that they would be few in number." See Attina Grossman, *Jews, Germans, and Allies* (Princeton University Press, 2007), p.133.

9. Just weeks before he died, President Roosevelt appointed Earl Harrison as the US representative on the Intergovernmental Commission on Refugees. In June 1945, President Truman sent him to perform an inspection of the DP camps. In what came to be called the Harrison Report, which was submitted to Truman, Harrison clearly stated that the deplorable conditions he found on his tour of the DP camps warranted that a separate and distinct category be created for the Jews, who had suffered so greatly at the hands of the Nazi regime. Because of Harrison's findings, President Truman took a much more active role in supporting improved conditions and separate DP camps

for surviving Jews, as well as a more liberal immigration policy in favor of the DPs. Changes were slow, though, and they didn't occur until the Truman Directive was issued the following December. In his directive, the president said, "The pressing need . . . is to act now in a way that will produce immediate and tangible results. I hope that by early spring. . . immigration can begin immediately. . . . I am informed that there are various measures now pending before the Congress which would either prohibit or severely reduce further immigration. I hope that such legislation will not be passed. This period of unspeakable human distress is not the time for us to close or to narrow our gates. I wish to emphasize, however, that any effort to bring relief to these displaced persons and refugees must and will be strictly within the limits of the present quotas as imposed by law. The attached directive has been issued by me to the responsible Government agencies to carry out this policy. . . . This is the opportunity for America to set an example for the rest of the world in cooperation toward alleviating human misery." His executive order did not substantially help immigration to the United States, but more Jews were admitted than before. See https://www.jewishvirtuallibrary.org/jsource/Holocaust/truman_on_dps.html.

10. From the *My Day Project,* November 7, 1945. The Eleanor Roosevelt Papers Project is a university-chartered research center associated with the Department of History of George Washington University.

11. That prayer is at the root of anti-Semitism. It has been argued time and again that Jews are not to be trusted because the prayer is a loophole through which contracts are broken and obligations not met. It is, on the face of it, exactly that; however it has to do with breaking a personal obligation and prepares the soul for the coming year by giving it a clean slate. Paradoxically, Beethoven was inspired by Jewish liturgical music, and the melody from *Kol Nidre* inspired him to write a few bars of it into his *String Quartet in C Minor.* Hitler's love for inspirational music led him to listen to Beethoven and send his troops into battle listening to the *Ninth Symphony* in particular to raise their morale.

12. Mrs. Rosenthal is referring to the report by Earl G. Harrison, the man appointed by President Truman to look into the condition of the Jewish DPs at the camps.

13. Nicknamed "The Voice of Doom," Gabriel Heatter was a famous radio announcer whose dramatic broadcasts during World War II always started with, "There's good news tonight . . . ," offering optimism to boost the listeners' morale before delivering the devastating war news that often followed.

14. *Gerichtskasse*: German term for a court's cashier office.

15. UNRRA: United Nations Relief and Rehabilitation Administration for repatriation and support of refugees under Allied control after the end of World War II. Among their responsibilities was relief coordination at camps housing displaced people.

16. Bindermichl was a Displaced Persons camp located in a suburb of Linz in Austria, in the American zone.

17. While serving under General Eisenhower as military commander of Bavaria, General Patton, during an interview with American journalists, declared that there was too much attention being paid to denazification and made light of the situation by comparing the Nazi party's loss to that of a loss between the Democrats and the Republicans in the United States. After he was formally reprimanded by Eisenhower for making those comments, Patton assured the president that he would uphold the Potsdam Agreement in which the Allies agreed to eliminate Nazism in all of its forms from German life. Ten days later Patton was removed from his command of the Third Army. Just two months later in December, General Patton was killed in an automobile crash that many have speculated was not an accident.

18. *American Jewish Chaplains and the Shearit Hapletah: April–June 1945* by Alex Grobman. "The chaplains were American military personnel who were among the first Jews from the United States to meet survivors."

19. The Zebra Club was an exclusive club for personnel with three stripes or more, or as my father put it, "Upper 3 Graders Club."

20. *Parigot* is slang for "a French person from Paris."

21. *The Difficulties of Mr. Hofmannsthal*, a comedy about Austrian aristocracy.

22. General John C. Lee was known as Jesus Christ Himself both because of his initials and his highly egotistical nature combined with an intense religious fervor. The general was the first person to go against army segregation policy, offering all physically fit African American soldiers in the Services Supply Corps a chance normally given to otherwise white divisions in the infantry during World War II. "Lieutenant General John C. H. Lee, General Eisenhower's deputy commander, ETO, provided a perfect solution when he suggested using the African American servicemen in the theater as volunteer infantry replacements. Since African American soldiers were already in the ETO in service units, and seemingly under utilized, Lee theorized that these men were a solution to the Army manpower dilemma. Lieutenant General Lee invited 'a limited number of colored troops who have had infantry training' to accept 'the privilege of joining our veteran units at the front,' allowing the men the opportunity to 'fight shoulder to shoulder to bring about victory.'" US Army Center For Military History, *http://www.history.army.mil/html/topics/afam/aa-volinfreps.html*.

23. While I completed the research for this book at Columbia University and we were discussing Paris one day, my mother made note of something quite curious about the large apartment overlooking the Bois de Boulogne, where her cousins Marie and Nathan Lévitan lived. On a family visit in 1968 when we were invited to lunch, she complimented Marie on her stylishly appointed living room at their flat on Rue de Franqueville. It reminded her of Radio City Music Hall. As she looked around, she commented on her exquisite taste in Art Deco furniture and the wonderful view from her window. Flattered, Marie disclosed that behind the perfect veneer of their home was a more suspect past. During the war, a German general took possession of the apartment after the family's escape. When the Lévitans returned after liberation, in August of 1944, they found their home in perfect condition; not a thing was missing. This was odd, because during Möbel Aktion, under the auspices of Alfred Rosenberg, the Nazis systematically emptied upwards of 38,000 Jewish homes in occupied Paris alone. They looted everything

from art to cultural artifacts to furniture and musical instruments, including thousands of pianos. Marie elaborated that before his escape, the general gave specific orders that the contents of the apartment be left alone. Before the war, the Lévitans had an Austrian cook who worked for them and who remained in the service of the general during the war. She must have been some cook if he ordered the apartment to be left untouched!

Although the general's name is lost to history, another fascinating detail surfaced that until recently remained one of Paris' great secrets. The Lévitans owned a famous furniture store chain whose motto was "Un meuble signé Lévitan est garanti pour longtemps" (A piece of furniture made by the Lévitans is guaranteed for a long time). It was furniture for the laboring classes. During the occupation, French radio was taken over by the Vichy government and Radio Paris became a propaganda vehicle. People all over France, including my father, turned to the BBC on their short-wave radios for real news. The BBC broadcast in French and took advertising slogans like the Lévitan ditty and changed the words to, "Le triomphe des Allemands n'est pas garanti pour longtemps" (German victory is not guaranteed for long).

Behind the façade of a city under siege was an outpost of the notorious concentration camp, Drancy. The Nazis requisitioned the Lévitan building located on Rue du Faubourg Saint-Martin and turned it into an internment camp for people of mixed "racial" origin from 1943 to 1944. It became a slave labor camp in the heart of the city, where hundreds of internees "were made to sort, clean, repair and pack furniture and other objects of value that had been methodically looted by the Germans from tens of thousands of Jewish apartments in the occupied zone of northern France . . . sent off by the trainload to Germany," according to the *Glasgow Herald*, October 23, 1940. The first priority for the stolen property during Möbel Aktion was given to military and Nazi hierarchy who often came to shop at the warehouse as if they were shopping at a department store, while the rest was distributed to German civilians as a means to compensate them for losses incurred by Allied bombings or to help raise money needed to immigrate to the Reich's newly acquired territories.

Even though conditions were somewhat better than at Drancy, they were still deplorable. Internees were permitted the occasional visitor, packages were allowed to be delivered or could even send mail, but prisoners rarely saw the light of day, and discipline was harsh. Many were eventually deported to other concentration camps and exterminated. After the occupation, the building was returned to the family and its past was hidden under layers of grime and old paint, until a recent renovation uncovered clues. That is when noted historian, and my distant cousin, Jean-Marc Dreyfus approached the building's new owners and told them of its sordid past. The new home of Paris' largest advertising agency was once Lager Ost-Lévitan.

24. *New York Times*, May 25, 1940.
25. A *prestataire* is a civilian auxilliary recruited for noncombatant defense work, according to Vicki Caron in *Uneasy Asylum: France and the Jewish Refugee Crisis, 1933–1942* (Stanford University Press, 1999).
26. Mel Brooks was, in fact, a customer at Bon Marché. My mother, who often worked at our uptown store on the Upper East Side in New York, waited on him and his wife, Anne Bancroft.